Talking *and* Learning *with* Young Children

SAGE was founded in 1965 by Sara Miller McCune to support the dissemination of usable knowledge by publishing innovative and high-quality research and teaching content. Today, we publish more than 850 journals, including those of more than 300 learned societies, more than 800 new books per year, and a growing range of library products including archives, data, case studies, reports, and video. SAGE remains majority-owned by our founder, and after Sara's lifetime will become owned by a charitable trust that secures our continued independence.

Los Angeles | London | New Delhi | Singapore | Washington DC

Talking and Learning with Young Children

MICHAEL JONES

Los Angeles | London | New Delhi
Singapore | Washington DC

Los Angeles | London | New Delhi
Singapore | Washington DC

SAGE Publications Ltd
1 Oliver's Yard
55 City Road
London EC1Y 1SP

SAGE Publications Inc.
2455 Teller Road
Thousand Oaks, California 91320

SAGE Publications India Pvt Ltd
B 1/I 1 Mohan Cooperative Industrial Area
Mathura Road
New Delhi 110 044

SAGE Publications Asia-Pacific Pte Ltd
3 Church Street
#10-04 Samsung Hub
Singapore 049483

Editor: Amy Jarrold
Assistant editor: George Knowles
Production editor: Nicola Marshall
Proofreader: Thea Watson
Indexer: Silvia Benvenuto
Marketing manager: Dilhara Attygalle
Cover design: Wendy Scott
Typeset by: C&M Digitals (P) Ltd, Chennai, India
Printed in India at Replika Press Pvt Ltd

Library of Congress Control Number: 2015935347

British Library Cataloguing in Publication data

A catalogue record for this book is available from
the British Library

ISBN 978-1-4739-1239-7
ISBN 978-1-4739-1240-3 (pbk)

At SAGE we take sustainability seriously. Most of our products are printed in the UK using FSC papers and boards.
When we print overseas we ensure sustainable papers are used as measured by the Egmont grading system.
We undertake an annual audit to monitor our sustainability.

For Andreas, Eva, Dani, Brendan, Savash, Ayaan, Jasmine, Jayden, Ibrahim and Layla. And for Rachel.

CONTENTS

About the Author   viii
Acknowledgements   ix

Introduction: Talking successfully with children   1

1   How and why do children learn to talk?   11

2   Babies and adults communicating and
    learning together   32

3   Towards first words   50

4   Talking with two-year-olds   68

5   Different experiences of talking at home   83

6   Quality talk in early years settings   101

7   Talking effectively with groups of children   118

8   Pedagogy and practice that influences talk   145

9   Communicating complex ideas   172

Glossary   187
References   193
Index   200

ABOUT THE AUTHOR

Michael Jones has worked as a speech and language therapist, as a teacher in primary and special schools and as an advisory teacher for children with speech and language difficulties. He led the Every Child a Talker (ECaT) project in three areas of the UK.

Michael currently provides training internationally and publishes widely on the subject of early language development.

ACKNOWLEDGEMENTS

Many thanks to Mary Field, Kelly Yuen, Katja O'Neill, Judith Twani, Lisa Pepper, Sam Randall, Steve Grocott, Debbie Brace, Bhavna Acharya, Dee Gent, Sally Roberts, Lucy Jenkins, Trevor Stevens, Edmund Gentle, Maggie Harris, Catherine Croft, Kathy Brodie, Emma Huxter, Jay Begum and Mine Conkbayir.

Thanks to Chapel Street Nursery School, Luton and The Rainbow Centre, RAF Marham for the cover photographs.

Special thanks must go to Sue Thomas, Sadie Thornton and Tina Cook, who co-led the Every Child a Talker (ECaT) projects with me in Luton, Bedford Borough and Thurrock. Along with the many practitioners in the settings who were involved in these projects, they provided me with so many ideas, insights and inspiration. Jeni Riley gave me hours of her time, in person and via the phone and email, with inspirational discussion and support with this book. And to Amy Jarrold and George Knowles at Sage for expertly steering me through the whole process.

And to Professor Hazel Dewart, sadly no longer with us, who showed me that the study of child development can be an intellectual activity, a deeply emotional experience and sometimes highly entertaining!

INTRODUCTION: TALKING SUCCESSFULLY WITH CHILDREN

What is this book about?

This book explores how children learn to communicate using language, how they use language to learn and the role of adults in the process. From the moment they are born, children use a powerful inner force for communicating and a drive to make sense of their environment and the people in it. If adults show the child love, affection and involve him in the right type of early interaction, spoken language emerges that the child can use to communicate ideas. With continued adult support, most children by the age of three-and-a-half have an almost complete set of communication, language and speech skills. This book focuses on how children learn language within the context of social relationships: initially with their parents and other family members, then later with professional adults who assist in their language development and learning within early years settings, and with other children.

We examine how adults help children learn by involving them in positive interactions, meaningful conversation and by helping them play, explore and talk with each other. Every child's experience is different, so we look closely at how adults help children from diverse backgrounds, including those with additional learning needs, to develop the language and the confidence to communicate that they will need to achieve well in school and build positive relationships throughout life. There are many examples of practical strategies and activities that come from my experience in working with young children, families and practitioners, and from my involvement in the England-wide Every Child a Talker (ECaT) project.

Who is this book for?

This book will be valuable for students and those already working with young children, including those in leadership and advisory roles. It aims to inspire students and practitioners to develop their skills when talking with children, to influence how adults plan for talk in their settings and to give an insight into how language develops in the home.

How the book is structured

Early chapters link key research findings with successful practice, using examples of children and adults talking and learning together. Later chapters focus on case studies of successful approaches that support language and learning in early years settings. Points for reflection and discussion and practical tasks help the reader reflect on the implications of research findings for pedagogy and daily practice with children. Each chapter concludes with suggestions for further reading in research and practical approaches. Words in italics throughout the text are technical terms specific to the study of language and child development, and are explained in the Glossary.

A note about terminology and children's ages

Throughout the book, professionals working with children are referred to as 'practitioners'. The establishments that children attend are referred to as 'settings'. Day nurseries and childminders are described as providing 'childcare', in recognition that children will often spend most of their day in these settings. The term 'early years' is used to refer to children's chronological age from birth to five years. Children's ages are described in years and months; e.g. a child aged three years and four months will be 3;4. Children are referred to as either 'he' or 'she'.

Learning a language and introducing some more terminology

There are many ways that human beings communicate messages face to face, with talking being the most widely used. *Communication* is the way that people convey messages to each other, including talking, using gestures and sign language. *Verbal communication* involves what is understood by the speaker and the listener (*verbal comprehension*), and how they talk with each other (*verbal expression*). Our *interaction* with other people, how we respond to each other while communicating, may involve *conversation*. Conversation is a series of turns, where each speaker has a chance to participate in sharing messages.

When communicating with babies or children who are in the early stages of developing language, we focus on the interaction between child and adult. As language emerges, we tend to look closely at how we use words, i.e. our conversation. However, underlying all of our communication with children is a belief that our interaction should be as positive as possible. By using the word 'positive', I assume that we are using language to support children to enjoy communicating, so that we can build their enjoyment of talking for pleasure as well as a way to learn.

Let's imagine that we are learning Japanese by visiting Japan and being immersed in the language, with little or no help from anyone who speaks English. Talking successfully with a Japanese person can only happen if we both have an understanding of spoken *language*, i.e. how we use verbal symbols to express a meaning. As well as knowing that we are being spoken to in Japanese, as opposed to, say, Vietnamese or Thai, we need to understand how individual *speech* sounds are used in that particular language to make up words, i.e. the phonological system. We need to know when one word ends and another begins, and to link words that are spoken to the objects, people or ideas that they relate to.

Every language has thousands of *vocabulary* items, including nouns, verbs and adjectives. At the very beginning, it is fine to use vocabulary items singly, but this will only allow us to communicate very basic ideas. At this stage, we will rely very heavily on our understanding of *non-verbal communication*, including understanding the other person's gestures. If we really want to understand the true message behind the words that are being used, it is essential to be able to read the messages that are being conveyed by the speaker's facial expression and, crucially, tone of voice, which indicates how the speaker is feeling. We need to know the rules of how words are linked together, including word order, to convey ideas such as when something happened, to whom and why. Broadly speaking, we can refer to this as *grammar*. To really understand ideas, we need to have experience. For example, you can't possibly understand what a Japanese person is saying about the Japanese Tea Ceremony unless you have experienced it, ideally in real life or at least from pictures or film.

We need to know all that in order to understand someone else. To make ourselves understood, we would need to know how to pronounce individual Japanese speech sounds and how to put them together in words. At exactly the same time we would need to know how to convey our meaning (*semantics*), including linking the words together in an agreed way, using accurate Japanese grammar. You have to know what you are talking about and constantly check your Japanese listener's face to literally see if he understands. If he doesn't understand, then you need to have the skills to use more basic non-verbal communication, such as gestures. This is the all important use of *pragmatics*, where we use different ways to convey our message. When you have done all that, then you have successfully asked about the toilet and understand where to find it!

If that sounds like hard work, then let's think about miracles. Children are little miracles, because they will have all of these skills by the time they are three years old. What is even more miraculous is that they will have learned all this without anyone sitting down with the specific aim of teaching them how to talk. All this understanding and expression will have been learned naturally through talking with other people, and particularly with adults. This learning journey starts at home and continues in childcare, pre-school and school. It is a truly amazing achievement.

So let's start as we intend to go on: with children talking.

Adam, Lucy, Michael and the bananas

On a visit to a busy nursery school, I was involved in a fascinating conversation with two three-and-a-half-year-old children. They were sitting at the snack table, peeling a banana each and chopping it up. I had never met the children before, but as a visiting advisor I had been invited to join the children at the snack table and 'have a chat' with them as they prepared their food, ate it and then cleared the table. I am indicated as MJ.

Adam (to Michael):	Do you like toriander? (Coriander.)
Michael:	Yes I do.
Adam:	My mummy buys toriander.
Lucy:	What's toriander?
Adam:	It's dreen and loots lite a plant. (It's green and looks like a plant.)
Lucy:	My dad drinks beer.

Adam:	My dad don't lite beer. He drints Tote. (Coke.)
(To Michael):	Do you like nanas?
Michael:	Yes. I like bananas. I like lots of fruit.
Adam:	What's truit?
Lucy:	You know. Pums and stuff like that.
Michael:	Pums?
Lucy:	Yes. They are purple and got a stone inside.
Michael:	Oh plums!
Lucy:	Yes. Pums.
Adam:	My lite pums. My mummy don't buy me pums.

This conversation lasted about a minute, but contains the essence of this entire book: that language learning and using language to learn come from having effective interactions within a social setting. These very young children have already achieved an enormous amount in the 36 months since they were born. They are able to ask an adult and each other questions. Adam asks two types of question: for information about my food preferences, checking to see if I like the same as he does; and for clarification about a misunderstood statement. Lucy is an equally sophisticated communicator. She is able to ask another child a question and give a clarification, even though the child she is talking to is not pronouncing all his words clearly.

Both children are still developing their ability to make single speech sounds (*articulation*) in a way that is acceptable in the area where they live (*pronunciation)* and to combine them to make words (*phonology*), with Lucy being ahead of Adam in terms of how intelligible she is. If we chose to analyse this brief exchange in more depth, we would find a wealth of information about both children's phonology. We would note that Adam, for example, is regularly substituting /t/ for /k/. This is not uncommon in children of this age, and does not present a significant obstacle to Adam communicating his message. Lucy, on the other hand, is developing her use of /pl/ initial consonant blends, so that 'plums' become 'pums'. This did briefly impede our understanding, but Lucy's expert description of a plum 'repaired' the conversation, so that the children could bring it to a satisfying conclusion.

These little children are highly sophisticated communicators for the following reasons:

- They are able to engage an unfamiliar adult in conversation
- They can talk in abstract about something that is not there for them to look at and handle

- They can talk in this way while using their hands to do something else (and eat at the same time!)
- They understand how to 'repair' a conversation when it starts to break down because of potential misunderstanding

What is most remarkable about these children is that Adam is being brought up in an Italian-, Hindi- and English-speaking home environment and Lucy's parents only speak French with her at home. What the children say, the ideas that they communicate and how they talk, are the tip of a very large iceberg of communication that has been expanding rapidly over 36 months. However, as practitioners, we will only ever be party to a minute fraction of that talk and communication. This is often because of the nature of daily life in settings, where children are together in large groups with relatively few adults to talk with them in detail.

The role of the adult

I was very restrained during this conversation. I made a conscious decision to say as little as possible, to see how the children were able to talk to each other. What I chose to do, and most importantly what not to do, were the crucial factors in determining how this conversation would evolve. The decision to respond simply to Adam's initial question with 'Yes I do' gave him the space to lead the conversation where he wanted it to go, i.e. about what he knew most about: his home life and family relationships. By controlling my automatic adult reaction to probe Adam with questions, I allowed him to maintain the role of leader of the conversation. This encouraged his friend Lucy to enter the conversation as an equal and to contribute information that kept the conversation going.

There can be so much to discover, even in the shortest of conversations! But what I was bursting to find out, after we had finished talking, was why this little boy, who was talking to me for the first time, asked about coriander, when we were involved in cutting up bananas? Why did he know about coriander at all, when most children of his age talk about more well-known foods such as apples and oranges? I was intrigued to find out, so asked the practitioners. It emerged that fresh coriander is a popular ingredient in Indian cooking. Adam is very close to his grandmother, who regularly cooks for him and often adds some chopped coriander onto Adam's food. The previous day, Adam had asked if he could have some coriander on his rice at nursery, which led to a discussion about food, including whether anyone else liked coriander or other types of green-leaf vegetable. This reveals Adam's question to be a logical extension of his own exploration of the whole subject of food, modelled to him by adults in a naturally occurring group discussion the previous day.

But where was the learning in our 'chat'? Both these children made 'errors' of grammar and pronunciation. Wasn't it a wasted opportunity to extend the children's language, particularly bearing in mind their need, as *bilingual* learners, to progress in their ability to understand and speak English? Had I been a student being observed by a tutor or a practitioner being observed by an inspector, I may have been roundly criticised for not capitalising on an important learning opportunity. Granted, by dropping the word 'fruit' into the conversation, I moved onto an interesting subject, before Adam brought it firmly back into the realm of his family. But that was basically it, in terms of my 'teaching' input.

Many practitioners feel under pressure when communicating with children. Pressure develops through the lack of time to have the type of intense, in-depth conversations that they know children need in order to learn. Practitioners also feel under pressure to make every conversation count: to use each opportunity for talk to move children forward in their knowledge and understanding of other curriculum areas, e.g. mathematics. Such a practitioner would have taken control of the conversation, asked more questions and used more complex vocabulary. He might even have used this as an opportunity to improve the children's pronunciation by modelling correct usage. This is laudable, but by behaving in this way it could have denied both children several equally important lessons:

- It is fun to talk for the sake of talking
- People value what I have to say
- I can use language to explore my own ideas
- I talk best when adults listen to me and are interested in what I have to say
- I can compare my life experience with another child
- I am becoming more confident as a talker with adults and with other children
- Other children also have speech that can be unclear at times, but how you talk is not as important as the message you want to convey
- I am learning how to be a good communicator in a social setting
- I am learning how to be a good communicator in a setting where there are several children for every adult
- I am successful as a communicator in another language other than those I speak at home

The scope of this book

Adam and Lucy are sophisticated learners. Their journey as language learners is by no means over, but, like most three-and-a-half-year-olds, they have covered most of the ground. They have developed most of the skills that they will need to become successful communicators, including acquiring the fundamentals of pronunciation and sentence construction: in English and another language. We use the terms 'develop' and 'acquire' advisedly. Theories of language development have evolved over the centuries. Simple notions of imitation developed into behavioural theories of reinforcement by reward. Chomsky's theory that children have a built-in capacity for language acquisition – to create for themselves or 'acquire' the rules of speech and grammar – gives an insight into how humans have an inbuilt drive to learn how to talk. Theories that stress the importance of children developing language to use socially in communication point to the vital role of adults interacting with children: to help them understand the meanings of words and how to use them to talk with other people. The view taken in this book is that all of these theories play a part in explaining children's development as communicators.

We examine in detail how children from birth to 18 months, which can broadly be defined as 'infancy', acquire skills and develop communication through social interaction. Observations of children learning at this age provide us with insights into how most children manage to learn to develop their understanding and expressive language skills so rapidly. This occurs through a combination of children's rapidly developing neurological system (*maturation*), physical growth and intellectual or *cognitive development* and opportunities to explore their immediate world and close relationships. Central to this process is the interaction between infants and their parents and key caregivers. Positive interaction promotes wellbeing and security, as part of the establishment of early relationships. These adults provide the essential experience of many thousands of interactions and play experiences.

Between two and three years of age, we see a rapid increase in children's ability to communicate and understand sophisticated ideas. This growth in communication and learning is linked to children's increasing experience and their drive to explore the wider physical world and the world of ideas. However, not all children welcome being exposed to new and exciting experiences, particularly some two-year-olds, as they move tentatively towards embracing independence, or children with *speech and language delay,* who can find talking with unfamiliar adults and other children very challenging. With children's increasing independence, the adult's role changes from providing total nurture and protection, to encouraging and allowing the child to explore. Language and conversation play a large part in helping the child to make sense of family relationships and the outside world, including the abstract world of stories.

Young children's experience of growing up in families is diverse, and this is reflected in how children communicate and talk. Some children have two parents, some have one. Some are brought up in extended families, while some children spend their early lives away from their natural parents in a number of different care situations. Many young children are exposed to more than one language at home, or speak a language different to the one used in the setting. The biggest influence on how quickly and successfully children learn to understand and use new languages is how well children and adults are able to share talk together. Children have differing rates of development, and problems with speech and language learning are evident from very early on when children have *developmental delay*, e.g. Down syndrome. Children who do not have developmental delay can experience speech and language difficulties for no apparent reason, or because of physical difficulties such as hearing impairment. However, being unable to communicate effectively, and particularly when away from the family, can impede children's confidence and impact on their learning.

Communication and language can also be adversely affected by the impact of reduced experience, and the term 'language impoverishment' was introduced in the UK to describe the impact of children's lack of experience and reduced exposure to talk at home. Concern about the extent of language impoverishment led to the introduction of the England-wide Every Child a Talker (ECaT) project. Children who suffer neglect, which often includes limited exposure to interaction and conversation, are particularly at risk of language delay.

Talk at home differs from talk in settings. The biggest difference is created by the ratio between children and adults. With the exception of children coming from very large families, or those in the care of childminders, there will always be more children per adult in a setting than at home. At a basic practical level, practitioners need to organise themselves so that they can help children thrive socially and learn effectively. Key UK research in the 1980s indicated that conversations at home were often much longer, richer and mutually more satisfying than in settings. Ongoing research looking in detail at strategies for young children's learning in early years settings indicates that effective talk is crucial. Adults' collective beliefs about how children learn – their *pedagogy* – has a direct impact on children's wellbeing, communication and learning. The collective pedagogy that practitioners follow in a setting influences the environment that they create for children and the opportunities for talk and learning that take place within it. A central theme of this book is exploring how practitioners can involve children in conversations where adults and children can talk for long enough about subjects of shared interest, that develop children's thinking and learning in a mutually satisfying way.

Pedagogy influences how the adults plan the curriculum that children will be involved in, but also influences how adults balance child-initiated activities with those that are adult-led or highly structured. Observation, recording progress and planning for children's learning are central tools in early years settings. What children say and how they respond to adults during play provide valuable evidence of progress and insight into how individual children learn. This also informs planning for future activities. How practitioners observe and record influences what they find out, and we explore ways to make observations and recording as natural as possible, so that adults can maximise opportunities for interaction and conversation.

There are several types of settings in the UK: nursery schools and nursery classes that are led by teachers in primary schools; day nurseries and childminders that provide care from early in the morning until the parents return from work; pre-schools that operate from their own premises; or 'packaway' settings, where staff are able every day to turn an empty hall into a creative environment for 30 children. Whatever the setting, judgements about children's progress in language development and relationships between children and adults are at the heart of deciding how well children's needs are being met (Ofsted, 2013).

While children learning English as an additional language (EAL) have been attending settings in urban areas for many years, practitioners in many rural areas are now working with children who are in the very early stages of learning English. This book does not devote specific chapters to focusing on children learning EAL, but many examples are from families where a number of languages are being spoken and learned by the children and their parents. Reference is also made throughout the text to children with additional speech and language learning needs.

And what are our hopes for children as they reach their fifth birthdays? In the UK, most will be involved in primary education, where in many cases the majority of learning experiences are led by adults. These experiences will have very clear, pre-planned outcomes. When children talk in class, how much they talk and what they talk about are also clearly defined. Children who start primary school are often expected to have a specific level of knowledge and sets of skills that include being able to talk about what they know, in a group. This book suggests that, as children move from the early years into the world of the primary curriculum, their social development, including their ability to use language to learn in groups, is as important as the level of skill that they can show.

CHAPTER 1

HOW AND WHY DO CHILDREN LEARN TO TALK?

This chapter will

- Give a brief overview of the main theories on how and why children develop language
- Introduce a perspective that places interaction and conversation between children and adults at the heart of communication, language development and learning in early years

Example 1.1 Amy and the combine harvester

Amy was seven years old when she decided that she was going to learn French, and now has a degree in French Language and Literature. It all began while she was on holiday in France with her parents and four-year-old brother, Ben. The very first French word she wanted to learn was 'moissonneuse-batteuse' (combine harvester). This was the

(Continued)

(Continued)

largest thing she could see at the time, as she looked out from the garden of her hotel to the combine harvester in the field across the road.

At bedtime, Amy and her Mum were having a chat. Amy looked worried.

Amy: I'm never going to learn French.

Mum: Why not?

Amy: 'cos I can't remember how to say the word for that big tractor thing! It's so hard to learn one word … so how can I learn lots and lots?

Mum: There is an easier way. You know that song you learned in nursery, 'Frère Jacques'? Let's sing it.

Frère Jacques, frère Jacques/Dormez-vous? Dormez-vous?

Well 'dormir' means 'to sleep' and 'dormez-vous' means 'Are you sleeping?' 'Bien' means 'good' or 'well'. So if I tuck you in, give you a kiss and say, 'Dormes bien ma cherie', What do I mean?

Amy: Sleep well, my cherry?

Mum: It means 'Sleep well, my darling'. (Tucks her in and gives her a kiss.) Dormes bien, ma cherie.

Amy: And can Ben learn to speak French, too?

Mum: Yes, of course. And we can start tomorrow by telling him 'The Three Bears' in French.

Amy: And …

Mum: No more questions. Dormes bien, ma cherie.

Amy: Dorma ben, ma cherry.

It's not unusual that Amy and her mother should be thinking about how to learn language. Anyone learning a second language will use the knowledge that they have already gained from developing their first language, whether they are consciously aware of that knowledge or not. This example highlights the key perspectives in a debate that has involved philosophers, psychologists, linguists and educators for centuries, as they seek to answer two questions: 'How do children learn to talk?' and 'How does a baby with no verbal language at birth come to possess an almost complete set of communication and language skills by their fourth birthday?'

Amy assumes that if she starts by learning, one at a time, the names of the biggest objects she can find, and keeps repeating their names until she can pronounce them correctly, then she will learn, in double-quick time, all there is to know about French. She imagines her mind as an empty box that has no French in it, just waiting for her to fill it up with key vocabulary. Amy's conceptualisation of language learning is not as naive as it may seem: repetition is an important part of developing language, and when children begin using words, at around 12 months of age, they do generally use one word at a time. But children will not get very far if they only imitate what is said to them, or merely repeat words to themselves. Amy has advantages that will support her learning, including a drive to learn and a good role model who understands the language and knows how to teach it. However, one suspects that unless Mum steps in and makes the whole process rewarding, through praise and encouragement, then Amy will give up and concentrate on her other holiday projects, like how to do 'cat's cradle' or perfecting the art of using a skipping rope.

Amy's mother has absolutely the right approach to language teaching:

- Let's find some words that we can use meaningfully as part of daily life, e.g. 'sleep'
- Let's say them as part of a pleasant experience, e.g. as part of our cosy bedtime routine
- Let's learn a song that links words to ideas. If the song has a catchy tune and some actions, then it will be easy to remember and the key words will be repeated many times
- Let's share a simple story, in French, that the children already know, so that they can link new words to familiar ideas

So we have the feeling that French is going to make sense for Amy, and that the process of learning will be fun and, most importantly, will take place as part of a loving relationship. As a teacher of language, it is likely that Amy's Mum will have thought carefully about how she will introduce French to her children; i.e., that the children can be helped to develop language if the process is meaningful and fun and based around activities and ideas that are relevant for the children's intellectual levels. Amy's seven years of experience in becoming a successful communicator and talker in English have given her an intuitive 'feel' for how language works, as well as the ability to talk about it. This knowledge will provide her with strong foundations for learning French. What is remarkable is the fact that Amy absorbed all of this knowledge of English without anyone sitting down with the express purpose of teaching her how to talk. So how can we explain very young children's extraordinarily rapid growth in knowledge and skills?

The role of imitation and rewards

From the 1950s, learning theory has proposed that language, like all other aspects of children's learning, is largely the product of imitation and reward. The theory put forward by *behaviourists* suggests that, for example, babies hear a variety of common speech sounds around them and when they accidentally use some of these sounds, parents respond with delight and praise, which rewards the child and spurs him on to repeat the behaviour (Skinner, 1957). The child then starts to regularly repeat these sounds because they are rewarded, or 'reinforced', for doing so. The process of giving rewards for behaviour is known as 'extrinsic reinforcement'. As well as being rewarded by praise from adults, children also receive internal rewards or 'intrinsic reinforcement', from feelings of achievement and wellbeing from communicating successfully. Vocabulary, speech sounds and grammar are introduced in the same way, so that children eventually learn to use the language, sound system, grammar and *accent* that their parents use.

> ### Example 1.2 Tanaz, Fouad and the Scottish, Iranian and Geordie accents
>
> Tanaz (4;7) and her brother Fouad (3;2) live in Newcastle, with their Scottish mother and Iranian father. They occasionally visit Scotland but have never been to Iran. Both children are being brought up as English- and Farsi-speakers at home. Mum has a pronounced Scottish accent when she speaks Farsi and English, while Dad has an equally strong Iranian accent when he talks in both languages. Both children attend a local pre-school, where the majority of staff and children speak with a distinctive regional 'Geordie' accent.
>   When Tanaz speaks English or Farsi, she does so with a Scottish accent, while her brother speaks both languages with a Farsi accent. When Tanaz plays 'being in pre-school' at home, which involves her pretending to be various members of staff, she uses a Geordie accent.

It is inconceivable that an adult should sit a very young child down and try to teach them how to speak with a particular accent. In order for Tanaz and Fouad to have developed their respective accents, we can assume that some form of imitation must have taken place, though probably not at a conscious level. So imitation is important. Yet the behaviourist model of imitation and reward can only explain a relatively small part of the process. It can't explain, for example, how Tanaz and her brother have developed different speech patterns, because they have never been rewarded for talking like a Scot or an Iranian or a Geordie. They will have learned their accents naturally, through listening to the accents of those around them.

Imitation and reward feature in many daily activities that are planned by adults for young children. These include singing and rhyming sessions, where children are encouraged to imitate, repeat and memorise as many songs and rhymes as they can. Looking at this valuable experience from a behaviourist standpoint, the children are receiving external, extrinsic rewards, in the form of praise from the adults, for joining in the session, and making progress towards mastering the tune and the words. The children also experience internal, intrinsic rewards from feelings of wellbeing they gain from being part of a fun group activity, as well as pleasure from the process of learning the tune and words.

We need only to think of the popular 'ABC Song' to further illustrate this point. Tanaz and Fouad are learning a version sung to the tune of 'Twinkle, Twinkle Little Star', ending with the lines, 'Now I know my ABC/ Aren't you very proud of me?' Their parents are rightly very proud of their children's accomplishment, and respond by exclaiming, 'Well done! You are so clever! Show Granny what you can do!' The song may not make too much sense at the moment, but the children are developing a feeling that learning to talk, as part of learning in general, is something that their parents value. A year later, the parents will not be reacting in the same way when Tanaz sings the song. In fact, they may choose to ignore her as a way of getting her to stop doing it! However, they will be equally excited when she comes home and says, 'I can speak French!' and sings the first two lines of 'Frère Jacques'. This example gives credence, in part, to the behaviourist view that adults systematically reward learning by providing praise for certain behaviours and by ignoring others.

But can we realistically explain children's rapid growth of language by imitation and reward alone? Learning to communicate meaning is not the same as learning the words to a song by rote. Young children – or older children learning English as an additional language, or those with speech and language delay – could learn the words of the songs without being able to make any sense of the meaning of the words (as do adults apparently 'learning' words of pop songs, only to realise that they have totally misinterpreted the songs' actual lyrics!). However, unlike learning songs and nursery rhymes, language has to make sense if we are to understand what is being said to us and for us to be able to say what we mean. And how do we explain what is happening when children spontaneously say, 'My goed to the shops' for 'I went to the shops'? It is most unlikely that they would have heard their parents use a sentence like that, and the children wouldn't be praised for doing so. We need to see imitation and reward as only one part of our model of language development.

Point for reflection and discussion

How much do you use praise and rewards in everyday conversation with children? ('Praise' does not have to involve words, or physical rewards such as stickers. It could be your smile, or making an effort to stay with the child even though other children are calling for your attention.)

When Amy was three, she said to her granny, 'Granny. A baby cat is a kitten.' Grannie replied, 'Goodness, you are a clever girl for knowing that. Come and tell Granny lots of other things that you know about.' Amy got a big hug and a kiss, too. Did Granny need to tell Amy that she was a 'clever girl'? What impact might this have had on Amy?

How much do you praise children for knowing about language or for having learned something new? Is it necessary?

 Practical task

Adults often praise children by saying, 'Well done' when a child has learned something new, e.g. completed a new puzzle. Sometimes, we say this when children have learned a new word, e.g. colours, shapes or numbers. Experiment with other ways of praising and rewarding children for developing their language. Choose a child who is quiet and possibly unsure about talking. Use the style of praising used by Amy's granny by overtly praising and rewarding the child's efforts and knowledge of new words and ideas, e.g. by spending a bit more time talking with them or praising their 'cleverness'. This might increase a quiet child's sense of wellbeing and be a powerful 'intrinsic motivator'. (NB: Don't go 'over the top' by being loud and enthusiastic. Talk in a calm and interested voice, which is what quiet children prefer.) Observe the child's reaction.

Noam Chomsky and language as a genetically determined 'organ of the mind'

Seven-year-old Amy, our second language learner in Example 1.1, already knows, at an intuitive level, how language operates. This gives her a distinct advantage when it comes to learning French. Her parents have never sat her down and told her about the facts of language: e.g. that 'horse, cat, dog' are all nouns, but 'run, jump, climb' are all verbs, or that verbs have participles. By being successfully involved in the process of becoming a fluent English-speaker, Amy has reached the point where she has an informal understanding of these rules of English grammar. She 'just knows' about these rules.

At school, Amy's teacher wrote a string of words on the board: 'brown the cat little chair the on is sleeping', and asked the children to use all of these words to make up a sentence that made complete sense (but making sure that the words 'brown' and 'little' are next to each other). Most of the children in the class could do this very quickly. Some wrote, 'The little brown cat is sitting quietly on the chair', while others wrote, 'Is the little brown cat sitting on the chair?' However, the children learning English as an additional language (EAL) were unsure about where 'little' and 'brown' should go in relation to each other. If you were to ask Amy, 'How did you know that "little" comes before "brown" and not the other way round?' she would reply, 'I just know.' However, there is no harm in Amy's mother explicitly explaining the rules of English grammar when describing how her new language operates, e.g. 'In English we say "I walk" but in French they say "Je marche." "Je" means "I" and "marche" means "walk"'.

Example 1.3 'sheeps' 'falled over': examples of overgeneralisation

Ryan is 3;4 and from an English-speaking family. He enjoys talking and has a very large vocabulary. The following examples are from conversations with his father:

Dad: I saw five sheep. How many did you see?

Ryan: I seed three sheeps.

Dad: England were great. They won the football match.

Ryan: Yeh. England winned at football.

Dad: Which train do you like best? I like the red one best.

Ryan: My blue train is bestest.

Dad: Whoops! Teddy just fell over.

Ryan: That teddy falled over.

Dad: Teddy fell over.

Ryan: Yeh. He falled over.

Dad: He fell over. Not falled. He fell. Ryan, say 'fell over'

(Continued)

(Continued)

Ryan: Fell over.

Dad: Now say teddy ... fell ... over.

Ryan: Teddy ... fell ... over.

Dad: Good boy! Well done! What did teddy do?

Ryan: Teddy felled over!

The phenomenon illustrated here, known as *overgeneralisation*, occurs when children try to apply a regular rule of grammar to a verb or part of speech that is irregular.

However, six months later, with no formal teaching at all, Ryan spontaneously began using 'fell', and never used 'falled' again.

Example 1.3 illustrates parts of linguist and philosopher Noam Chomsky's theory that all children have what is a uniquely human capacity to 'acquire' language, by 'creating' new sentences, using vocabulary that they have learned. His theory emphasises the central role of the child in creating language for themselves, as opposed to learning by imitation and direct teaching. He argued that children's *language acquisition* follows set patterns, as they acquire, or gain, the rules of grammar in their first language. Chomsky used the universal phenomenon of overgeneralisation to illustrate how children create their own rules of grammar, based on logical assumptions they make from hearing adults talk. He argued that they do this by using an innate *Language Acquisition Device (LAD)*, which is an 'organ of the mind' operating separately from other brain functions (Chomsky, 1975). Like physical organs, it grows due to a uniquely human genetic blueprint, i.e. it is *genetically determined*.

Chomsky argued that children's language acquisition cannot be explained solely by imitation. If children only imitated what adults said, then how can we explain Ryan's use of completely unique sentences such as 'That teddy just falled over'? He certainly wouldn't have heard that sentence from his parents. According to Chomsky, Ryan's Dad is exceptional, because Chomsky suggested that, in general, much of the spoken language that children are exposed to is imperfect and even 'degenerate' (Chomsky, 1965). This is largely due, Chomsky asserts, to the stops and starts, revisions and hesitations that are a feature of conversation. Yet, children are somehow able to construct and apply their own rules of grammar to understand what is said to them and to express themselves in what seems to be an entirely logical way.

Linguists influenced by Chomsky, listening to Ryan in Example 1.3, might analyse his expressive language, or 'performance', including what would be described as Ryan's 'errors'. From this they could make assumptions about what Ryan actually understands about the rules of English grammar, i.e. his 'competence' (Fletcher, 1985). Competence and performance expand as the child's LAD grows, as illustrated by Ryan automatically dropping his use of 'falled' in favour of 'fell'. Chomsky used children's move from immature to mature use of grammatical rules to argue that the LAD expands as the child matures, and in doing so allows the child to acquire understanding and use of new grammatical features, as part of an entirely automatic growth in brain structure (Chomsky, 1980).

Chomsky's ideas led to a major shift in the study of children's language, moving the focus of interest from the role of the child's environment, and specifically the behaviour of the adults in that environment, towards a theory that emphasised the child's contribution to the process of acquiring rules of grammar. This is described as a 'nativist approach', with its emphasis on what is essentially innate, or determined by genetics. While Chomsky was operating in a purely theoretical context – he didn't actually work with children – he influenced a generation of researchers, who sought to explore his theoretical model through detailed analyses of conversations between adults and children. Roger Brown and his dedicated team of linguists, for example, focused on the language of two children known as Adam and Eve. Brown concluded that children are active and creative in their language acquisition, and that children's acquisition of the rules of grammar follows a sequence that is essentially universal (Brown, 1973).

Chomsky and adherents to his theory emphasise that language acquisition is an innate feature of human development, i.e. genetically determined. They also argue that much of children's language is acquired despite the seemingly chaotic nature of what they hear being said to them and around them. But there are some important considerations that suggest that the child's LAD, should it exist, can only partly explain how most children come to be fluent speakers and communicators so quickly. For example, why do Japanese children learn Japanese and not English? There must be an element of imitation. How do we explain other aspects of language, such as the rapid growth of children's vocabulary? Again, there must be an element of imitation. And is the language that children hear directed to them really as unsystematic as Chomsky suggests, particularly when we discover that his opinion was based on analysis of how adults talk to each other, and not to children?

As we explore below, research based on analysis of interaction between young children and their carers shows that adults and older children systematically adjust what they say to babies and young children, to ensure that children are fully involved in conversations and can understand exactly what is being said to them. Furthermore, adults actively change the way they talk to individual children as the children's language use matures. This shifts our thinking towards an exploration of what the 'adult' does that is so helpful for the developing child. Chomsky's theory and behavioural theory may explain, to a certain extent 'how' children learn to talk and acquire the rules of grammar, but an essential question is, 'why do children do it at all?'

 Points for reflection and discussion

Much of our understanding of the correct usage of spoken grammar is intuitive and we may not be able to explain it unless we have actually studied grammar. Many so-called 'rules' of English written and spoken grammar are hotly debated. Yet, most children seem to absorb these rules effortlessly, through sharing conversation and reading informally with adults and older children.

To what extent do you expect children naturally to 'pick up' the rules of grammar?

Are there any fun activities and resources, including interactive websites or apps, which could help all children in the setting become aware of English grammar?

 Practical tasks

Spend time talking with a child like Ryan in Example 1.3, who overgeneralises and says things like, 'I swimmed'. Try, like Ryan's Dad, to see if he can learn the mature form of the verb, e.g. 'I swam'. You might do this by saying, 'Oh, you went swimming?' Does it make any difference? (NB: The child should have English as his only language.)

Make regular observations of this child talking spontaneously. Does he change to using mature forms of verbs? How long did it take? Did it happen naturally, or did someone teach him how to 'speak properly'?

Now observe a child who is learning EAL. Does he use overgeneralisations in his use of English verbs? If not, what does this mean? For example, might it be because he already has a 'feel' for grammar in his first language and is learning English grammar by thinking about it, as opposed to naturally 'acquiring' the rules? (Beware: this could turn into a massive area for theoretical study!) This type of observation illustrates just how difficult it is to make generalisations about how children or individual children are learning to talk. However, speech and language therapists are trained to do this, based on observations of individual children, and to make recommendations for how to help them.

Why do children learn to talk?

Important is grammar. That sentence makes no sense, because the word order is incorrect.

Full blue notions wake anxiously. That sentence is grammatically correct, but makes no sense either, because it has no obvious meaning. 'Meaning' is one of the most important words used in this book, because it points us towards the essential reason why humans talk, i.e. in order to communicate meaning. During the 1970s, linguists moved away from a wholly theoretical focus on language acquisition to explore, through detailed observations, how children and their carers actually communicate. This led to the establishment of what is often described as a 'non-nativist' perspective, based on the premise that the environment, and specifically the way that adults *interact* with young children, has a major impact on how communication and language develops (Saxton, 2010). This perspective is also referred to as 'empiricist' or 'empirical', in the sense that it is based on the interpretation of observable, empirical data, as opposed to pure theory (Stilwell Peccei, 2006).

M.A.K. Halliday and the uses of language

Linguist M.A.K. Halliday rejected Chomsky's theory of acquisition of grammar. He suggested that children learn to talk in ever more complex ways as a result of using language to fulfil different functions, and particularly to convey meaning to other people (Halliday, 1975). He proposed that there are seven main 'functions' or reasons why young children use language to talk to other people:

- Instrumental: to get what I want, e.g. 'Want teddy'
- Regulatory: to control what others do to me, e.g. 'No buggy!!'
- Interactional: to make contact with other people and build relationships, e.g. 'Hello, Daddy!'
- Personal: to say how I feel, to express my opinion and to talk about myself, e.g. 'My like biscuit,' 'Me big boy'
- Heuristic: to find out about my environment, e.g. 'What that dog do?'
- Imaginative: to tell stories, make jokes and create imaginary worlds
- Representational: to convey facts and information

Halliday's perspective is that children use language in different ways as they mature, physically and cognitively, and gain experience. His work helped create a balance in the study of language development, between focusing on grammar and exploring children's growing ability to use talk in different ways. Halliday's ideas reflected a growing interest in the study of pragmatics, how children use language and their understanding of non-verbal communication to convey messages and understand other people. This influenced the exploration of how children with additional learning needs could be supported to use language socially and to learn. For example, as the understanding of Autism Spectrum Disorder (ASD) increased, psychologists became aware that some children might acquire the skills of using accurate grammar and phonology, but be unable to use them in a meaningful way. A specific language impairment, Semantic-Pragmatic Language Disorder, was also identified, where children have particular difficulties with understanding the meanings of words and how they are used to communicate ideas, although their grammar and pronunciation are relatively well developed (Bishop, 2000; Bishop and Norbury, 2002). Therapists with an increased understanding of the functions of language were able to support children with speech and language difficulties to extend how they used language, as well as focusing on their grammar, vocabulary and phonology (Dewart and Summers, 1989, 1995).

Introducing interaction: 'Motherese' and Child Directed Speech

In the 1970s, Catherine Snow made recordings of mothers playing with their infants in a laboratory setting. She then analysed in detail how each mother and child pair, or 'dyad', behaved as they played. Snow and subsequent researchers confirmed that, far from being fragmented and difficult to make sense of, the language that the mothers used with their babies and older children is designed not only to make sense, but changes systematically as children's language develops (Snow, 1977). Initially, the mothers' speech patterns contained highly exaggerated tones of voice, and a type of made-up vocabulary, including words like 'diddums', 'boo', 'wasamatta?' and 'there, there'. Snow observed that this type of talk had an identifiable structure that was used by many of her adult subjects. This suggested that there was a particular *register*, or style of speaking, that was being used specifically with babies. This register became known as 'Motherese'.

Mothers in these studies generally used Motherese to arouse their babies, and specifically to make them laugh and smile, or to calm baby down when he became overstimulated or fretful (Snow, 1977). As well as observing a specific register, analysis of film and transcripts showed a pattern of behaviour between mother and child that showed that the interactions involved a mutual turn-taking. Analysis of turn-taking showed that the majority of mothers in the studies responded to their children's sounds and movements, as well as trying to start verbal sound play with their babies (ibid.). Typically, baby would make a sound and mother would respond, then baby made another sound, which led to another response. Snow found that the mothers also gave meaning to apparently meaningless sounds emanating from the babies: so-called 'vegetative' sounds, such as burping or gurgling. It was suggested that these positive adult reactions, which are usually highly exaggerated in tone of voice and pitch, give babies a sense that making vocal sounds is not only pleasurable, but will create an enormous response from adults (Soderstrom, 2007). As we explore in detail in Chapter 2, extensive research in the field of adult–child interaction suggests that these types of playful encounters are not only important for communication and language, but crucial in developing the child's emotional wellbeing as part of the process of building early social relationships.

What was initially called 'Motherese' is now widely referred to as *Infant Directed Speech (IDS)*, in recognition that fathers and other carers also use this specific register, or style of talking, when playing with infants (Soderstrom, 2007). Extensive research into interactions between carers and children shows that adults alter their register as infants move towards using their first words, so that adults and children engage in less verbal play and have more exchanges that can be accurately described as 'conversation'. It was more appropriate to label the type of register that adults use with children who are now talking as *Child Directed Speech (CDS)*. Detailed analysis of CDS shows that it has an identifiable structure, including simplifications to vocabulary, changes in grammatical complexity and length of sentences. Significantly, it was found that the main reason for adults changing the way in which they talk is to achieve understanding (Fletcher, 1985).

Example 1.4 Child Directed Speech (CDS) with a child at different ages

(a) Two-year-old Isabelle is getting ready to go outside with her grandma:

Grandma: Give me my shoes, please. (Isabelle picks up her own shoes.)

Grandma: No. Not yours. I mean my shoes. (Isabelle stands still, looking slightly confused.)

Grandma: Pass me Grandma's shoes. Not Isabelle's shoes. No. Grandma's shoes.

Isabelle: Grandma shoe.

Grandma: That's right. Give them to Grandma. Well done. Good girl.

(b) Isabelle at 3;6 is getting ready with Grandma again.

Isabelle: Grandma, where your shoes? You put them downstairs? My shoes are over there.

Grandma: Yes. Mine are downstairs. Isabelle, have you seen my bag?

Isabelle: It upstairs. In the spare room.

Grandma: Can you get it for me please?

In Example 1.4a, Grandma gives her instruction in a mature adult form. When Isabelle clearly does not understand, she changes her register. The meaning is exactly the same, but instead of using 'my' and 'yours', she uses 'Grandma's' and 'Isabelle's' to refer to who owns the shoes. Grandma does this automatically, in order to quickly get the result that she wants, i.e. 'I want my shoes, but I also want my granddaughter to develop her language and enjoy talking with me.'

In Example 1.4b, Grandma's language reflects how Isabelle is now talking. She now uses 'my' and 'your' correctly, so Grandma no longer needs to use the simplified register that avoided these words. Again, Grandma's change in register is automatic, as she matches her use of language to Isabelle's.

Are Infant Directed Speech and Child Directed Speech necessary?

Across cultures, within communities and within families, there are wide differences in parenting styles, including ways in which parents interact with their young children. The extent to which using IDS and CDS influences language development, or whether they are needed at all, remains a subject of debate. Some linguists have argued that IDS and CDS are unimportant for language development, citing examples of children developing language despite the fact that their parents claim that they never used CDS when talking with their young children. Shirley Brice Heath, in her classic anthropological study of two communities in the US, observed that many children in one of the communities seemed to grow up without any CDS speech being addressed to them at all (Heath, 1983). Another study, involving interviews with parents in Kuwait, suggested that the parents claimed not to have used CDS. However, when these same adults were observed talking with their children, it was clear that they did adjust the way they spoke to their children by, for example, simplifying the vocabulary that they used (Haggan, 2002). This suggests that the main motivation of the adults in changing how they spoke with children, even if they were not aware of doing so, was to make sure that the children understood the meaning of what was being said to them (Pine, 1994).

> ### Example 1.5 Cultural influences on parents talking and playing with babies
>
> While leading a session on language development with a group of parents, I came across some very contrasting views. One mother from a West African country, with two children aged three and

seven, expressed a view that she had been right to pay attention to her children as babies only when they were hungry, needed changing or were either too hot or cold. She said that she didn't pick them up when they cried for any other reason, as this would 'spoil' them.

This caused a heated discussion among the parents about different parenting styles. The central issue was whether or not babies should be picked up and comforted when they cry. The parents were from many cultures, but the general view was that as a parent you make your own decisions about how you bring up your children. This includes how much you play and talk with them, though you will be influenced by the advice that your parents and parents-in-law give you.

A father from Ghana spoke to me after the meeting and expressed his own views about culture and parenting. As a father living in the UK, he knew that he was expected to play with his children and use what he described as 'baby talk'. However, he felt uncomfortable doing this because he worried that this type of interaction would make him 'lose my authority over my children' and that they would become 'undisciplined'. He much preferred to sit down at a table and teach them how to do puzzles, to read and to write their names. He also took them to the park, and the whole family attended church and regularly took part in large gatherings of family and friends. All of the family enjoyed singing together whenever they could. He felt that the time he spent with his children was helpful for their general learning, including language development, and would prepare them for doing well in school. He said that his wife felt the same, but pointed out that had the family been living in Ghana, much of the childcare would have been carried out by the grandparents, who would probably have spent a lot of time playing, singing and laughing with the young children, while the parents went out to work.

This example illustrates that parenting is an intensely personal and emotional experience. Parents' views on childhood and how they should respond to their children, including how they talk and play with them, will be influenced by their own experiences. This will include their experience of growing up within a particular culture. From my experience, some parents, and many fathers, are very self-conscious about using IDS, but still play and communicate with babies and very young children in a natural, positive and pleasurable way.

The discussion about the relative importance of IDS and CDS is fundamental for this book. If one takes the view that the quality of interaction with a young child has a minimal influence on language development, then we can assume that the best way to lead a child to the point where she is a competent communicator is to talk to her, from birth onwards, as if she were an adult. Yet, most adults who are successful at talking with children – i.e. adults who children respond to positively, understand and learn from – adapt how they talk to make sure that children understand what is being said to them. My personal and professional opinion is that young children need to spend time communicating with adults with whom they can build a close relationship. This time can involve IDS, but the important element of the time spent together is that child and adult should enjoy being together, so that a positive emotional bond is formed that includes communicating and talking in a pleasurable way. Adults need to feel comfortable in the way that they are sharing talk with children. By 'comfortable' I mean that they are able to communicate and explore ideas with children in a style that the child enjoys, responds to and learns from. This influences the child's growing sense of wellbeing and pleasure in using language. This topic is explored in detail in Chapters 2 and 5.

 Points for reflection and discussion

Do we need to use IDS when talking with babies and very young children? Do we need to use CDS with children who are older?

How can we support colleagues and parents who are not communicating successfully with children, because their language is 'too advanced'?

 Practical tasks

Talk with an older child with speech and language delay, ideally engaging him in conversation when you are doing something together, e.g. completing a puzzle or playing with playdough. Did you automatically simplify your language, and particularly your vocabulary and your questions when talking with him? What was the impact of doing this?

(This skill of 'tuning in' to the right level when talking with children at different stages of developing language comes with experience, as well as observing colleagues who are successful at communicating with children. We explore this in detail in chapters that follow.)

Try talking, for a short while only, with children as if you were talking to adults. Did you find this difficult? How did the children respond?

Spend time talking and playing with a baby. Experiment with using IDS and, for a short while, drop the exaggerated features of IDS and talk in a matter of fact way, as if you were talking with an adult.

Could you talk in IDS? How did you feel about it? Did it feel natural, or something you might need to practice? Was there a change in the baby's reaction when you changed the way you spoke? What might this mean?

Language development and learning in general: Bruner and scaffolding

While Chomsky's is a purely theoretical viewpoint and Snow's early observations were made under laboratory conditions, linguists and psychologists recognised that language development takes place within the very real world of everyday life. There was also a growing recognition that language does not develop as an isolated skill, but that children learn to talk as part of a process of intellectual growth, or cognitive development. Developmental psychologist Jerome Bruner was in the vanguard of exploring how children and adults talk together, and how these experiences influence learning, and language development in particular.

Bruner proposed that the development of cognition and language are influenced by how children and adults share experiences (Bruner, 1975). Through the minute analysis of interactions between children and their parents, he was able to show that children use language in order to communicate with other people, and that through this they learn the rules of language, as well as how to share meaning effectively. This 'parent–child interaction' is the context within which adults help children with their learning and language development. They do this by *scaffolding* learning: by showing children how to learn new skills based on what the children already know, while using language that is adapted to support the children's understanding (Bruner, 1983).

The notion of adults scaffolding children's learning was influenced by, and an extension of, Lev Vygotsky's concept of the *Zone of Proximal Development* (1978). This can be described as the distance between what the child already knows and what they could learn with the support of a mature and experienced helper (Conkbayir and Pascal, 2014). For example, this could take place when an adult shows a child how to complete a puzzle of a street scene. The child fits in a car shape first, because he finds that relatively easy to do. The adult, seeing the child struggle with the bus shape, picks up the bus and places it almost to within its corresponding hole. He encourages the child by pointing to the bus, saying, 'I think the bus fits in there. You have a go.' The child now sees where the bus should go and how it fits in place, so the next time he tries the puzzle he is able to fit in the car and bus with little effort, while saying 'bus' to himself. The adult had successfully scaffolded the child's learning by providing support without actually doing the task for the child, as well as by sharing related language that the child absorbs.

Bruner argues that the help that adults give to children through their social interactions, including meaningful conversation, provides a support system for children's general learning, and language development in particular. He describes this as being an external Language Acquisition Support System (LASS). Through engaging children in meaningful activities, accompanied by appropriate language, adults effectively promote language and learning (Bruner, 1983). Many of Bruner's observations took place in the home, and he is credited with influencing a generation of researchers who based their work on his pioneering techniques for collecting and analysing data (Conkbayir and Pascal, 2014).

Adults as teachers of language and social norms

Much of adult interaction with children is informal, spontaneous and takes place as part of play and being involved in routines of everyday life. However, there are instances where adults set out to teach very young children how to talk and behave. Jean Berko Gleason, for example, studied how parents teach their children social routines, such as saying 'hello' and 'bye bye' and how to respond when given a gift (Berko Gleason and Weintraub, 1976; Blank Grief and Berko Gleason, 1980). The findings from this research reinforce the idea that adults have a clear vision for the types of language skills they want their children to learn and use, within the norms of their particular community. These norms are often shared from a very early age. Adults also set out to teach children particular aspects of vocabulary, e.g. colours, shapes and numbers, and set great store by children having achieved such language milestones. Similarly, parents often teach their children songs and rhymes. Indeed, as we explore in Chapter 5, it may be possible to predict children's overall educational progress from the type of 'Home Learning Environment' that parents create for their children, including the quality, quantity and types of interactions and conversations that they experience (Melhuish, 2010).

Language 'acquisition', language 'development' and language 'learning'

Children receive a lot of information about language from adults talking with them. In order for children to develop language effectively, they need the adult to share experiences with them, where the children can be actively involved. If adults adapt the way they talk to an appropriate level, using vocabulary that is relevant, then children will have enough information to remember what has been said to them, and to use it to help them in their learning. Empiricists would suggest that, rather than children possessing a specific Language Acquisition Device that functions purely to help them with rules of grammar, language develops as part of learning in general: i.e., as a consequence of brain growth and maturation, physical development and sharing meaningful experiences with adults and other children.

The distinction between the acquisition of skills and the development of language processes is an important one. If we use the term 'acquire', then we agree with the idea that children gain skills automatically through a process of maturation. If we use the term 'develop', then we assume that language emerges through a process of children interacting with their peers and adults, as the child matures. The term 'learning' includes language development, but also refers to the process of general cognitive growth, again made possible by appropriate interaction with adults and other children. If one describes children 'learning' a language, this suggests a large element of conscious thinking on the part of the child, e.g. Amy in Example 1.1 about the nature of language and how to go about learning it. For the purposes of this book, we refer to the 'development' of communication and language, in recognition that it is an active process that involves children and other people interacting together. When interaction is at an appropriate level and meaningful, it facilitates, i.e. provides support for, the acquisition of the skills needed to communicate, such as the grammar and pronunciation specific to the child's family and community. These skills often emerge automatically with time. How they are used depends on the type of experience children have with communication. In the same sense, children who grow up as bilinguals, by speaking one language at home and then later having to speak another, will 'develop' their first language and then 'learn' the second. They 'acquire' the grammatical rules of one language and then consciously 'learn' the rules of a second.

Conclusion

This whistle-stop tour of the 'how' and the 'why' of language development brings us to an important conclusion: that what adults believe about language development is the biggest influence on how they talk with children. This in turn has a direct influence on how children develop as communicators. These beliefs are shaped by our own experience: within our own childhood, bringing up our own children, working with other peoples' children and through study.

The perspective that we explore throughout this book is that the most productive way of approaching the question 'How and why do children develop language?' is to look at speech and language development within a social context and ask, 'What is it that children and adults do together that helps children learn to talk effectively?' This perspective, that children develop as communicators, talkers and learners through interaction and conversation, is based on the following principles:

- Children are born with an inner drive to make sense of the world. This drive includes developing language and using it to learn
- The type of interaction children are involved in, with adults and other children, facilitates or hinders language development
- Imitation (even if it is largely unconscious) and rewards (even if they are essentially 'intrinsic', e.g. through a sense of wellbeing) play a part in facilitating language development.
- Interaction must be pleasurable for all involved
- There is interplay between genetically determined forces within the child and external experiences, supported by sensitive adult interaction. This facilitates children's language development and their learning about language, their place within the family, the community and society
- Language development is a holistic experience where understanding, speech and expressive language develop as part of the child's growing ability to communicate and use language to learn

The message developed in the following chapters can be encapsulated in one sentence:

Conversation is the place where children develop as talkers – through learning about language, themselves, the world and their place in that world.

 Points for reflection and discussion

A big question (and it is very big) concerns children who for some reason are finding language-learning difficult. Can we expect them to acquire grammar through conversation only, or should we plan to involve activities that set out to teach them the rules of grammar?

  This could be a very important discussion to have with a psychologist or speech and language therapist who is working with a child with additional language-learning needs.

Further reading

Conkbayir, M. and Pascal, C. (2014) *Early Childhood Theories and Contemporary Issues: An Introduction*. London: Bloomsbury.

Crystal, D. (2007) *How Language Works: How Babies Babble, Words Change Meaning and Languages Live or Die*. Harmondsworth: Penguin.

Levine, L.E. and Munsch, J. (2010) *Child Development: An Active Learning Approach*. London: Sage, particularly Chapter 9, 'Language development'.

McDonagh, J. and McDonagh, S. (2008) 'Learning to talk, talking to learn', in J. Marsh and E. Hallet (eds), *Desirable Literacies: Approaches to Language and Literacy in the Early Years*. London: Sage, pp. 1–17.

Saxton, M. (2010) *Child Language Acquisition and Development*. London: Sage.

Stilwell Peccei, J. (2006) *Child Language: A Resource Book for Students*. Abingdon: Routledge.

CHAPTER 2

BABIES AND ADULTS COMMUNICATING AND LEARNING TOGETHER

This chapter will

- Outline how a baby's emotional, social, communication and cognitive development are interrelated
- Explore how babies from birth to nine months develop the foundations for talking
- Give examples of projects that support parents and practitioners to form intuitive relationships with babies

The title of this chapter has been chosen carefully to suggest that, like any partnership, the growing relationship between baby and parent, and later baby and other carers, is a two-way process. This involves both partners getting to know each other, including their likes and dislikes, and how best to communicate. An important role for parents and practitioners is to adjust how they respond to a baby's rapidly expanding social, communicative and cognitive needs, in a way that will encourage the baby to become a confident and competent communicator and learner.

Our examples in this chapter, from observations made on home visits to a family that I knew well, illustrate just how rapid the baby's development is, and how parents are able to adapt to the baby's rapidly changing ability to communicate. Though the examples are short, they contain a wealth of information that we will explore throughout the chapter.

Example 2.1 Natasha at two days old: a baby's fixation on her mother's face

Three-year-old Natasha's Mum and Dad are looking back through video clips they made of Natasha when she was a newborn baby.

Baby Natasha had just come home after being born in hospital. She spent most of her first week sleeping, and only woke up for a feed and to have a quick look around. It is this looking that has been captured on film. There is a period of about a minute when Natasha locks her gaze onto her mother's face. Mum says, very quietly, 'You're looking at me, aren't you? You know who I am, don't you?' As she says this, you can just make out baby Natasha moving her mouth and ever so slightly moving one of her hands. As Mum stops talking, baby stops moving. You can hear Dad off camera saying to his wife, 'Are you talking to me, love?' and Mum replies, a little tersely, 'I'm talking to the baby, you twit!'

Dad's interjection kind of kills the moment, but both adults have a laugh, which startles the baby. This 'love session' goes on for five minutes, and then baby falls asleep. Naturally, the proud parents didn't film many clips of Natasha crying, though there are a few that show how Mum was able to stop baby from crying by giving her a feed.

Looking back on these early days, Mum is very definite that she could recognise the different types of cries that Natasha used. She also says that as soon as Natasha was born, Natasha recognised her mother straight away – including recognising her mother's voice. 'Recognised'? 'Used'? Is Mum really suggesting that this two-day-old baby can do things consciously, and has detailed knowledge about who her mother is? Like many first-time parents, Natasha's Mum and Dad were relatively unprepared for parenthood when Natasha was born. They had attended antenatal classes and had read a few books on what to expect from their baby in early infancy. However, this short vignette shows that Mum used her intuition. This gave her insight into exactly how babies operate, and what her baby needed in order to have a great start as a communicator, and to be a healthy and happy child. This concept that babies need to be talked to and responded to came naturally to Natasha's mother, as part of her belief system about childhood.

Looking at each other: 'intersubjectivity' and communication

Since the 1970s, researchers have been involved in the microanalysis of film of mothers and infants in face-to-face interaction. Andrew Meltzoff, Daniel Stern and Colwyn Trevarthen, for example, have all written extensively about the importance, from birth, of early parent–child interaction (Beebe et al., 2003). Meltzoff sees the baby's ability to imitate some of the parents' facial movements as an indicator that the infant already has an understanding that the parent exists as a separate entity, but has emotional states similar to the baby's own (Meltzoff, 1999). The parents' role is important in the very early 'scaffolding' of cognitive development by supporting the baby's emerging awareness that there is an environment that exists outside of themselves and that 'mummy is just like me' (Meltzoff and Gopnik, 1993). This, Meltzoff suggests, is the beginning of the child's *Theory of Mind*, i.e. that 'other people have thoughts and feelings the same as my own'.

The concept of Theory of Mind is explored extensively in research about children with Autism Spectrum Disorder (ASD). Children with ASD, it is suggested, have a fundamental difficulty in seeing the world from someone else's viewpoint or, in some cases, recognising that other people have thoughts that influence what they say or do. This aspect of their disability can make other people's behaviour seem random and unpredictable and create high anxiety (Baron-Cohen, 1995; Attwood, 2008).

Example 2.2 Natasha at four months: early steps in the dance of communication

Mum has a visitor: it's her friend who is expecting a baby. Natasha is sitting in her baby bouncer on the floor in front of the television, studying the rapidly changing images. Mum and friend start talking, and immediately Natasha turns around in their direction and starts kicking her feet up and down, which makes the bouncer rock. This is the cue for Mum to make Natasha show off her latest 'clever trick'.

Mum (moving the bouncer and baby away from the TV): You like that don't you? You like to hear people talking!

(To friend): Watch this. I know how to make her laugh.

(Mum makes a grab for Natasha's tummy and tickles her.)
Tickle … Tickle … TICKLE!!

(Natasha cries, instead of laughing.)

Mum (soothing voice):   Oh, sorry! Silly Mummy did it too quickly and took you by surprise. Let's start again.

(Keeps tickling Natasha's tummy and exclaiming, 'Gotcha! Gotcha! Gotcha!' until Natasha laughs.)

Mum (to friend):   This is the best bit, watch this.

(Mum stops tickling.)

Natasha (looks at Mum intently):   Ah!

Mum: Gotcha, gotcha, gotcha!!

Natasha (watches Mum intently):   Ah!

Mum: Ah! AH! (Tickles Natasha.) You clever girl! Who's Mummy's clever girl? Clever girl! You knew Mummy was going to do it, didn't you! (Natasha smiles.)

Daniel Stern suggested that there are two different functions for the type of exchanges that we see between Natasha and her mother in Examples 2.1 and 2.2. Shortly after birth, the spontaneous imitation of baby and mother ('simultaneous exchanges') lead to emotional bonding and a feeling of 'oneness', i.e. 'I am a unique individual.' Other exchanges, as in Example 2.2, where mother encourages baby to communicate that she wants to be tickled again, are 'sequential' and 'alternating' exchanges, that support language development (Stern, 1985, 1998).

These types of play sessions, where the baby's initial action or vocal sound provokes an adult response, which in turn is responded to by the baby, have been described as *proto-conversations* (Snow, 1977; Trevarthen, 1977; Bruner, 1983). As in the term 'prototype car', meaning one car that is built to test out how it handles or whether it needs adaptations before it goes into full production, the proto-conversation is a 'road test' for later, real conversations. The proto-conversations that Natasha and her Mum engage in, including Mum's use of Infant Directed Speech (IDS), have many of the features of more mature conversations, including eye contact, waiting, listening and turn-taking.

Trevarthen regards the infants' imitating behaviour as *innate*, e.g. when Dad sticks his tongue out at his newborn daughter and she automatically responds. This behaviour is seen as important in beginning the process of forming emotional bonds, which will be a foundation for the child's language development, as well as helping the child feel part of the family and wider culture. When describing the concept of *primary intersubjectivity*, when child and adult look at each other, Trevarthen suggests that the concentration of adult and child on communicating with each other represents the first level of the foundations for communication. This includes being involved in intense eye contact, imitating facial expression and copying each other's vocal sounds. The baby's ability to imitate facial expression is far from random, but serves a specific purpose, which is to engage the parent in communication (Trevarthen et al., 2003).

Secondary intersubjectivity: looking at objects together

Example 2.3 Natasha at five months: reaching and laughing

Natasha has a favourite object that she knows she is not allowed to touch. It is a small helium-filled balloon attached to a stick, stuck into the earth in a plant pot on the windowsill. It belongs to her mother, and for the past month Natasha has enjoyed being held close to it so that she can look at it. Today, Natasha is being held by her grandfather, and they walk over to look out of the window. Natasha grabs the stick with the balloon on it and tries to put it in her mouth.

Grandad: Ah! You've got the balloon. Give it to Grandad! (Natasha tightens her grip on the stick.)

Grandad: Come on Tash! Let Grandad have it!

(Natasha drops the stick on the floor, and leans backwards to indicate that she wants to be put down on the floor.)

Grandad (bending down to retrieve the stick): There we are. Let's put it back in the pot.

(Natasha reaches for the stick. Grandad puts it back in the pot. As he walks away from the window, Natasha starts to cry. Grandad picks up Natasha's bottle of water and offers it to her. Natasha turns her face away from the bottle and squirms. Grandad finds a rattle and Natasha grabs it, shakes the rattle and hits Grandad on the nose. Mum enters the room and takes Natasha.)

Mum (to Natasha, smiling and with a high voice): What's going on? You know you're not supposed to have that balloon. Grandad didn't know. Are you messing Grandad around? You little monkey. Poor Grandad is not used to you and your little ways!

There has been a significant change in the way that baby Natasha behaves and communicates. Natasha now has an awareness of objects in her environment, and what she can do with them. This awareness has led to what is known as *secondary intersubjectivity* (Trevarthen and Hubley, 1978) or 'joint attention' (Baldwin, 1995), where the baby and an adult can look at an object together. This creates important opportunities for her to share attention with an adult and for the adults to talk about objects of joint interest, in what Trevarthen calls the 'Triangle of Attention' (Trevarthen, 1979). This stage of development comes about through a combination of physical and neurological maturation and cognitive development. Natasha can now clearly see an object that she has decided is interesting. She can reach for it, grab it, take it to her mouth and decide that she does not want to let it go. The involvement of the adult provides huge potential for Natasha to hear language being used meaningfully in a context that is very interesting.

Example 2.4 Natasha at nine months: pointing to show what she wants

Natasha is in her high chair in the kitchen. Dad is just finishing warming up her favourite meal of puréed broccoli and carrots.

Natasha (shouting loudly):	Uh! Uh!
Dad (not looking in her direction):	Yes, I know. You want your lunch!
Natasha:	Uh! Uh!!
Dad (looking at Natasha):	What is it? What is it? Are you hungry?
Natasha (pointing to a box of baby biscuits on the counter next to Dad):	UH! UH!! UH!!!
Dad:	I know! That's where the baby biscuits are! But you are not having one until all this lovely broccoli and carrot has disappeared into your big fat tummy (Tickles Natasha, who squirms and keeps pointing. Dad offers a spoonful of purée. Natasha spits it out and turns her head away.)
Dad (pointing to a banana):	Look at this great big banana that I've got for you.

(Continued)

(Continued)

(Natasha does not look at the banana, but keeps looking at the box of biscuits.)

Dad:	No Tash. You're not having a biscuit. Mum will go spare if she finds out you've had two of them.
Natasha (kicking her feet up and down. The sides of her mouth have started to curl downwards and she has closed her eyes):	Ah! Ah!!
Dad (rushes to the fridge and comes back with a pot of strawberry yoghurt. Dad holds it up by his own face and points to the pot):	Look, Natasha, here's your favourite yoghurt!

(Natasha looks at the yoghurt, looks at her Dad's face and stops protesting.)

Imperative pointing

Natasha's pointing for what she wants, or *imperative pointing* shows us that she understands how to communicate with her Dad in a very sophisticated way. Her thought processes may go something like this:

> I know what is in that box. I know that Dad knows, too. If I move my hand and stretch out my index finger or whole hand, Dad will not look at my finger, but will look in the direction of where I am pointing, until his gaze reaches a solid object. If he ignores me, then I will make a sound with my mouth. If he does not give me what I want, then I will make a loud sound with my mouth and start to squirm until I get what I want, or something equally as good.

This type of pointing emerges from the repeated experiences of joint attention/secondary intersubjectivity as described above. Judith Coupe-O'Kane and Juliet Goldbart, writing about children with profound learning disabilities, highlight the development of pointing as being one of the most important milestones in communication that precedes talking (Coupe-O'Kane and Goldbart, 1998). This is no exaggeration. Natasha's pointing shows a clear understanding of adults' behaviour and how to influence that behaviour. She is at the pre-verbal stage of communication in terms of her verbal expression – i.e. before she starts to use recognisable words – but her verbal comprehension, her understanding of language, is growing rapidly. Crucially, she is growing in her realisation that she can use non-verbal signals, including pointing, screwing up her face in disgust or refusal, and crying or laughing to show that she is displeased or pleased. The communication may be non-verbal, but in a few months her pointing will be supplemented with, and eventually replaced by, words. Furthermore, this pointing behaviour suggests that, should the parents be interested, this little girl's communication could be enhanced by her parents teaching her how to use signs, such as those from Makaton or British Sign Language, to communicate more successfully (Jones, 2014).

Non-verbal communication

It stands to reason that children in the pre-verbal stage will be developing non-verbal skills: after all, they as yet have no words to express themselves. The understanding of other people's non-verbal signals is crucial for all successful communication, and this process begins from birth. Sioban Boyce, who worked for many years as a speech and language therapist, describes non-verbal communication in detail (Boyce, 2012). The baby's interpretation of facial expression and tone of voice are particularly important. Boyce describes how children in their early years need to have many hundreds of experiences of watching the faces of people talking and of linking people's facial expressions to the tone of voice that they use. This gives children essential information about what is being said. This includes understanding the message, as well as the emotional content of the message, which is conveyed by tone of voice and facial expression. Boyce distinguishes between 'eye gazing' and 'eye contact'. A newborn baby will gaze fixedly into her mother's face, and will soon gaze fixedly at bright lights, balloons and the mobile hanging above her cot. Eye contact is more subtle, and involves looking at a person's eyes, making contact when their eyes meet and then looking away when it is appropriate.

The baby particularly needs to see these faces when other people are talking. Not just talking to the baby, but just as importantly when people are having conversations with each other. For this reason, Boyce attaches particular importance to family mealtimes, where a baby can watch people looking at each other, reaching and passing, offering, refusing politely, being offered again, refusing more firmly, giving in, discussing, agreeing, disagreeing, being quiet and watching, being told off, being praised, spilling things and the effect this has, clearing away, bringing, being pleased, being disappointed, being bored, asking questions ... the list goes on and on, and the experience is just what young children need. If young children

are regularly involved in mealtimes, then they will be able to observe people doing all of these things with each other. At first, all the words have no
meaning, but because mealtimes are rituals, with language that is repetitive and predictable, language will gradually start to make sense.

The involvement of the baby in play and talk, often in quite ritualised
ways, can become such an important aspect of the baby's life, that when
it stops it can be quite a shock. The Still Face Paradigm experiments show
this in graphic detail (Tronick et al., 1979). Edward Tronick and colleagues
devised an experiment where a mother talks and interacts with her baby
using IDS, in the natural way that the baby is used to. At a given signal,
the mother stops talking and adopts a completely still face. Babies under
seven months became confused and very quickly stopped making the vocal
sounds that they had previously been using in response to their mothers'
interaction. When this experiment was repeated with babies over seven
months, the baby actively tried to get the mother's attention by making
noises and movements, clapping hands and trying to touch her. In fact,
they were using all the tricks that they had learned in the past few months
while playing and being engaged in IDS with their mother. Some babies
began to cry, at which point the mother was, quite rightly, unwilling to keep
up her still face and went to comfort her child. This research points towards
the establishment of a deep relationship between the mother and the child,
which is firmly based on interaction. This interaction involves the mother
in exaggerated forms of vocal play. The baby responds to this stimulation in
positive ways, using vocalisations, which the mother, in turn, responds to.
Many of these interactions are predicable, revolving around games such as
hand-clapping and peek-a-boo and using silly sounds and pet names for the
baby. The temporary removal of these familiar interactions, and the distress
that this causes the child, shows how important early playful interaction
has become for the child's emotional wellbeing.

The growth of love, attachment and babies' brains

The growth of intersubjectivity, from gazing into the parent's face to sharing a joint interest with another person, is a sign of the child's cognitive
development and the strengthening of the foundation of communication
and language. It takes place within a highly emotional relationship
between parents and child. So far, we have made the assumption that both
parents are very much 'in tune' with their baby, in the sense that they are
able to interpret what their baby needs and wants, and are enjoying sharing the adventure of her emerging skills and abilities. This mutual enjoyment grows from the baby and her parents sharing a sense of wellbeing.
Underlying the developing relationship between parents and child is an
understanding that a baby needs to be played with and talked to, and that
this play and talk will change as baby rapidly develops. For many parents,
this comes from an intuitive response to baby. It is through the process of

bonding and *attachment* that the growth of the intense communication described above takes place.

Sue Gerhardt is a psychoanalytic psychotherapist and the author of *Why Love Matters: How Affection Shapes a Baby's Brain* (Gerhardt, 2015). Her work, which is based on *Attachment Theory*, has had a major influence of the way that children are cared for in day nurseries and other day care settings. Attachment Theory was brought to international attention by British psychologist, psychiatrist and psychoanalyst John Bowlby, who stated that a baby and her mother (or someone very close to the baby who does most of the caring) needs to become attached to their baby so that they can form a bond with each other (Bowlby, 1953). Gerhardt argues that, not only is this process of developing attachment essential for the baby's wellbeing, but it is also vital for the baby's brain development. She cites evidence that suggests that connections between *neurons* are made and strengthened in the baby's brain as a result of being involved in play and language. Positive experience in early play and social communication in infancy, it is argued, has an important role in brain development and particularly optimising the number of connections between neurons.

Gerhardt places particular emphasis on the need for parents to work hard to become 'attuned' to their baby's needs. Her view is that most parents are instinctively aware of what their baby needs, e.g. in the newborn phase, recognising the message that the baby is trying to communicate when the baby uses different types of cries. Parents then become sensitive to the baby's needs and are able to help the baby regulate her feelings. In other words, the baby has learned, 'I can make a noise that gets me food and attention, but because my parents understand me and respond, I don't need to make such a fuss. This makes me feel calm and loved.' This ability to self-regulate is very important for children because it helps them to learn to be calm and not to be overwhelmed by stress. Gerhardt argues that what babies require is to be cared for by someone who is sensitive to their needs and 'emotionally available', i.e. someone who is mature enough and comfortable with their own emotions so that they can give time and affection to the baby (Gerhardt, 2015). The intimate and positive relationships that children form with their parents help them to form attachments with other relatives, e.g. grandparents. Later, children can form attachments with the adults in a childcare setting and make friends with other children.

Maggie Harris, Specialist Health Visitor for Perinatal and Infant Mental Health, in a personal communication with the author, describes the importance of this early interaction and attachment as follows:

> It is now recognised that positive, sensitive experiences in early play and social communication in infancy enable the optimum neuronal pathways to develop in the infant's brain. In addition, if the carer is consistently emotionally attuned to the infant, then positive emotional connections are reinforced and can contribute to the development of a secure attachment.

Loving and communicating in the real world

Thus far, in the description of the early life of the baby and his parents, I may have given the erroneous impression that parents and baby should spend endless amounts of time interacting peacefully with each other, devoid of outside interruptions or stress. This is an unreal image. Naomi Stadlen, in her book *What Mothers Do: Especially When it Looks Like Nothing* (2004), recognises that parenthood can sometimes be extremely busy, stressful and even chaotic. However, Stadlen reinforces the view that the early relationship between mothers and their babies is vital, and that this relationship develops within the framework of the wider family and daily life. Stadlen also reinstates the term 'mothering', as opposed to 'parenting', in recognition of the vital role that mothers play in babies' lives. This is not to diminish the role of fathers, but acknowledges that it is the mother–baby relationship that is most crucial in the very early stages of life.

Families come in all shapes and sizes, and while parents may have been able to give significant amounts of time to nurturing their firstborn, this is going to be less likely when second or subsequent children are born, or when the baby enters childcare. However, Gerhardt's concept of 'being emotionally available' is an important one, particularly when we consider the differing styles that parents have when interacting with their babies. In Examples 2.1 and 2.2, we see that Natasha's mother uses quite significant amounts of IDS and gives the overall impression that she is emotionally responsive to her baby. We can also feel that adult and child gain a huge amount of pleasure from being together. Mum has an intuition that her baby is an active communicator, as well as knowing intuitively how to behave in order to create excitement and a sense of relaxation. In Examples 2.3 and 2.4, we see grandfather and father being just as attuned and responsive to Natasha, but not using IDS. They are communicating in an effective way, but not using the same register as Natasha's mother. Yet, the two men are making themselves emotionally available by showing that they are willing and able to share time with the child and to interact with her. This points us to the reality that adults differ in the way that they communicate with children. What is important is that adults attempt to respond to the child's efforts at communication, and share whatever time they have together in a positive way.

Early Years Consultant Debbie Brace also recognises that everyday family life is busy. Her concept of 'Being in the Moment' has proved to be an important factor in helping parents become attuned or to 'tune into' their children (Jones, 2013). 'Being in the Moment' is a state of mind where parents feel that they can give their total attention to the child, even if only for a brief period. This is typically when adult and child are involved in intimate moments, such as changing a nappy, bathing and feeding, putting down to sleep or when the child is waking up. These regular events during a baby's day can add up to a significant amount of time. If parents and child are able to share moments of calm, this can support the baby to self-regulate and not feel desperate for attention. The baby will know that in those particular few minutes, even if it is having her nappy changed, her parent will be focusing on her feelings. These moments are important because they convey a message of emotional bonding. This approach to communication and attunement is similar to that of paediatrician and psychoanalyst Donald Winnicott, who recognised that early experiences within the busy family are crucial for the child's long-term emotional wellbeing (BBC Radio 4, 2013). Debbie Brace stresses the importance of this early emotional connection and communication on establishing the foundations for language (Jones, 2013).

Challenges for early relationships and communication

Our assumption so far has been that the baby has a drive to make sense of the world and actively seeks to build relationships with other people. However, there will be circumstances where the baby is unable to do this immediately after birth. This may be due to the need for intensive care, which can restrict the amount of interaction that parents can involve their children in. In some cases of developmental difficulties, the baby – e.g. with Down syndrome – may be unable to respond to the parents' initial attempts to build a relationship though interaction (Slonims et al., 2006). Children who later receive a diagnosis of Autism Spectrum Disorder may have responded differently to their parents' attempts at interaction when they were babies (Trevarthen and Daniel, 2005; Apicella et al., 2013). In these cases, parents may be able to access support to help them and their child build their early relationship as the basis of attachment and bonding and early communication.

It is also possible, from the baby's point of view, that some parents will seem very difficult to interact with. This could be because the mother was unwell after giving birth, or may suffer from post-natal depression, which can have the impact of reducing all communication, including with her baby (Cummings and Kouros, 2009). What seems most crucial for the baby is the extent to which the parent or caregiver is emotionally available and present for her, and can help her to regulate her states of hunger, pain and longing for connection (Emde and Easterbrooks, 1985). Emde further suggests that some parents can have difficulty with helping the baby because of difficulties with regulating their own feelings.

The work of T. Berry Brazelton and his colleagues has been instrumental in developing the knowledge and skills of professionals such as neonatal healthcare specialists, so that they can provide support to parents and babies who need help with establishing their relationship. The Brazelton Institute's Neonatal Behavioral Assessment Scale is designed to help parents, healthcare providers and researchers interpret the messages that the baby is giving through his behaviour. This helps adults understand what they will need to offer the child in terms of nurture, i.e. caring for the child in order to support her growth and development (Brazelton and Nugent, 1995).

Supporting the creation of attachments in baby rooms

Elinor Goldschmied and Sonia Jackson, in their influential book on good practice in care for young children, *People under Three: Young Children in Day Care* (2004) describe children's need to develop relationships with a few adults. Taking into account Goldschmied and Jackson's recommendations and subsequent research into best practice with very young children in childcare, many settings now adopt a 'Key Person' approach. Each adult in the team is designated as 'Key Person' for a small number of children in the setting, e.g. for three children in a baby room. This practitioner will have key care responsibilities for the child, as well as making detailed observations, recording progress and communicating with the parents of the practitioner's 'key children'.

One suggestion for helping very young children develop attachments with practitioners who care for them is to involve the children in special times during the day known as 'Islands of Intimacy'. Here, the Key Person finds calm moments to spend with a child when they can play together, e.g. exploring the contents of a basket with interesting objects that the child can handle. The Key Person might also make up a bag containing objects that are personal to the adult, e.g. a favourite book and small toys from when she was a child, car keys, her favourite socks and a laminated picture of her cat. Playing with these objects and talking about them with the child can help the child to get to know his Key Person as part of the process of becoming attached (Goldschmied and Jackson, 2004).

Catherine Croft and colleagues in Thurrock, Essex, extended this concept to include bags containing photographs and objects that are personal to the child, e.g. favourite toys from home and photographs of relatives (Croft, 2009). These were used during quiet moments, known as 'Island Time', when the child was able to look at and handle the objects and photos with a responsive adult. One child in a baby room that I was visiting, took great pleasure in pointing to her peg where her 'Island Time Bag' hung. This was a signal that the child wanted to explore with an adult some of the objects inside. One of her favourite items was a photograph of her Mum and Dad, which she would smile at and point to.

Bonding in the baby room: implications for babies in childcare

Attachment Theory and the work of Brazelton, Gerhardt and others have had a major impact in the field of childcare, including projects such as The Northamptonshire Baby Room Project (Lawrence and Stevenson, 2011a, 2011b) and Luton's Baby Matters (Jones, 2012a). These training programmes have been influenced by the understanding that children who have a secure attachment to their parents will be able to form attachments to other people, including relatives, or the staff who will be caring for them in childcare settings.

In addition, childcare practitioners need to be sensitive to children's emotional needs. Maria Robinson states that practitioners need: 'Kindness and loving affection, understanding and a degree of self-awareness' (Robinson, 2003). Trevarthen and colleagues state that: 'Infants require consistent and close adult attention, for rest, protection and nurturance and to benefit from playful communication' (2003: 41–42). Sally Featherstone makes it very clear that the most important feature of a setting that cares for babies should be the priority that staff give to developing attachment and attunement (Featherstone, 2011).

CASE STUDY 2.1

The Baby Room in Lewsey Nursery, Luton: 'We just know.'

I have visited this Baby Room in Luton on several occasions as part of a personal exploration of effective care and interaction and to see the impact of Luton Borough Council's 'Baby Matters' training programme.

On this particular visit, the children were aged from nine months to two years. There were four staff and 10 children during the morning, which included regular scheduled mealtimes (breakfast, mid-morning snack and lunch). The children were engaged in free play, either on their own, with other children or one-to-one with adults, in a free-flowing session where the adults responded to the children's exploratory play. This developed into a spontaneous drumming session, where one child was interested in a large tambour and several other children wanted to join him. The adults moved to this small group. One child, Dylan, had arrived late and had been crying for most of the session so far. One of the adults (Dylan's Key Person) stayed with Dylan and tried to engage him in various activities. He remained on the verge of crying and seemed not to want to become involved in taking part.

The drumming activity came to an end and moved into a planned, adult-led, foot-painting activity, involving the children changing into 'all-in-one' waterproof suits and taking off their shoes and socks. Dylan was reluctant to join in and so he sat on his Key Person's lap and watched the other children having noisy fun.

(Continued)

(Continued)

After spending 15 minutes on his Key Person's lap, Dylan began yawning. A conversation took place between the practitioners about Dylan's responses up to that point. The conclusion was that he was 'not his usual self' and that the Key Person should monitor him for another half an hour. Another conversation took place, and it was decided that Dylan was possibly 'feeling poorly'. Dylan ate his mid-morning snack, but shortly afterwards he was sick. His Key Person telephoned his mother, who immediately came to collect him.

Later, I asked the staff how they knew that Dylan was not well, as opposed to feeling tired, a bit grumpy or hungry. They all replied, 'We just knew.' When I asked about 'just knowing', I was given the following ideas:

- We have learned about his personality by interacting with him and observing him over the past few months
- We know when he is feeling tired
- We can tell when children are feeling unwell from our experience as practitioners
- We spend a lot of time talking with parents to find out whether children's negative reactions, such as crying and being fretful, are part of the process of separation from parents, or because of other factors like lack of sleep the night before, teething, etc.
- We try to meet all children's needs by being sensitive to their changing emotions, learning and physical needs
- We just know from experience and are keen to learn

This response to children's emotional, social and learning needs was professional, in the sense that the staff had a strong commitment to providing the best care that they could, including thinking about the environment and the resources in it and how these could be used for the children's maximum benefit. My overriding impression was that these adults were willing to make emotional bonds with the children. These bonds were in addition to those already forged by the children with their parents, and were providing the children with a firm foundation for language development and learning in an environment away from home.

Instinct, intuition and 'just knowing'

We noted above that Gerhardt views much of the mother's behaviour in the process of attachment as being 'instinctive' (Gerhardt, 2015).

This implies that this ability to interact is somehow biologically pre-determined, in the same way that the infant's drive to walk is instinctive to our species. This may be the case. However, if we use the term 'instinctive' with parents and practitioners – e.g. 'It's part of human instinct to become attached to babies and to play and talk with them' – we run the risk of alienating many parents who, for whatever reason, are experiencing difficulties with forming a positive relationship with their baby. Organisations such as Debbie Brace's 'Baby Talk and Play' and 'The Northamptonshire Baby Room Project' focus on involving parents or practitioners and babies in practical activities that help adults and children experience the positive emotions involved in playing and communicating successfully with each other. Experiencing these feelings in positive interactions helps the parents to feel when subsequent interactions are positive and successful. This can build an emotional intuition, as well as an intellectual conceptualisation, of what adults need to do in order to be successful early communicators.

For these reasons, the terms 'intuition' and 'intuitive' may be more appropriate to describe the type of adult interactions needed for successful communication. These words imply something that can be learned from experience, or an emotional state that can be reached through experience, as opposed to 'instinct' and 'instinctive', which imply a behaviour that is biologically determined. The staff in the baby room in Case Study 2.1, for example, had learned most of their skills through training and while working with babies, under the supervision of an experienced member of staff who led the team. The practitioners all enjoyed their work, while their experience and commitment had led them to a point where they were able to make intuitive judgements about children's emotional needs, communication and learning.

Conclusion

The development of an intimate and positive early relationship between the baby and his mother is crucial for the child's emotional development and his ability to form positive relationships with other people. Through these early relationships, the baby develops understanding of key aspects of non-verbal communication, including how to interpret facial expression and tone of voice, and develops the early communication skills that will influence later language development. Babies are also aware that other people have thoughts and that their behaviour can be influenced, e.g. by the baby pointing at an object. The baby also learns key skills that are crucial for successful conversation, including how to take turns in an exchange, as we explore in detail in Chapter 3.

Points for reflection and discussion

Given the importance attached to the baby's early relationships in childcare, what practical steps can be taken to ensure that babies are able to form attachments to staff in childcare settings?

Not all parents recognise the use of Infant Directed Speech as a valid form of communication with their children. How can we influence parents who are not familiar with IDS and intimate play with their babies, so that they can:

(a) Appreciate the importance you give towards attachment and early communication?
(b) Adopt some of these interaction styles at home?

How can we support parents who are experiencing difficulties with forming a positive relationship with their children?

How can we support colleagues who would benefit from help to become more intuitive in their interactions with babies in their care?

 Practical tasks

Observe parents or carers when they are together with their babies. Is there any interaction, and is it enjoyable for both parents and child?

(To be fair to the parents, it will need to be in a situation where there is a chance for parent and child to be relaxed – not the waiting room in a doctor's surgery, or when getting on or off a bus with a buggy and lots of shopping! It could be when parents are collecting the baby from childcare, or sitting in the park, or while sitting together on a train.)

How can you tell that the parent/carer is showing affection towards the child?

If things have not gone well, how would you have handled things differently? What advice would you give that parent/carer?

This activity helps us appreciate (if we haven't had the experience of parenting ourselves) that parenting is not the same as caring for a child in a childcare setting, where there are set routines, resources and no need to go on public transport or shopping! Most parents do not have prior experience of caring for children before they have their first child, so they may need support and guidance and affirmation that they are providing the best experiences for their babies.

Further reading

Conkbayir, M. and Pascal C. (2014) *Early Childhood Theories and Contemporary Issues: An Introduction.* London: Bloomsbury.

Gopnik, A. (2009) *The Philosophical Baby.* London: Bodley Head.

Gopnik, A., Meltzoff, A.N. and Kuhl, P. (1999) *How Babies Think.* London: Weidenfeld & Nicolson.

Saxton, M. (2010) *Child Language Acquisition and Development.* London: Sage.

Useful websites

Baby Talk and Play

www.babytalkandplay.co.uk (accessed 25 May 2015)

The website of educational consultant Debbie Brace, supporting positive relationships between parents and their very young children.

Makaton

www.makaton.org/aboutMakaton/ (accessed 25 May 2015)

A UK charity promoting the use of selected signs from British Sign Language to enhance children's communication, including those with additional learning needs.

The Northamptonshire Baby Room Project

www.northamptonshirebabyroom.org (accessed 25 May 2015)

A national training project for practitioners working with young children and professionals working with parents.

Siren Films

Providing training films and accompanying notes on many aspects of early child development, e.g. on attachment: http://sirenfilms.co.uk/product/attachment-in-practice/

and on early communication: http://sirenfilms.co.uk/product/born-to-talk/ (accessed 25 May 2015)

For a discussion about babies' and toddlers' early learning and the significance of their responses to the 'Still Face Paradigm' experiments, visit: www.youtube.com/watch?v=bG89Qxw30BM (accessed 25 May 2015)

Talk to Your Baby

www.literacytrust.org.uk/talk_to_your_baby (accessed 25 May 2015)

A useful website with information about early communication. Although it is primarily aimed at parents, there is a wealth of information and practical ideas for practitioners.

CHAPTER 3

TOWARDS FIRST WORDS

This chapter will

- Outline the phases that babies go through to reach the babbling stage, and how this gradually emerges into using first words
- Introduce two main theoretical approaches to the significance of babbling
- Explore how adult interaction with babies and toddlers supports progress towards first words

From cooing to babbling to 'scribble talk': the facts

Phase 1: Vegetative sounds to cooing

From birth to around eight weeks, the baby makes what are variously known as 'vegetative sounds' or 'reflexive vocalisations'. As these terms suggest, the oral sounds that baby's emit are often the result of bodily functions, e.g. burping. The baby's lips and tongue are largely involved with sucking and swallowing at this stage. 'Cooing' develops from around two months, where babies make sounds with their mouths that consist mainly of vowels like 'ih' and 'uh'. Here, air is passing through the baby's *vocal cords* and causing them to vibrate, creating *voice*. When the baby's mouth is open, this produces a vowel sound. Neurological and physical maturation is rapidly taking place, where the developing nervous system allows the baby to have more conscious control over movements. At the same time, organs and structures such as the baby's larynx ('voice box') grow and change shape, and the baby's muscles become stronger. This leads to a rapid change from automatic movements to those that come increasingly under the baby's control.

As the baby's vocal tract and muscles of breathing, lips and tongue develop, he begins to make more sounds. This is pleasurable for the baby, and often takes place when he is lying on his back. This allows the baby's tongue to rest naturally towards the back of his mouth, creating the contact that produces these 'back sounds' such as 'g' and 'k'. Many parents report that their baby does most cooing early in the morning, after a good sleep, when baby is relaxed, and without being aware that adults are present. Some babies make these sounds when they are laid down to rest, and it seems to have a soothing impact on them.

Phase 2: Sound play

Jean Stilwell Peccei describes the phase between four and six months as 'vocal play' and when 'children start testing their equipment' (2006). There are changes in pitch and we begin to hear a variety of sounds which are typical of adult speech. This is the start of the phase where the baby develops control over his lips, tongue and voice. The word 'control' is an important one, because it highlights the active role the baby plays in using whatever aspects of physical development are becoming available through maturation and physical growth, in the same way that they experiment with their hands and later their feet.

Phase 3: The babbling phase proper

At about six to eight months, our baby will be sitting up and making newer sounds, including the nasal 'm', where the lips are closed, air passes through the vocal cords causing them to vibrate and then passes down the nose. This is often recognised as the babbling phase proper, because the child is using a much wider range of sounds, including sound strings like 'ma-ma', which mamas and mummies all over the world are waiting for. If you are a father from a country where you will be referred to as 'Papa', then you won't have to wait much longer, but fathers in the UK need to be patient because the strings of 'da-da' and 'ta-ta' come a little bit later, when baby is able to use sounds where he can position his tongue up against his palate, with his mouth open.

Once the baby can pull himself into the standing position, at about 10 to 11 months, we have a definite sense that he is using a wide range of sounds, individual syllables and strings of syllables, such as 'aba-aba' and 'dad-dad-dad'. His 'intonation', the way that words rise and fall and are stressed as we speak, is beginning to sound like talking. What is particularly exciting for adults is that we assume that, by making these sounds, the child is in some way trying to communicate with us, and we respond as if the sounds have meaning. At this stage the baby is communicating that he wants to 'talk' with the person he is with, rather than trying to use actual 'words'. Many parents will copy the sounds that their children make, and this becomes part of the way that parents and children interact together.

Phase 4: Interactive babbling and 'scribble talk'

Here we see a dramatic shift in babbling. Not only is the baby using many more sound combinations, but he changes from making sounds to primarily give himself pleasure, to using them to communicate with other people (and sometimes with pets!). The baby also attempts to imitate sounds that parents make, and particularly when involved with adults using the exaggerated interactions of Infant Directed Speech (IDS). At this point, interaction with parents can become more sophisticated, where the child seems to 'talk' to adults using many of the features of conversation, such as using appropriate intonation, looking at the other person talking, taking turns and trying to copy what they have said. This is illustrated in a hilarious clip on YouTube known as 'The Talking Twin Babies', where two boys of about 15 months of age appear to be having a highly sophisticated conversation while using only babbled sounds (www.youtube.com/watch?v=_JmA2ClUvUY accessed 25 May 2015). David Crystal describes this stage, which directly precedes the infant's use of first words, as 'scribble talk' (1989), which they use when talking with themselves or as part of 'proto-conversations', as described in Chapter 2 (p. 35).

Babbling all over the world: an international language or just bodily functions?

The French musician Thierry 'Titi' Robin performs a song, 'La Rose de Jaipur', featuring a Hindi-speaking singer singing a lullaby and talking to a baby (Robin, 2000). The baby is probably about six months old and begins by making 'ahba' and 'ahah' vocalisations typical of that age. This presumably is a baby who is being brought up in a Hindi-speaking community. What I find remarkable is that I have heard babies of the same age making exactly the same sounds in France, Spain, Thailand, Cambodia, Greece and the UK. It is a widely held view, known by linguists as the 'Continuity Hypothesis', that babies all over the world make more or less the same sounds in babbling, and then gradually drop certain sounds in favour of those that feature in the language that they hear addressed to them and around them. This hypothesis accepts that the baby's repertoire of sounds used in babbling will grow as the baby's anatomy matures, but emphasises the part that the child's social environment plays in changes to the sounds babies make. The baby pays close attention to the reaction that he gets from his parents, and goes on to use the sounds that the adults take most delight in, including those that the adults copy in play. When children in the later babbling stage use sequences of syllables such as mama/papa/amma/abba/dada, parents all over the world delight in assigning particular meaning to these sounds and judge these to be the baby's first words. If we accept this hypothesis, then we recognise that parents have a very important role to play in moving the baby from making automatic vocal sounds to using speech and language meaningfully (Yule, 2014).

The alternative view, the 'Discontinuity Hypothesis', suggests that babbling has absolutely no relationship to language development. According to this hypothesis, infants produce sounds in no particular order and, as they grow, may drop certain sounds only to pick them up again in later months. Over time, infants will re-learn sounds and develop words in a specific language, irrespective of what sounds they made while babbling. When children finally reach the age where they are able to develop their home language, it is argued, they develop speech sounds in an orderly manner (Locke, 1989).

The reason why babies move through phases from cooing to babbling, in a more or less universal fashion, probably lies in a grey area between the two theories. The baby develops the ability to make sounds due to his maturing nervous system and developing vocal tract and musculature. As with other physical skills, such as crawling, cruising round the furniture and eventually walking, the infant is driven to practice his developing oral skills. As children's physical development is roughly identical across the world, it makes sense that babies should make similar sounds. However, once again, it is what adults *believe* about their baby's behaviour and how they respond that really counts. If parents respond to their baby's babbling as if it has some meaning, then the baby will associate making sounds with a positive response, and will be very likely to continue babbling. Whether this leads directly to the child's first words is a matter of opinion, but interaction with babies during this pre-verbal stage is highly beneficial for babies and parents. One crucial reason for responding to babbling as if it has meaning is that these early interactions help the baby to develop a feeling for the rules of interaction, i.e. the all-important understanding of the non-verbal cues needed for successful conversation, once the child develops verbal language. As was described in Chapter 2 (p. 39) these rules include how to gain attention through talking, how to initiate and maintain eye contact, how to identify a speaker's emotions through their facial expression and tone of voice and how to take turns in a conversation.

Difficulties in the babbling stage

Not all babies pass through the babbling phase in a uniform way. There is evidence that children with hearing impairment begin to babble, but the sounds that they use may be fewer than children with normal hearing. This may be due to impaired *auditory feedback*, i.e. where the children hear themselves making sounds. It is suggested that the children do not hear themselves making sounds, which prevents them from gaining pleasure from hearing themselves babbling (Oller and Eilers, 1988). Detailed observations of children with profound hearing impairment who have been fitted with *cochlear implants* at a time when normally hearing children are well beyond the babbling phase, suggest that as soon as the child's hearing improves, the child starts babbling (Robinshaw, 1996). I have witnessed this phenomenon when working with a three-year-old boy with profound hearing impairment and severe additional learning needs. He had been fitted with a cochlear implant six months previously. Up to that point, he had made few vocal sounds. However, when his cochlear implant was fitted, he began to babble. When his parents disconnected his implant each evening before he went to sleep, his babbling immediately ceased. This would suggest that as he could no longer hear himself making sounds, i.e. he no longer had auditory feedback, his pleasure in babbling also ceased.

Children who are later given a diagnosis of Autism Spectrum Disorder (ASD) may have shown early babbling behaviour, but failed to use it as a form of interaction with other people. It is also possible that infants with autism may be less motivated to use babbling socially, or that babbling may be delayed because the child's speech production is delayed. Recent research analysing the babbling behaviour of babies suggests that children with autism may actually use different babbling sounds to babies who grow to have normally developing communication (Warren et al., 2010). Some children with speech and language delay may stay at the babbling phase for longer than other children, or at the time of referral for speech and language therapy may still be in the stage of 'scribble talk'. The absence of babbling or remaining within a particular phase may represent a potential sign of cognitive delay (as in Down syndrome), difficulty with interaction (as in ASD) or speech and language delay. Practitioners working with babies who are known to be at risk of developmental delay should focus on stimulating these babies by encouraging early interaction and babbling. Equally, practitioners who engage babies in vocal play and encourage them to use babbling as part of IDS will be strengthening the foundations for children's speech and language development.

Points for reflection and discussion

What is your view on the importance of babbling for later language development?

How do you and your colleagues respond to babies who babble?

How do you communicate with parents about the possible significance of babbling for communication?

 Practical tasks

Observe a baby babbling. If you are working with them, make a recording of them babbling and keep it for your records. Compare this with their vocal sounds a few weeks or months later. Has there been any change?

If you are observing the baby as a stranger, e.g. in a public place, can you identify which phase they are in?

Do these babies also use pointing or forms of non-verbal communication at this stage? Do you have a sense that they might be using babbling as a means of communication with you or with their carers?

How does the baby respond if you copy their babbling or 'scribble talk'?

Can the baby copy your sounds, e.g. as part of an interactive game?

Declarative pointing: from 'I want that!' to 'Let's talk about that'

Example 3.1 Isaac at 11 months, looking and pointing at pigeons

Isaac is in the late babbling stage, using sequences of sounds and syllables in what seems like a conversation. Up until now, his use of pointing had been 'imperative', i.e. meaning 'I want that.' Physically, he is crawling and very keen to pull himself up to standing, by holding onto furniture and other people.

Isaac lives with his family on the second floor of a block of flats and he is very keen on pigeons. The first thing he hears when he wakes up

(Continued)

(Continued)

in the morning is a pigeon cooing, as they often roost on the balcony outside his bedroom window. Mum shoos them away whenever she sees them, as they are prone to make a mess. She shouts and waves, 'Shoo! Shoo! Go away pigeons!' and as they fly away, their wings make a flapping noise. Consequently, Isaac is a bit of a pigeon expert. Pigeons excite him because they are big, active and noisy, and he associates them with his Mummy getting very excited and raising her voice and waving her arms around. Mum often picks up Isaac and looks out of the window with him and comments on the birds flying in the sky or landing and taking off from the trees.

One morning in his nursery, Isaac bumped heads with another child and started to cry. A practitioner, Kristina, picked him up and tried to comfort him by looking out of window, in the hope that there was something exciting going on outside that would distract him from being upset. A pigeon landed in a tree outside the nursery fence. Isaac immediately forgot about his bump, began pointing at the pigeon and shouting, 'Deh! Deh!' To which Kristina replied, 'Yes. Look at that pigeon. He's a big one, isn't he?' This was a key moment in the development of Isaac's communication.

This was the first observed example of Isaac using 'declarative pointing', i.e. with the message, 'Look at that. That is interesting. I know what that is. Please talk to me about it.'

Kristina and Isaac stayed looking out of the window at the pigeon until it flew away two minutes later, at which point Kristina said, 'Look, Isaac. The pigeon is flying away now. Say, "Bye bye pigeon." Wave bye bye.' Isaac waved 'bye bye' and noticed that another practitioner was getting the mid-morning snack ready. He waved his hand in the direction of the snack table, while babbling and squirming, which meant that he was fully satisfied and wanted to be put down near where he could see what food was going to be on offer that morning.

The type of pointing that Isaac was using with Kristina differed significantly from imperative pointing. 'Proto-declarative' or 'declarative' pointing indicates that the infant wants to share an interest with another person. By using this point, the child recognises that the adult has a mind, i.e. that they can see the same thing and that she, too, can think about something that is of interest to the child (Camaioni et al., 2004). As discussed in Chapter 2 (p. 34), this Theory of Mind is crucial for effective communication. A child who realises that someone else can think about the same things as them is a child who will use all the skills they currently have to share an interest. Isaac currently is not using identifiable single words, but can use 'Deh!' – declarative pointing, excited facial expression and tone of voice to engage the adult in what he hopes will be an exciting piece of interaction.

Kristina's response to Isaac exemplifies how to maximise a child's comprehension, expression and emotional wellbeing. If adults are able to respond verbally to children when they use declarative pointing, then the interaction will be meaningful, with the potential for increasing the child's pleasure in communicating successfully. The child takes the lead when they start pointing, and this increases the likelihood that he will understand much of what is said to him in the interaction that will follow. Isaac didn't point to the plane flying high above the tree that the pigeon was sitting in. He is interested in planes, but it was the pigeon – a creature that he has some detailed knowledge of – that attracted his attention. Kristina had already lifted him up, and Isaac's cheek was resting against hers. As a result, they would be looking in almost exactly the same direction. When Isaac pointed, and said, 'Deh! Deh!' Kristina could make a well-informed guess about what Isaac was referring to.

So here we have an adult and child completely emotionally and linguistically in tune with each other, with the adult able to respond to what the child is pointing at. What Kristina said was ideal, too. She used the word 'pigeon' as part of a comment, in response to Isaac's pointing. This is an example of 'scaffolding', where the adult is aware of how to support the child towards his next step in learning, in this case by providing the words he needs to frame his emerging ideas.

Declarative pointing is an important indicator of the child's use of communication for making social relationships. Children with a diagnosis of Autism Spectrum Disorder (ASD) may use imperative pointing to get what they want, but not use pointing to draw an adult's attention to something in order to talk about it (Baron-Cohen, 1989; Baron-Cohen et al., 1992; Loveland and Landry, 1986; Dawson et al., 2004; Clements and Chawarska, 2010). Children with significant developmental delays may be taught how to use pointing to indicate what they want, but it may be some time before they are able to show that they want to be involved in sharing ideas about an object of interest by pointing or other non-verbal means, e.g. facial expression, eye pointing or excited body movements.

 Points for reflection and discussion

Development in the pre-verbal phase can be rapid, but can also last for several months before children use their first words.

What monitoring tools do you use to observe and record the changes in children's non-verbal development, such as imperative and declarative pointing?

Are you able to have the types of spontaneous interactions with children like the one between Kristina and Isaac in Example 3.1?

Practical activities

Helping children develop joint attention is an important aspect of working with children with delayed communication, as a precursor to developing language through conversation.

If you are aware that a child you are caring for possibly has developmental delay, look closely at how they are using pointing. If the child is having support from a speech and language therapist, ask about activities and approaches that can develop joint attention and using either imperative or declarative pointing.

Something Special and the growth of singing, talking and using signs with babies

In 2003, the BBC began airing a televison programme aimed at children with additional communication and learning needs. *Something Special* is now one of the most popular TV programmes for children in the UK between the ages of 18 months and three years, and older children with additional learning needs. The programme was developed from a belief that young children benefit from associating repetitive language with familiar experiences, and that their understanding and expression is facilitated when adults and children simultaneously speak and sign. The presenters, Justin Fletcher and his clown character Mister Tumble, use Makaton signs while simultaneously saying and/or singing key words selected for each programme. As a result, the concept of using signs from either Makaton or British Sign Language (BSL) has become part of the experience of most young children and their families.

Many settings across the UK involve children in regular singing and signing sessions, where they use agreed signs to accompany key words in children's popular songs. In addition, practitioners often use key signs as they talk with children, as part of play and everyday activities, e.g. at snack time. Here, words like 'more', 'finished' and names of foods can be introduced naturally and in a meaningful context. Signing and talking simultaneously with young children, to emphasise key words in context, is an important tool in helping children in the early stages of language development. There are also positive implications for using signing with older children, to introduce key mathematical concepts, the language of emotions and literacy (Jones, 2010, 2012b). Signing is also used with older children who have additional language learning needs as a way of developing their understanding and to facilitate their expressive language development.

Staff in the baby room at Isaac's nursery regularly use signing to reinforce children's understanding, but also to help children express themselves. The development of Isaac's use of declarative pointing took place during a phase when he began to use signs spontaneously to indicate his wants and needs, and to enthusiastically imitate adults' use of sign. 'More' was a very popular sign, which he regularly used in relation to bananas, which were his favourite food. Whenever he made the sign for 'more', to indicate 'I want another banana,' the adults would copy his sign and say, 'Oh! You want some more? (Using the sign for 'more'.) You'd like another banana?' (Using the sign for 'banana' at the same time.) Regular involvement in this type of exchange was highly significant in Isaac's communication and language development. By being responsive to Isaac's attempts at communication through signing, vocalisatons and pointing, the adults were sharing verbal and non-verbal interaction within a meaningful context. These successful interactions gave the child and adults pleasure and a sense of positive wellbeing. These experiences facilitated his progress into the next phase of his communication: the emergence into using first words. However, as we explore below, the process was to take some time.

 Points for reflection and discussion

Many settings use signs, often from the signing system Makaton, as part of singing sessions with children. Signing and talking, using key signs, is particularly effective when all practitioners agree to use selected signs as part of everyday communication with children at the stage before language emerges. What is your approach to signing? How effective is it?

How can you encourage parents to talk and sign at home?

Supporting children into their first words

Example 3.2 Isaac at 18 months: how long does the pre-verbal stage last?

Isaac is 18 months old and his parents are worried because he hasn't said his first words yet. Isaac's cousin Rebecca, who has just turned two, started talking when she was 13 months old and hasn't stopped since. Isaac's mother feels that, after a promising start, Isaac's progress in language development seems to have ground to a halt.

Mum is assuming that all children begin to talk in the same way as Isaac's cousin Rebecca, who one day pointed to her favourite soft toy

(Continued)

(Continued)

and said 'frog'. Mum has heard from many friends and relatives that girls are quicker at developing language than boys. This leads her to assume that Isaac will take longer to use his first words, because he is a boy. She also wonders whether the staff should stop using speaking and signing, because Isaac may have become 'lazy' because he can get his needs met by using basic signs. Should she be worried? What evidence is there that Isaac is making progress? Why isn't he talking yet, and what can be done to help him say his first words?

Isaac can point to his nose, ears, mouth, eyes, hair, tummy and various other body parts belonging to himself and other people. He is becoming interested in books, and particularly non-fiction photo books with colour photos of familiar objects or animals on each page. He can recognise photos of himself and close family members, including cousin Rebecca. If Mum asks Isaac, 'Where's Rebecca?' he will point at the photo. If she says to Isaac, 'Rebecca. That's Rebecca.' He will say, 'Ah!' To Mum's mind, that's just imitating, and can't really be classed as a 'word'. Mum, quite rightly, sees a 'first word' as a recognisable set of speech sounds that the child regularly uses to represent an object or person. For example, Rebecca said 'doh doh' to mean 'frog' and did this for a few months until it became 'dot'. Then it was 'foh', and now she is two years old and she calls it 'fod'.

Records of observations made in the baby room show that, for about six months, Isaac has been nodding and shaking his head to agree when you ask him a question, or refuse when you offer him something. He can wave 'bye bye' to people and passing trains and buses if you tell him to. (He's a very big fan of trains and buses. He lives near a railway station and near a busy bus route.) He is very keen on music and singing, and has several favourite action songs that he likes to sing along to. When singing, Isaac will 'dah, dah, dah' along to the song and claps and uses actions in the right places. He is watching people more when they are talking, and listening more to what they say.

Example 3.3 Incidental talk as part of a walk back home from the park with Dad

Isaac's Dad finished his studies and took an eight-week break before starting work. The family's first action was to cut Isaac's nursery place to mornings only, as Dad had a lot of time on his hands. So Dad set up a daily routine for himself and Isaac, while Mum was at work. Dad got Isaac his breakfast every morning before getting him dressed and taking him to nursery. At midday, they would take a slow walk home and have lunch. After lunch Isaac had his nap, and after that father and toddler usually went out on a little trip. Their favourite destination was the local park, as Isaac was very keen on the swings and the slide, but they might equally go for a ride on a bus or visit the local shops. There was a nice route to the park across the canal, where they could stop on the bridge and watch the trains. They took the buggy with them, but Dad encouraged Isaac to walk as much as possible. It was early summer, so the weather was reasonably warm.

Here are examples of language addressed to Isaac by his Dad:

Hold Daddy's hand. Let's cross the road. Are there any cars coming?

No. That's dirty. Put it down.

Up you get.

(They meet a neighbour): Hello! Who's that? Say 'hello'. (Dad to neighbour): Did you see Spurs last night? Shocking. That ref got it all wrong.

(To Isaac): Wave bye bye.

Look at that dog. What's that squirrel doing over there? Up you get. Careful!

You go and see those pigeons.

Up you get. Are your hands dirty?

Shall we buy a drink?

Pass the ball.

Don't take your shoes off.

What's wrong? Oh dear!

Can you hear a train? Shall we go and see one?

Hold Daddy's hand.

Let's go up the stairs. Or shall we go in the lift?

There doesn't appear to be any cohesive structure to the language that Dad directs towards Isaac. In truth, Dad hasn't really thought about Isaac's communication much, so he just does what he normally does – which is to talk about whatever Isaac is interested in and what needs to be done to get from A to B without too many accidents. But Dad doesn't talk all the time. What he talks about is related to what Isaac is doing. Isaac is looking at the pigeons, so Dad talks about the pigeons. Isaac falls over, so Dad tells him to get up. Isaac stops and listens to a police car siren, so Dad says, 'What's that?' It's true that Dad's language is mainly made up of comments about what Isaac is doing, and quite a lot of instructions. However, all of his language is contingent, i.e. everything he says is related to what the child does. This provides the all-important element of meaning to whatever is said. Furthermore, Isaac has a predictable structure in his life, which allows for repetition of experiences and repetition of contingent language.

In Example 3.3, we only included what the father said. Isaac did have a chance to respond to Dad's questions and comments, and below is another example that shows that Isaac is actually talking, and has been doing so for a few months. He may not be using the elusive 'first words' that his parents have been waiting for, but Isaac is almost there. Let's take another look at what was said on another walk, but this time with Isaac's contribution.

Example 3.4 Isaac and Dad walking in the rain

Dad:	Watch those puddles. (Isaac falls over.) Up you get.
Isaac:	Deh.
Dad:	You're all wet?
Isaac:	Deh.
Dad:	Show me. There?
Isaac:	Deh.
Dad:	Never mind. We'll change you when you get home.
Isaac (pointing to a flock of pigeons on the grass):	Deh!
Dad:	Eh? You want to see the pigeons?
Dad (talking to their neighbour):	Alright there? (To Isaac.) Say hello. (Isaac smiles at the neighbour.)
Dad (to neighbour):	Bad news about Spurs. We gave it away in the second half. Can't stop for a chat. I've got to get Isaac home. Wave bye bye. Come on then.
Isaac (pointing at a squirrel):	Deh!

Dad:	Eh? You can see a squirrel?
Isaac (pointing at a pigeon):	Deh!
Dad:	What? You can see a pigeon?
	Put that stick down. It looks a bit dirty.
Isaac (protesting):	Bah! Bah!
Dad:	Eh? Oh alright, we can take it home. (Isaac falls over and starts crying.)
	You've fallen over? Up you get. You want Daddy to help you? Daddy pick you up.
Isaac (lifting arms up):	Uh! Uh!
Dad:	You want Daddy to carry you? Quick then. Up we go!

Contingency, making meaning and cognitive development

It may seem just an everyday walk back home from the park, but this is a very important learning experience. Everything that Dad says to Isaac is meaningful. Isaac points to a pigeon and says 'Deh!' so Dad replies with 'What? You can see a pigeon?' which is an example of recasting. Recasting is a strategy that many adults use with young children, often without thinking about it. It is highly effective because it:

• Confirms for the child that the adult is listening and interested
• Acknowledges that the adult has understood
• Gives the child an accurate model of how he should talk
• Increases the child's sense of achievement that he has communicated successfully
• Encourages the child to talk further

What Dad says is contingent on Isaac's talk, responding to the meaning and scaffolding the child's development by giving him the words to express his thought. When they arrive at their block of flats, Dad gives the choice between going in the lift and walking up the stairs. While they are in the lift, Isaac likes to press the buttons, and already knows the correct button to press for the second floor. Each of these experiences, repeated daily, provides the necessary linguistic form for Isaac's growing awareness of his surroundings and thoughts about how he can act on his environment. For example, Isaac associates pressing a particular button with his home, and his father consistently says, 'Isaac press the button? That's right, number two.' Isaac is linking the word 'press' with the idea that pushing a button creates a movement in the lift. We should not be surprised to learn that 'pressabutton', 'two' and 'lift' will feature in Isaac's first 50 words and phrases that he will later use regularly.

Mum and Dad didn't notice the dramatic change in Isaac's communication because they assumed that Isaac would be like his cousin Rebecca, i.e. using one word to clearly represent an object. Isaac's route to talking was a bit different. Practitioners at nursery began to observe that Isaac had become more involved in singing and signing sessions. When his Key Person sang a line of a song and left off the last word, Isaac would join in with the other children and have a go at filling in the gap. His Key Person noticed that he was laughing and smiling more and waving 'bye bye' without being told to do so. Crucially – and this was a new feature of his interaction – Isaac began to imitate spontaneously almost everything that was said to him.

Is it a coincidence that all this has taken place at nursery since Dad had begun collecting Isaac at lunchtime? For quite a while Isaac had been building up his physical skills, including walking without falling over, climbing on the sofa, jumping on his bed, climbing on the slide at nursery, picking up sticks and filling a bucket with small stones. He was very keen on walking. The daily walk home and the walks to the park in the afternoon had given him the time he needed to really explore walking. While he was doing this, he had the time to look around and see lots of his favourite things, like birds and sticks and trains, and to go on the swings and slide. Most importantly, he had an adult with him who was able to give a natural running commentary on what Isaac was doing and looking at. Isaac had all the non-verbal skills he needed for talking: he understood about conversation and taking turns and looking at people while they are talking to him. What probably had happened was that Isaac's early progress in expression had slowed down while he focused on developing his physical skills. Once he had mastered these, he was able to focus exclusively on what was being said to him. Equally, there had been a rapid expansion in his verbal comprehension due to his experiences at nursery and at home, including the use of signing. Being with his father and sharing meaningful experiences in a prolonged and unhurried fashion was the catalyst for Isaac's move from babbling towards using first words.

One meaning or two? What was Isaac's first word?

Looking again at the dialogue in Example 3.4, it seems that 'deh' was Isaac's first word. He used 'deh' to signal a range of meanings, as well as to imitate the last word that his Dad said to him. 'Deh!' means 'Look over there!' and 'Tell me about that,' but it also means 'Yes,' as in the short exchange:

Dad: You're all wet?

Isaac: Deh.

Dad: Show me. There?

Isaac: Deh.

But Isaac has other words, too: he only uses 'Uh! Uh!' (while making eye contact with an adult and with his arms raised) to signal 'Pick me up!' He only uses the expression 'Bah! Bah!' when he is protesting about something. These expressions, which Isaac uses regularly to communicate specific meanings, are 'proto-words', i.e. they are used instead of words. These proto-words are used regularly to convey not just one meaning, but a range of meanings. However, from this point onwards, the floodgates were opened. During regular book-sharing sessions with Dad, Isaac now consistently imitated what his Dad was saying. He stopped using proto-words like 'deh!' and recognisable single words began to appear in his streams of scribble talk. Whenever he used imperative pointing to indicate that he wanted something, he now accompanied it with 'dat' ('that'). A typical exchange between Isaac and Dad would now sound like this:

Isaac (pointing
to a box of juice):   Dat.

Dad: You want some juice?

Isaac: Yeh!

Dad: You want some juice?

Isaac: Doo.

Dad: Good boy! Here it is.

Everything that had been going on in Isaac's life thus far had been building up to his use of first words. The words that he eventually used were just the tip of an iceberg of social, cognitive and communicative development, with the following features beneath the surface:

- Understanding that talking is meaningful
- Having keen interests in objects and events in his life
- Knowing that a picture represents an object or person (symbolic understanding)
- Knowing that words can be used to represent objects or actions or people

- Making sense of questions ('Where's your nose?' etc.)
- Understanding pointing
- Understanding facial expressions
- Understanding tone of voice

Adult behaviour and attitudes

Isaac's parents were busy people. Mum had a full-time job and Dad was a student. This meant that they had to be very focused on using their time and energy in the best way possible. The day nursery staff were doing a great job, but parents are fundamentally their child's first and main teachers. The parents and practitioners between them had built up Isaac's non-verbal skills and understanding of language. If we imagine that we are able to ask Isaac to reflect back on what has helped him to be a happy and successful communicator thus far, these might be his responses:

- Having an adult being with me, who has time to talk with me
- Adults responding to me
- Adults creating a routine for my day
- Adults talking about what I am doing
- Adults allowing me to learn at my own pace
- Being allowed to 'talk' using a stream of sounds, and my parents recognising that this is me trying to communicate, as well as me role-playing being a talker
- Adults recognising that I am 'almost there'

Conclusion

Along with taking their first steps, children's use of their first words is one of the most eagerly awaited milestones in a young child's development. Children take different paths to first words, and some can take a lot longer than others. It is important that practitioners are able to plot progress in non-verbal development as well as the types of sounds that babies make and use. Practitioners working with children at this age should use every opportunity they can to encourage children's social use of sounds. Parents may benefit from information and the modelling of positive reactions to their children's emerging communication, so that they are able to support their children's progress towards first words, and beyond. If settings have invested in developing using signing, e.g. by attending training and introducing singing and signing sessions, it is important to ensure that all practitioners sign consistently and regularly with children. This will then encourage parents to adopt signing and simultaneous talking at home.

 Points for reflection and discussion

How detailed is your system for monitoring children's progress at the stage just before first word use?

Do you feel confident that it will have sufficient detail for you to have an informed discussion with parents?

Thinking about Isaac's Dad's use of language with his son, would you adopt the same approach (lots of comments and 'contingent' chat about what Isaac is doing)? Or would you use other strategies, e.g. adult-led activities to boost his vocabulary?

Why?

 Practical tasks

Imagine that Isaac's Dad asks you for advice about how to develop his son's language. What would you suggest?

Further reading

Crystal, D. (1989) *Listen to Your Child: A Parents' Guide to Children's Language.* London: Penguin.

Yule, G. (2014) *The Study of Language,* 5th edn. Cambridge: Cambridge University Press.

CHAPTER 4

TALKING WITH TWO-YEAR-OLDS

This chapter will

- Illustrate the rapid expansion of children's speech and language and their ability to convey complex meanings
- Introduce three theoretical approaches that explain this rapid expansion
- Explore how adults can effectively involve young children in conversation

Being two years old

The phase between 24 months and 36 months marks a rapid growth in physical ability and social development. The child's drive to explore and learn – about herself, other people and the world she lives in – is linked to her rapid growth in verbal comprehension, expressive language and pronunciation. This drive is tempered by the need to have adults close by to provide support, guidance and reassurance. Two-year-olds' 'tantrums' are a topic of great debate, including what causes them, how they can be avoided and whether they exist at all. One key issue for young two-year-olds who experience tantrums is their difficulty in fully expressing what they mean and how they feel, which generates enormous frustration. Twelve months later, many children will have experienced a dramatic increase in all aspects of language and communication. With this growth of language, children feel more confident about talking with adults, as well as developing relationships with other children (Lindon, 2012). Adults have an essential role to play in this period in order to support the child's social and language development, and particularly to assist children through periods of emotional turmoil, until they have sufficient language to express how they feel.

A particular feature of this stage in development is children's fascination with involvement in repetitive play and actions. Studies of what is described as children's *schema* play highlight ways that children use objects repetitively: to explore how they can be used and as a reflection of their growing cognitive development (Louis et al., 2008; Nutbrown, 2011). Children often have a fascination with spinning objects, throwing them, putting them into containers and taking them out again. Children are equally drawn to repetitive physical activity, including swinging, spinning and climbing on and jumping off low objects such as the sofa indoors and logs and stones outdoors (White, 2014). These activities provide many opportunities for developing children's language, particularly if adults are able to become involved in play and conversation with them for extended lengths of time, e.g. while children are on the swings and slide in the playground or garden.

Using spontaneous conversation to develop language

Example 4.1 Connor at two: talking about planes, birds and spiders

Connor has just had his second birthday. He is sitting on the back doorstep of his house, looking out onto the garden, talking with his father. His six-month-old little sister, Lauren, is playing with Mum on a blanket nearby. In this example, [ubudubuduba] represents the various sounds of 'scribble talk' that Connor uses between single words. An aeroplane flies overhead:

(a) Connor
(pointing excitedly):   Look! Bei! (Plane!)

Dad: Yes. It's a plane.

Connor: Bei! [Ubudubuduba] Updeh! (Up there!)
                         Bei! [Ubudubuduba] Updeh!

(Continued)

(Continued)

(Dad is looking at baby Lauren, so he doesn't respond.)

Connor:	Bei! Updeh! Updeh! Bei! (Repeated four times until Dad responds.)
Dad:	Yes. There's a plane up there in the sky.
Connor:	Bei! Updeh! Dai!! [Ubudubuduba]

(This exchange continues for two minutes, until a bird flies past and lands on the bird table.)

(b) Connor

(pointing excitedly):	Look! Bed! (Bird!)
Dad:	Yes. There's a bird. It's eating.
Connor:	Bed! Deh!
Dad:	Yes. It's a bird over there. He's eating seeds.
Connor (hears a pigeon in the tree and points excitedly towards it):	Look! Bed! Updeh!
Dad:	Yes. It's a pigeon over there. He's over there in the tree.
Connor:	Bed! Deh! Dee! (Tree.)

(This exchange continues for two minutes until Connor sees a butterfly.)

(c)

Connor:	Look! Baida!!! (Spider!)
Dad:	It's a butterfly. It's not a spider. It's a butterfly. Connor, say 'butterfly'.
Connor:	Baida! Bai!

(d) Connor's Mum brings baby Lauren to Dad. Lauren has Connor's cuddly toy rabbit in her mouth.

Connor (protesting and pointing to his sister and the rabbit):	Bebi!! Babi!!! Mine!!! (Baby. Rabbit! It's mine!)
Dad:	It's OK, Connor. I'll get your rabbit off Lauren. (Dad tries to take the rabbit, but Lauren hangs onto it.)

> Connor (now
> shouting and crying):   Babi!! Mine!!
>
> (Connor grabs the rabbit and Lauren starts crying. Dad gives Lauren a leaf to play with. She puts it in her mouth and stops crying.)
>
> Connor (to himself):   [Ubudubuduba] Bebi [Ubudubuduba] Babi [Ubudubuduba] mine!

Children at this age have particularly strong likes and dislikes. Connor's three main fascinations are animals, anything that flies and crawling insects. Most animals are referred to by the sound they make, apart from his favourite toy animal, which he always refers to as 'babi' (rabbit.) Planes and helicopters are 'bei' (plane) and insects are 'baida' (spider). Birds are 'bed'. Connor spends a lot of time looking upwards and seems incapable of allowing a plane, bird or butterfly to pass overhead without him commenting on it. He particularly enjoys throwing objects, and one wonders whether his pleasure in seeing stones, pine cones, wooden blocks, apples and plums fly through the air explains his interest in planes and birds!

Example 4.1 shows the tenacity that young children have to make sure that an adult acknowledges that they know what something is called. Connor seems driven to look at every plane, bird, butterfly or bee that he sees or hears. He seems equally driven to point at each flying object and tell someone that he has seen it and knows what it is called. It is fortunate that Connor's Dad is able to respond, because he uses the seven minutes they have together, before being interrupted by the baby, to respond and move his son's language development forward.

In exchange 4.1a, Dad acknowledges that he has heard Connor and repeats his son's comment, but using an adult form of English. He uses this 'recasting' naturally, without thinking about it, as part of his way of talking with Connor at that particular stage in his language development. Isaac's Dad in Example 3.4 uses the same technique, again without giving any thought to how he is talking. Recasting is a highly effective means of communicating with young children. Practitioners often use recasting as part of their particular interactive style that they have developed, either from experience or as a result of training.

In exchange 4.1b, Dad decides to add to Connor's comment by mentioning that the bird is 'eating'. Connor ignores this, preferring to explain that the bird is 'deh' (over there). Dad realises that Connor is not interested in talking about the birds eating, so when Connor reacts to the pigeon cooing, Dad introduces the word 'tree'. Connor immediately picks up on this new word and repeats back 'dee!' This suggests that he wants to focus on talking about where the bird is, rather than what it is doing. In 4.1c, Dad sets out to teach Connor a new word: 'butterfly'. Up to this point, Connor used 'spider' to name all creepy crawlies or flying insects, but Dad correctly judged that he would be able to teach his son a new word. Connor responds by calling the butterfly a 'spider butterfly'. Connor continued to do this for a few days, until he spontaneously called all butterflies 'bai', while spiders, ants and bees continued to be 'baida' for another six weeks. Suddenly, he was able to refer to each creature with a different name (ant = 'at', bees and wasps = 'bee' and only spiders were now called 'baida').

This was a seven-minute interaction that happened naturally and spontaneously. The father responded intuitively to his son, and clearly got pleasure from moving Connor's language development forwards. It's very unlikely that the father set out to use his time to develop his child's language in a systematic way: it was just something that seemed right at the time. Both conversational partners felt pleasure, and the end result was the learning of a new word, 'tree', and exploring a new concept: that spiders are creepy crawlies, but other creepy crawlies can have names, too. Dad had also been 'teaching' his son, in the sense that, just for a few minutes, he wanted to see if he could introduce a new word, 'tree', and make this an active part of Connor's expressive vocabulary. Successful communicators with young children are able to identify when using this type of interaction is appropriate, and make the most of these spontaneous moments to develop vocabulary and as part of scaffolding children's learning.

In broad terms, speech and language therapists and other professionals working in early years apply a 'one word at one year and two words at two years' rule: signifying that children would be expected to use their first words at about 12 months and begin combining words at about two years of age. On the surface, one might then assume that Connor's language development is progressing rather slowly. However, this extract from everyday life shows that Connor has already amassed a huge amount of knowledge about communication, understanding of language and expression. This example and others in this chapter illustrate three very important concepts that may help to explain the rapid growth in language that takes place during this period, i.e. the 'Naming Insight', the 'Word Explosion' and 'Word Mapping'.

Explaining rapid vocabulary development

Connor is showing that he understands that all objects can be named. He has had this Naming Insight (Barry, 2008; Bloom, 2000) from at least age 10 months, when he began responding to his mother asking him to point to various parts of his body. At the same time, he was able to understand and want to use simple signs like 'finished' and 'more'. Having this awareness contributes to young children developing an understanding of people's names, nouns and simple verbs, and to focus on them when they are involved in talk or when listening to talk in their environment. For example, Connor at 11 months knew that the words 'shoe' and 'socks' referred to anything that went on his feet. So, when his Mum complained to Connor's Dad one morning 'I can't seem to find Connor's sock anywhere!' Connor immediately started to shout and pull his other sock off. This Naming Insight allowed Connor to identify the individual word 'sock' within the stream of his mother's speech. Because most of Mum's talk with Connor was repetitive and based around every-day activities with Connor – including meals, changing clothes, getting dressed and undressed and getting ready to go out – Connor was able to focus on individual words that were associated with key objects and actions. Initially, he showed this knowledge through understanding what was said to him. By the time he was two, he was rapidly using these words spontaneously and through imitation.

Many children at age three have undergone a rapid expansion in expressive language development. They have progressed from using single words and making tentative attempts to combine words, to having an impressive vocabulary and expressing complex ideas. At three, for example, Connor was saying, 'Mummy. My no baby no more. My big boy now. Donnen she baby now. She poo in a nappy. My poo in a toilet now.' (Mummy, I'm not a baby any more. I'm a big boy. Lauren is still a baby, because she poos in her nappy, while I have graduated to using the toilet.) Up to about 18 months (and in Connor's case, 24 months), adults need to use highly repetitive language and involve children in thousands of exchanges focusing on the children's interests. The end result of this involvement is that children have gradually built up a bank of words that they begin to use spontaneously. Initially, each new word must be taught through a process of interaction, repetition and imitation. It seems like the child needs to hear a word hundreds of times before he begins to use it spontaneously. While this is true for children between 10 months and 18 months, this phase moves to a point where the child seems to need to only hear a word once and it becomes part of his regular vocabulary. Connor, in Example 4.1c, is about to move into this phase, as evidenced by his Dad's successful attempt at getting him to use the new word 'butterfly'.

The move from the slow phase of using new words to rapid expansion in vocabulary is referred to as the 'Word Spurt' or 'Word Explosion' (Bloom, 2000). How and why this happens – and whether it happens at all – is a matter of some debate (Bloom, 2004). One suggestion is that the child benefits from using 'Word Mapping'. This is the understanding of the concept that a group of similar objects can exist and that each of the objects within that group can be named. For example, Connor realises that 'insects' exist as a group of living creatures (though he doesn't need to know the word 'insect'). Originally, he refers to everything in this group as 'spider'. Eventually, he comes to realise, with help from his father, that each of these insects looks and behaves differently and can therefore be named differently. This understanding allows him to learn quickly and easily the name for 'butterfly' and then the name for any other creature that is small, crawls around or flies, or sometimes does both.

This suggests that Word Mapping was a significant factor in the rapid expansion of his vocabulary.

 Points for reflection and discussion

Many children at this age talk, like Connor in Example 4.1, with a great deal of intensity, as if everything they say is of vital importance. In the same way, their reactions can be very emotional and quite catastrophic if we don't understand what they say.

What are 'tantrums'? How much are they due to frustration at not being able to communicate effectively? Are there other forces at work that lead to these explosions of emotion?

 Practical tasks

How can we use children's fascination with 'schema' play to develop their vocabulary and use of language?

Play with a child who is involved in schema play, e.g. putting stones into a bucket until it is full and then emptying it out again. Drop a word or phrase into the play each time he drops a stone into the bucket, e.g. 'in it goes'. Observe his reaction. Does your language break his concentration or does he start imitating what you say?

Example 4.2 Connor at 2;6: in the garden with Grandad, talking about aeroplanes

[Ubudubuduba] represents all the padding sounds that Connor puts in to make his single words and two-word combinations sound like 'grown up talk'.

Connor: Dandad. Dandad. Pane.

Grandad: Yes. It's a plane.

Connor: Dandad. Pane [Ubudubuduba]. Upinagai. (Up in the sky.)

Grandad: Yes. It's a plane. It's up in the sky.

Connor:	Dandad. Dandad. Tonnor [Ubudubuduba] pane [Ubudubuduba] updere. Upingai.
Grandad:	Yes. It's a plane. In the sky.
Connor:	No. Tonnor [Ubudubuduba] plane [Ubudubuduba] updere.
Grandad:	It's a plane in the sky? Connor can see a plane in the sky?
Connor:	No! Tonnor, mummy, daddy. [Ubudubuduba] In pane. [Ubudubuduba] Updere! Upingai
Grandad:	I'm not sure what you are saying. Let's ask Mummy.

(Grandad seeks assistance from Connor's Mum. It transpires that he is saying, 'When I am a big boy I will go with mummy and daddy in a plane.' This firm conviction is based on a conversation that Connor had with his Dad two weeks previously while sharing a book about planes.)

Six months after our initial meeting with Connor, he is still thinking about planes and talking about them. On the surface, it might seem that his language development has not moved ahead significantly. He still uses 'scribble talk' to act as filler between single words and two-word phrases, and it appears that his vocabulary and the subjects he talks about are pretty much the same. Grandad is at a huge disadvantage, because he doesn't really know what Connor is talking about. This is because Connor is still quite difficult to understand, and as a result struggles to make himself understood with people who aren't familiar with him. It appears that he is still at the stage where he is driven to make comments about planes.

Grandad responds accordingly by using comments and 'recasting'. This, however, is not enough for Connor. He wants to share an extremely complex idea with his grandfather, i.e. 'I can't go on an aeroplane now, but one day, when I am bigger, I will go on one.' This shows that this little boy of 30 months has highly sophisticated thought processes. He knows that the metal thing in the sky, that at the moment looks tiny, is actually quite huge and is big enough to hold people. He is able to imagine himself as one day in the future being old enough to fly on a plane. He developed these sophisticated concepts because his parents understood his fascination with aircraft. They took him to the local library to borrow a non-fiction book about planes, which had illustrations of planes at the airport, people carrying luggage onto the plane and the plane flying in the sky. Connor had noticed a small detail on one page that sparked his imagination: a child sitting in a buggy holding a teddy bear, waiting in the queue to go onto the plane. This led to a conversation with his parents about whether children can go on planes, which concluded with the lines that Connor is to hear many times when he asks for something that is not appropriate yet: 'When you are a big boy.'

Talking with two-year-olds

Had Connor's Grandad, in Example 4.2, been aware of the message that his grandson was trying to convey, the conversation could have advanced in a completely different direction. He could have agreed with his grandson that, yes, he was still a bit young to fly in a plane, but certainly this would happen one day. Perhaps Grandad might have told a brief story about when he went on a plane and had his dinner of rice and vegetables and a cup of orange juice. This then might have led to Connor explaining what he might like to eat when he one day goes on a plane. But it was not to be, though doubtless there would be other opportunities for having that type of conversation.

This example of a missed opportunity reflects the challenge of talking with two-year-olds. They often have a lot to talk about, but adults who don't know them very well, or weren't present when the subject of the conversation took place, find it difficult to understand what the children are saying. This is much less of a problem for many children by the time they have reached three years of age, because their pronunciation and phonology is much clearer. Their vocabulary has expanded rapidly and they have more complex grammar at their disposal, both of which allow them to explain what they mean. In the meantime, it is very helpful for practitioners to know the context of what the child is talking about, i.e. what experiences he has been involved in when practitioners weren't with him. In early years settings, this can include asking parents what children did at the weekend, or asking parents to keep a short diary of things that happen at home.

Improving communication by improving adult interactive style

When we can't understand what a child is saying, it is a natural adult response to try and take 'control' of the conversation. One way to do this is to make sure that the adult always knows what will be talked about. A typical strategy, which can often become habitual, is mainly to ask children questions to which there can only be one correct answer, or either 'yes' or 'no'. This type of 'closed question' is not particularly conducive to enjoyable or effective conversation. In the following exchange, we have the feeling that the child is under interrogation:

Adult (pointing to a picture of a bus):	Tina. What's that?
Tina:	Bus.
Adult:	Good girl. What colour is it?
Tina:	Red.
Adult:	That's right. It's red. Is it big or small?
Tina:	Big.
Adult:	That's right. It's a big red bus.

The adult's aim here is to improve the child's language skills through teaching. While both child and adult are able to understand each other, the way that the adult engages the child in dialogue, i.e. his *conversational style*, is entirely controlling. Taking control like this gives the child no room to make comments, ask questions or otherwise use language in a natural way. If an adult uses this way of interacting as their main conversational style, then children are going to have limited benefit from talking with that person. There are many different techniques that adults can use to encourage children to become involved in conversation, and we explore these throughout the chapters that follow.

An important study from the 1980s, looking at adult conversations with children with hearing impairment and speech and language difficulties, provides an insight into how adults can communicate effectively with young children who are difficult to understand (Wood and Wood, 1984). The researchers were aware of the importance of adult conversation with children as a means to improve children's comprehension, expression and use of language. They were also aware that most children with severe or profound hearing impairment have two major disadvantages that prevent them from being involved in effective conversations, i.e. not being able to hear well and having significant pronunciation difficulties. This can lead to frequent misunderstandings and the need for the adult and child to constantly try to 'repair' the conversation by asking for clarification of what had been said.

The researchers viewed conversation as being a process where two people focused on the same ideas, by communicating together. In this study, 'success' was measured by the number of turns that each person took in the conversation. The more turns, and the longer the conversation, then the more 'successful' it would be. However, it is very difficult to keep minds fixed on a target when each participant has constantly to stop for clarification. This problem often occurs when the child is talking about something out of context, e.g. an event that the child, but not the adult, has taken part in. Although this study relates to children with hearing impairment, it reflects a similar experience for adults when talking with two-year-olds, so its findings are particularly relevant. In this particular study, the researchers wanted to see if they could influence the type of conversational style that adults used when talking to children, and whether this would have an impact on the effectiveness of conversations.

One finding that has particular relevance for talking with two-year-olds involves how adults responded when the children began a conversation about a subject that was out of context for the adult. For example, a child might walk into the classroom on a Monday morning and say, 'Me shops!' There were several possibilities for how an adult might respond, including telling the child how to 'talk properly', as in 'We say, "I went to the shops,"' or asking questions such as 'Did Mummy go with you?' or 'Who went with you?' or making comments such as 'I like the shops, too,' or 'Oh, the shops. Lovely!'

Telling the child how to 'talk properly' didn't allow the child to respond, and was likely to lead to him avoiding talking to any teacher who regularly talked to him like that! The question, 'Did Mummy go with you?' was likely to produce only single-word answers – either 'yes' or 'no'. Asking, 'Who went with you?' was equally likely to lead to a single word answer. In both cases where a question was asked, the child had answered the question, but the adult then needed to ask another question in order to get the conversation going again, possibly leading to the adult being in control. Equally problematic for the child was the adult assuming that when he said 'Me shops,' what he meant was 'I went to the shops.' This may not have been the case. He may have meant 'I want to go to the shops' or 'I'm going to the shops after school' or even 'I watched a TV programme about going to the shops.' The child didn't have sufficient language skills to be able to explain exactly what he meant, so the conversation broke down and in many cases was beyond repair!

The use of comments in this situation proved to be more effective than questioning. By making a comment that showed a personal interest, such as 'I like the shops, too,' the teacher showed that she had understood, at least in part, what the child had said. This comment then gave the child the space to answer in whatever way he liked, e.g. 'Me like shops.' This, in turn, gave the teacher the chance to make another comment, e.g. 'I went shopping yesterday.' This, in turn (literally), left a space for the child to follow up with their own comment, or possibly to use the word 'yesterday', as in 'Me shop. Yesterday.'

Using 'phatic comments', which indicate that you have understood and are making an emotional response, such as 'Really? That sounds interesting!' or 'The shops! Great!' is another technique for opening up the possibility for the child to respond. An adult who responds with enthusiasm – e.g. 'The shops! Wow! I love shopping!' or even 'Oh the shops! Lovely!' – is likely to generate an equally enthusiastic response from the child. Children who struggle to make themselves understood often develop some reluctance to talk. The use of phatic comments when responding to what they say conveys important messages to these 'reluctant talkers':

- I understand what you have to say
- What you say is exciting for me
- I'm interested in what you have to say
- Please tell me more!

From my personal experience, the use of commenting, and particularly using enthusiastic phatic comments, is by far the most effective way to involve two-year-olds with unclear speech – or older children with additional communication needs – in conversation.

The study by Wood and Wood (1984) showed that adults can change their style of talking with children, and doing this can have a significant impact on the children's ability to engage with them in conversation. This experience enhances children's language-learning, as well as promoting their self-esteem in relation to talking, which is an important component in learning to be a successful communicator. (We are assuming here that the adults have time to have such conversations with children. Not being able to find time to have uninterrupted conversations with small children can prove to be a significant barrier to effective talking and learning. Chapter 7 explores practical ways to have conversations with children in busy settings.)

Developing speech and language, developing confidence and developing learning

Example 4.3 Connor at 2;11 – sharing a book with a practitioner, Colette, in the book area of his room in nursery

One of Connor's favourite books is *The Big Red Bus* (Hindley and Benedict, 1996). It tells the story of a bus that blocks the road when its front wheel gets stuck in a hole. Various vehicles and their passengers arrive, but have to wait until a dumper truck comes along and fills up the hole. On the last page, we see a rabbit running across the filled-up hole.

(a)   A brief conversation as Connor and Colette are looking at the cover of the book:

Connor: My lite this boot. (I like this book.)

Colette: Is it your favourite? Is it your best book?

Connor: No. It not my bestest boot.

(Continued)

(Continued)

Colette: Oh. I thought it was your favourite. Mummy says you like it best of all.

Connor: No Tolette. My bestest boot is about panes. (Planes.)

Colette: So why don't you like this book so much?

Connor: Betos … Betos it dot no panes in. (Because it has no planes in it.)

(b) Adult and child have shared and talked about all the pages, and are looking at the rabbit on the last page:

Connor: My not dot a wabbit. (I haven't got a rabbit.) Tolette, you dot a wabbit?

Colette: No, but I have seen one.

Connor: My seen a wabbit too. My twoatid it. (I stroked it.) My twoatit it on hes tummy.

Colette: On his tummy? That's nice. I stroked a rabbit, too. I stroked it on his back.

Connor: My twoatid a dod on hes tummy. Tolette. Have you twoatid a dod?

Colette: Have I ever stroked a dog? Yes, I have. My sister has got a dog in her house. I stroke her a lot.

Connor: You twote you diter? (You stroke your sister?)

Colette: No, I stroke her dog! My sister's dog is a girl dog! I stroke my sister's dog!

This leads to a brief conversation about Colette's sister's dog, and how many brothers and sisters Colette has.

What has Connor learned and what can we learn about him? On the surface, we see that his phonological development has been rapid. He can't yet pronounce a [k] or [g] sound, so substitutes [t] and [d] instead. (This phenomenon, known as 'fronting' is very common in children of this age. Connor will continue to do this until he is five, when he will spontaneously use mature English speech patterns for most sounds in speech.) There has been an equally rapid expansion of the grammatical forms that he uses. He uses the past tense ('I stroked a rabbit') and he differentiates between 'his' and 'her' ('hes' – as in rhyming with 'fleas'). He is using an example of overgeneralisation when he says 'bestest', showing that he is trying to apply the rule in English that gives us 'longest/shortest/fastest' to the irregular 'better/best'.

This increased ability to express ideas allows Connor to communicate meaning, to use language to explore ideas and to learn. Sharing a familiar book provides the context for a discussion about what Connor likes, and allows Colette to ask a sophisticated but relevant question, e.g. 'So why don't you like this book so much?' This gives Connor the chance to formulate an accurate answer. In Example 4.3b, adult and child are able to explore experiences that are not directly related to the context of the story, i.e. about whether or not either has stroked a dog. This excerpt shows just how sophisticated Connor's use of language has become. For example, when he misunderstands what Colette means when she is talking about stroking her sister's dog, Connor is able to use exactly the same strategy that Colette had used previously to confirm meaning, i.e. turning Colette's statement, 'I stroke her a lot' into a question, 'You stroke your sister?' Adults often use this strategy when they are in conversation with each other, and Colette applies it without thinking when she is talking with children. One would presume that Connor picked up this technique quite naturally from being involved in conversation with adults. This is testimony not only to the child's complex use of language, but also to the way in which being involved in conversation with adults has shaped his ability to convey complex meanings.

Conclusion

We have the impression that Connor has changed rapidly in the past six months. Initially, his unclear speech restricted what he could talk about. This was particularly the case when trying to convey meaning to adults who found it difficult to tune into him, or when he was talking out of context. Now he is almost three, and able to use sophisticated linguistic techniques to explore ideas and to talk out of context. Example 4.3 shows us that Connor is a confident communicator, but also illustrates some of the skills that the practitioner needs in order to have effective conversations that are both natural and meaningful. The ability to be able to share ideas through talk, i.e. to talk in a way that is 'decontextualised', will be one of the most important attributes that will stand Connor in good stead as a communicator and learner in early years settings, in school and beyond. This theme is explored further in Chapter 9.

 Practical tasks

Engage children in conversation about something that they have done when you weren't there. Explore using the different types of responses described in the study by Wood and Wood. Observe children's

(Continued)

(Continued)

reactions when you ask closed questions, e.g. 'Was it nice?' or 'Did Daddy go with you?' or make enthusiastic comments about what they say, e.g. 'Oh. You saw a frog! Lovely!'

Does your reaction matter to older children with well-developed language, who might be able to 'repair' the conversation by correcting you when you misunderstand them?

How effective is enthusiastic commenting in helping younger children have a conversation with you?

Useful websites

Raising Children Network

www.raisingchildren.net.au (accessed 25 May 2015)

An excellent Australian website aiming to empower parents by increasing their understanding of children's development, including language development. It also describes theoretical issues and writes about research into language development in an accessible way, e.g.: http://raisingchildren.net.au/arti cles/language_development.html/context/1149 (accessed 25 May 2015)

CHAPTER 5

DIFFERENT EXPERIENCES OF TALKING AT HOME

This chapter will

- Explore the concept of adults' 'interactive style'
- Describe studies that highlight differences in children's experience of talking and learning at home
- Introduce the Effective Provision of Pre-school Education Project (EPPE) and the influence of a 'Positive Home Learning Environment'
- Begin an exploration of how practitioners can support children experiencing 'language impoverishment'

Since the 1960s, research has highlighted the wide variation in children's experience of talking at home and the potential influence this may have on achievement in school and beyond. Several studies, comparing the quantity and quality of conversations that children from different socio-economic groups are involved in, have had a major influence on opinion and government policy. This includes providing strategies and resourcing to help children whose experience of language at home has left them insufficiently equipped to achieve well at school.

Defining 'social class'

The studies that we refer to in this chapter focus on identifying aspects of language use within families that are defined as either 'High Socio-Economic Status' (also referred to as 'High SES', 'Middle Class' or 'White Collar') and those with Low Socio-Economic Status (also known as 'Low SES', 'Working Class' or 'Blue Collar') and families who are in receipt of welfare benefits. Families defined as 'middle class' will have parents who are working in a professional or managerial capacity and who are likely to have taken part in higher education. Parents in 'working-class' families will be involved in more manual jobs and may have left school with lower achievement than those in the middle-class group. The implications of being on welfare benefits, at least for the families involved in many studies, are that the parents may have had less educational success than those in working-class families and are broadly judged to be living in poverty. Whatever one's personal views on defining people in relation to their relative work status, these are the broad categories used in some influential studies of language and conversation in the home.

Studying language at home

'Naturalistic' studies use data based on recordings of children and adults talking while involved in everyday activities at home, in settings or school. Judging the quantity of talk is relatively straightforward, while deciding how to define 'quality' is more complex. Most research into the quality of talk looks at the reasons why adults and children speak to each other in any given exchange or 'speech act'. As most early studies involved mothers talking with their children, the term 'Maternal Interactive Style' was used to describe the way in which a mother talked with her children. In broad terms, mothers could be described as using either a 'child-centred' and essentially 'responsive' style (Wells and Gutfreund, 1987) or being largely 'directional' or 'controlling' (McDonald and Pien, 1982).

The key features of a 'Child-Centred Interactional Style' are where there is:

- Joint attention: adult and child are focused on what each one does and says
- Semantic relatedness: what the adult talks about is meaningful, because it is related to what the child does or says
- Appropriate complexity of adult language use, based on a desire to communicate effectively with the child

If adults use these features when talking with children, then they can be described as 'responsive'. The adult responds to what the child does and says and is able to adapt her language to ensure that the child understands her.

This leads to 'redundancy of meaning', where what the adult says to the child makes sense (Wells and Gutfreund, 1987). This gives the child 'processing space', allowing him to concentrate on thinking about responding to the adult, without having to give most of his time to interpreting the meaning of what was said to him (Lieven, 1984). The adult and child can therefore focus on learning through language and about language (Harris et al., 1986; Wells and Gutfreund, 1987).

The main features of a largely 'directional' or 'controlling' interactional style are where the adult mainly gives:

- Commands
- Requests
- Directives
- Instructions

There may also be an emphasis on 'prohibition', i.e. telling the child off, or an over-emphasis on being 'didactic', i.e. using talk mainly to tell the child how to do something (McDonald and Pien, 1982).

Although these descriptions are very broad, they are very useful and, in this chapter and those that follow, they provide the basis for our exploration of talking with children. Being able to describe accurately how adults talk with children can help to identify possible problems and provide ways to go about altering the adult's style. However, it is important to point out here that, as with any form of interaction, a balance needs to be struck between the various elements described above. In some situations, it is very important to be 'directional', e.g. where a child is doing something dangerous and needs to stop it. Likewise, an instructional approach is helpful when talking a child through a set of instructions for learning something new, e.g. how to put your jumper on. The adult who is skilled in talking with children has learned how to use various aspects of conversational style and knows when it is appropriate to use them.

Example 5.1 Child-Centred Interactional Style: Sarah at 2;9 with her Mum and a battery-powered puppy

Sarah is playing with her favourite toy, a small, fluffy, battery-operated puppy. When you switch it on, it stands on its hind legs and barks. Sarah is sitting on the floor in the living room. She is looking miserable:

Mum: What's the matter Sarah?

Sarah: He not work. He is brokened.

(Continued)

(Continued)

Mum: You think he's broken? Did you drop him?

Sarah: No. My not dropped him. He is just brokened.

Mum: How do you know? What do you think is the matter?

Sarah: He not bark anymore and he not jump up.

Mum: Shall I see if I can fix him? Can I have a go?

(Mum switches the dog on and off. He barks faintly, makes a vague attempt at sitting up, then stops.)

Mum: I think we need to change his batteries. I'll see if I can find some and then we can fix him.

Sarah: Put new batteries in him?

Mum: Yes. I think that will do the trick. I think we'll need a screwdriver as well.

Sarah: What?

Mum: A screwdriver. To open him up.

Sarah: A knife?

Mum: It's a bit like a knife. Let's go and find a screwdriver.

The conversation continued as they found the screwdriver, took out the old batteries, replaced them with new ones and got the puppy to work. Mother and child were both paying joint attention to the task in hand, which was of great interest to Sarah. Everything Mum said made sense, and allowed Sarah space to explore a new idea: about what a screwdriver is and what it is used for. When Mum, almost talking to herself, says, 'I think that will do the trick. I think we'll need a screwdriver as well.' Sarah does not understand, so Mum simplifies her language, which in turn opens up the possibility for Sarah to ask about 'screwdriver', which is a new concept.

The following example is an excerpt taken from a session that I recorded between a mother and daughter, Yolanda, in their home, finding out how the mother interacted with her daughter (Jones, 1988). This parent did not routinely involve her child in play and talk, so the session explored how the mother might use chat about everyday objects and activities, such as cooking and washing up, as a starting point in helping Yolanda with her significant language learning needs.

Example 5.2 Controlling/directional interactive style: Yolanda at 3;6 with her Mum and toy cooking-set

Mum (holding up a tray):	What's that?
Yolanda:	Uh. Uh. Uh. Spoon.
Mum:	No. It can't be a spoon. What is this?
Yolanda:	Uh.
Mum:	It's a tray. Say 'tray'. Yolanda. Look at me. Say 'tray'.
Yolanda:	Tray.
Mum (holding up a saucepan):	This is a saucepan.
Yolanda:	Saucepan.
Mum (pointing to a lid next to Yolanda's hand):	What have you got there?
Yolanda:	A take off.
Mum:	No. It's called a lid. Listen to Mummy. Say 'lid'. (Yolanda looks at the lid. Mum holds Yolanda's face.) Look at me, Yolanda. Say 'lid'.
Yolanda:	Lid.
Mum:	Can I have a plate please? Give me a plate.
Yolanda (giving the plate to Mum):	OK.
Mum:	What have you got in your hand now?
Yolanda:	A spoon.
Mum:	That's right.

This is an extreme example of an adult using a controlling or directional interactive style. The session was a challenge for both mother and

(Continued)

(Continued)

daughter as they were not used to playing together. Yolanda had effectively been brought up with very little verbal interaction, and what talk there was involved telling Yolanda what to do and what not to do. Yolanda had very severe language delay, almost certainly linked with her lack of involvement in verbal interaction.

Bernstein's Restricted and Elaborated Codes

Basil Bernstein was a British sociologist whose research in the 1960s examined the language used by groups of teenagers from working-class and middle-class families. These studies were to have a significant impact on educational thinking and policy. Bernstein used the term 'code' to describe the way in which people use language to show that they come from a particular group. Bernstein suggested that the working-class youths used what was described as a 'Restricted Code', as opposed to the 'Elaborated Code' used by their middle-class counterparts. A key difference in these codes was the use of vocabulary. The working-class subjects used a more basic vocabulary and were more likely to use non-specific words, like 'this/that/those'. The middle-class teenagers had wider vocabularies and as a result their language was more detailed. One suggestion from these findings was that certain working-class speakers may be restricted to talking about the 'here and now' (Bernstein, 1973).

Much has been written about Bernstein's work, including many ideas that he later suggested were unfairly attributed to him. He did not, for example, suggest that the language used by working-class children was 'deficient'. However, his work drew attention to the possibility that different experiences of talking in the home could in part explain why children grow up talking in different ways, and how this may have an impact on achievement in school and possible work choices. (Bernstein was a sociologist, and his use of the term 'code' differed from how it is used in linguistics. For example, children learning two languages who switch from one language to another, depending on what language the listener uses, are described as 'code switching'. Using words or phrases from two languages within the same sentence is referred to as 'code mixing'.)

Dialect, register and Standard English

We introduced the concept of *register* when describing how parents use Motherese or Infant Directed Speech (IDS) when playing with their babies and Child Directed Speech (CDS) when talking with older children (p. 22). 'Register' is often defined as the way in which someone changes the way they talk, depending on who they are talking to, as well as the social context. For example, I will use IDS with a baby and CDS when talking with a toddler, but immediately switch register to talk to a practitioner about that toddler. I know how to use CDS with older children and a different register when teaching teenagers. It's something that I am aware of and can now do without thinking about how to do it.

English 'dialects', on the other hand, are variations of English that have different vocabularies, grammatical variations and are often associated with a particular accent. Dialects usually originate from a particular city or region, and a listener who is not local can often find them difficult to understand. Cockney, for example, is a dialect associated with the East End of London, although slightly milder forms are used in different parts of London. Dialects are often very 'rich', in the sense that they may contain words and phrases that succinctly describe certain ideas (as we see in Example 5.3 below). However, dialects vary from what are regarded as the norm for talking and writing nationally.

'Standard English' is a more formal variation of English and is used in formal writing and by teachers in schools. It can vary across the world, so that North American English may have different vocabulary items or accepted grammatical norms (for example, it is acceptable in the USA to say, 'gotten' and 'have him come over here', instead of the Standard British English norms of 'got' and 'make him come over here'.

The three concepts of 'register', 'dialect' and 'Standard English' are very important for our discussion of how best to talk with children in settings, and how to support parents to develop their children's language at home. Some adults only use dialect and don't change their register, irrespective of who they are talking to. For example, one little boy I worked with, Johnny, who had considerable speech and language delay, had a mother and father who spoke in Cockney dialect at home. Whenever I spoke to Johnny's mother, she changed from speaking Cockney to using a register of English that was quite informal. For example, she would greet me with 'Alright, mate?' whenever she met me or talked to me on the phone. The little boy's father, on the other hand, insisted on using a highly informal register with me, which included quite a lot of swearing. His wife would constantly tell him off by saying, 'Don't talk to Mike like that. He's a pro.'

Johnny did not have language delay because his parents spoke Cockney, but because he had a hearing impairment. However, like Steven in Example 5.3 below, he copied the language of his parents. I spoke to him using the CDS register, and not Cockney dialect, because CDS was more effective for helping him understand me, and would enrich his vocabulary. One particular feature of both parents' language was their regular use of non-specific words such as 'thingy', 'whatsit' and 'whatnot'. This indicated to me that it would certainly be of benefit to Johnny if his parents made efforts to use a wider and more specific vocabulary when talking with him. I encouraged the parents to share storybooks with Johnny as a way of broadening his experience of hearing Standard English.

It is important to stress that I am not describing different dialects or the use of an informal register as in any way 'inferior' to Standard English. However, as children mature, they need to be exposed to, and involved in, using the variation of English that is used in school, which is Standard English. We return to this discussion in Chapter 8, when we explore the importance of practitioners being aware of different registers and when to use them, and setting standards for the type of English used by adults when talking with children in settings.

Example 5.3 Steven and 'the 'ump': an example of Restricted Code?

Steven is 4;9 and is in a Reception Class in a primary school. His teenage sister Caroline often has arguments with Steven's mother. Steven is from a working-class family in London and has a pronounced North London accent. Steven and his teacher have just shared a book, *Mrs Wishy-Washy*, about a set of farm animals that get a good scrubbing from Mrs Wishy-Washy and then immediately jump back into the mud (Cowley, 1998).

Steven: Mrs Wishy-Washy has got the 'ump with them animals!

Teacher: The 'ump?

Steven: Yeah. The 'ump. Good and proper.

Teacher: What's 'the 'ump'?

Steven: You know.

Teacher: I think I do. What do you mean?

Steven: Well my Mum always has the 'ump with Caroline when she won't get out of bed of a school day.

Teacher: Is it like when I get annoyed with some children in the class for throwing sand?

Steven: No. That's getting cross.

Teacher: How do you know I'm cross and haven't got the 'ump?

> Steven: 'Cos you tells us you are cross. My Mum says to Caroline, 'If you carry on like that, I'm going to get the 'ump with you good and proper.'
>
> Teacher: That sounds like getting really annoyed. I'd call that annoyed.
>
> Steven: I'd say so. Yes. Annoyed good and proper.

Is Steven showing that he comes from a background that uses Restricted Code? The term 'the 'ump' is typically used by working-class Londoners. It seems like a very good expression to describe a feeling that isn't quite 'getting cross', yet isn't the same as 'annoyance'. It's a particular feeling you might get when constantly having to chivvy a teenager to get out of bed on a school day. Steven is able to discuss the meaning of words, even if his vocabulary is not as advanced as other children in the class. However, we can see that the teacher is, quite rightly, using the discussion to teach Steven, by introducing new words into his vocabulary, in order to expand the way that Steven expresses himself.

 Points for reflection and discussion

Is Steven a child with restricted vocabulary? Is it right to say that his parents use 'Restricted Code'? The matter is not at all clear. However, what we do know is that many children in the UK fail in school because their language development is not adequate enough for them to access what is being taught. Having a restricted vocabulary and needing support to talk about ideas can contribute to difficulties with reading and writing in particular.
   What are your thoughts on this subject?

Talk at home: 'difference' or 'deficit'?

The Bristol Study was a longitudinal study, carried out throughout the 1970s, of the language development of 128 children between the ages of 13 months and starting school, using audiotape recordings of the children talking with members of their family at home (Wells, 1987). While researchers found a wide variation in how quickly individual children developed their language, recordings showed that conversation at home was often very rich and rewarding for both adults and children. This was irrespective of the families' socioeconomic background. Another study, reported on in the mid-1980s, compared conversations between mothers and their four-year-old girls at home, and the same children in conversation with adults in nursery schools (Tizard and Hughes, 2002). As in the Bristol Study, researchers found differences between the quantity and quality of conversations at home, and that these differences were related to the parents' socioeconomic background. When the research team looked at data collected from recordings between the same children and staff at nursery schools, they found that the quantity and quality of talk was greater at home than in nursery school. Wells also made comparisons between talk experiences at home and at school (Wells, 2009), and came to similar conclusions to Tizard and Hughes, i.e. that talk at home was often richer and more satisfying for the children, and ultimately more useful for their learning, than in settings.

These studies acknowledged that there were differences in the ways that many parents and children talked together, but looked critically at the idea that children from working-class homes were growing up in a language environment that was somehow 'deficient'. Their suggestion that children might be learning more from talking at home with their parents than with adults in settings was echoed by David Wood, in his influential book, *How Children Think and Learn* (1998). Wood suggests that many children are not experiencing learning difficulties at school because of a language 'deficit', but, rather, that certain children find it more difficult to explain to teachers what they mean.

Example 5.4 Talk at home: Jordan's Mum and the washing machine

Jordan is 2;3 and Evie 3;0. They live in a block of flats. Jordan is the son of Evie's upstairs neighbours. Their families are friends and the children often spend time together. Jordan's Mum works part-time in the kitchens at the local hospital, while Evie's Mum is a teacher. Jordan's Mum is in the kitchen, putting the washing in the washing machine. Jordan is looking for a banana to eat, while Evie, who has come up to play, wanders into the kitchen.

Jordan: Nana Mum!

Mum: It's 'banana'. And say 'please'. Evie says please, don'tcha darlin'? Hold on while I get this load of washing in.

Evie: My Mum got one 'chine like that.

Mum: Really? Bet it's quieter than mine!

Evie: My Mum hear your 'chine.

Mum:	It's a monster this one. Bang! Bang! Bang! Out the way, love. Look at that shirt. What a mess!
Jordan:	My want nana. Please!

(Mum ignores Jordan and carries on loading the washing machine.)

Jordan:	Mum!
Mum:	In a minute! In a minute! Look. I've only got one pair of hands. (Holds up her hands.) One, two. Pass me the washing powder will ya? If I don't get this load on, then it will rain soon and then we will have to dry all the washing indoors, and that's a right pain, that is.

(Jordan gets the powder out of the cupboard.)

Mum:	And the measuring cup an' all.
Evie:	My Mum got same one powder.
Mum:	Really?
Jordan:	My put powder? My press button?
Mum:	What about Evie? Can't she have a go?
Jordan:	No!
Mum:	Go on, meanie. You put in the powder. Evie can put in the conditioner, and you can press a button each.
Evie:	What's dishnah?
Mum:	What? Don't your Mum use it? It makes your clothes feel soft when they come out the washing machine.

This whole conversation, with the subsequent filling of the dispensers and the pressing of the buttons, lasted 10 minutes. Mum was busy, but she could see that the children were not going to give her any peace, so she involved them in the preparing of the washing machine. She also wants her son to learn to wait and to improve his pronunciation. Mum had not set out to give the children a lesson to boost their language and learning, but that was the end result of this short interaction. Granted, she is talking in her local North London *dialect* and accent, but that is irrelevant when we look at the information and ideas she shares with the children. Her washing machine is 'noisy' while Evie's is 'quieter'; you need to put washing 'outside' when it is not raining; if you dry it 'indoors' that is 'annoying' ('a right pain'); you can 'measure' the powder with a cup; you can use 'conditioner', too. No doubt Evie will have noticed the difference between the washing powder and the liquid conditioner. It is highly likely that when she next watches her Mum filling the washing machine she'll try and explain what she has seen upstairs. She may even try to ask a question about why her parents don't use conditioner. Jordan wasn't so involved in the conversation, but was listening intently, and negotiating with his mother.

While Evie's mother doesn't have such a pronounced London accent and doesn't use dialect when talking with her daughter, the content of the conversations at home will be similar. Evie's Mum is a teacher and will probably have a different way of explaining that she is busy, but the message will be the same, i.e. 'it's important to wait when you are asked to. You can join in with what I am doing, and talk about it too, but only if you are helpful.'

 Points for reflection and discussion

Jordan's mother in Example 5.4 uses a mild type of Cockney dialect and speaks with a London accent. For example, she says, 'Don't your Mum use it?' as opposed to the Standard English, 'Doesn't your Mum use it?' This doesn't stop Evie from understanding her. When she says 'don't' she leaves off the 't', which is typical of the London accent. Evie's Mum, on the other hand, does not use dialect.

By using dialect and a local accent, is Jordan's Mum limiting his ability to talk and learn?

Is her language and speech 'deficient' compared with Evie's Mum's Standard English?

The Effective Provision of Pre-school Education Project (EPPE) and the Home Learning Environment

The Effective Provision of Pre-school Education Project (EPPE) involved 3000 children and 141 settings in a longitudinal study. Its report describes the effects of early years education for children between the ages of three and four, as measured at primary school entry and when the children were aged six and seven years (Sylva et al., 2010). Among its many initial findings, and subsequent findings from further analyses of the data, the study highlighted the influence of what was termed the 'Home Learning Environment' (HLE). A 'positive HLE' includes parents involving their children in conversation, as well as singing songs, learning nursery rhymes and, when the children are ready, helping them understand the basics of number and letter-sound correspondence. A positive HLE was shown to have a long-lasting impact on children's ability to learn in early years and later in school (ibid.). In particular, these positive experiences with parents had the strongest influence on children's 'self-regulation', i.e. where children are actively engaged and thinking about their learning because they are highly motivated (Stewart, 2011). From the many findings based on the data from the EPPE project, one quote about children's home experience has great relevance here:

> For all the children, the quality of the home learning environment is more important for intellectual and social development than parental occupation, education or income. What parents do is more important than who parents are. (Sylva et al., 2004: 1)

We return to the EPPE project in Chapter 6, when we explore in detail effective conversation between practitioners and children.

The need for action

An influential study from the United States by Hart and Risley looked at 42 children from when they were aged eight months until their third birthday. In all, 13 families were judged to be middle class, 23 were working class and there were 6 where the parents were in receipt of welfare benefits (Hart and Risley, 1995). Their data, collected from recordings made at home, highlighted the wide difference in the amount of talk that children from different backgrounds were exposed to, and the quality of language and conversations that the children were involved in. One measure – the number of words addressed to each child per hour – showed that, on average, the middle-class children heard 2100 words, the working-class children heard 1200, while the children from families on welfare only had 600 words spoken to them. Data also showed that the middle-class parents spent twice as long engaged in conversation with their children as their counterparts on welfare.

Hart and Risley's study was cited in the influential UK report, *The Cost to the Nation of Children's Poor Communication*, from UK children's charity I CAN. This linked children's poor communication at school age with their having grown up in poverty and suffering disadvantage (I CAN, 2006). The report suggested that children were experiencing 'language impoverishment', caused by reduced interaction at home. Language impoverishment was mainly linked to families living on low incomes or in poverty. In some parts of England, as many as 50 per cent of children under five years of age were reportedly at risk of 'transient' additional speech and language difficulties, largely the result of language impoverishment. Such children did not have speech and language difficulties as a result of medical conditions or developmental delay, but had limited experience of language, caused by limited interaction and the reduced quality and quantity of language they are involved in or exposed to.

The report highlighted that this type of transient language difficulty can be reduced when settings create a 'communication supportive environment', and where skilled and appropriately trained practitioners work together. The report concluded that, unless action was taken, many children could have difficulties forming relationships and potentially limited achievement in schools leading to social difficulties and poor employment prospects.

A report on a national review of services for children with communication difficulties, *The Bercow Report* (Department for Children, Schools and Families (DCSF), 2008a), together with the I CAN report, spurred on the UK Government to respond. Between 2009 and 2011, over £50 million was made available to implement the Every Child a Talker (ECaT) project in settings across England. The project was aimed at reducing language impoverishment by improving practitioners' ability to communicate effectively with young children. This included implementing strategies, practices and activities that improve the environment for communication within the setting, as well as working together to influence how parents talk with children at home (DCSF, 2008b, 2009a, 2010).

Developing language in the setting to influence talk at home

CASE STUDY 5.1

Harry at 2;3 – moving from shouting 'Mine!' to saying 'Pick me up!'

Harry is from a 'vulnerable' family and has an assisted place at a pre-school. Part of the family's vulnerability is that Harry's parents experienced difficulties with developing a bond with Harry when he was a baby. This had an impact on Harry's ability to build a positive early attachment with his parents. Both parents have in the past been drug and alcohol dependent. Harry's mother had developed a highly directive interactional style with him, including the use of prohibitive language that included threats of punishment which were rarely carried out. This resulted in many altercations. Harry had limited play experience and showed signs of delayed speech and language, compared with other children of the same age in the setting. Harry was quite vocal: he shouted at other children and tried to engage staff by using 'scribble talk' and some single words. The main word that he used was 'mine!'

When Harry said 'Mine!' he might have been expressing one of several meanings:

It's mine! (And you can't have it!)

I want that! (So give it to me!)

It's me.

Pick me up! (Usually with arms stretched upwards towards the adult.)

Harry was spontaneously beginning to imitate some key words and phrases that adults used with him, and practitioners saw this as a sign of progress. Harry played alongside other children, but if another child took something from him, e.g. a plastic spade in the sand tray, he would shout 'Mine!' and start crying. If the child persisted, then Harry would hit him with whatever it was that they were trying to take from him. With support from a speech and language therapist, staff explored how to increase Harry's vocabulary in order to help him become an effective communicator, increase his wellbeing and reduce his aggression towards other children.

An initial approach involved adults modelling appropriate language whenever Harry said 'Mine!' when he wanted to be picked up. So, whenever Harry raised his arms towards an adult and shouted 'Mine!' the adult would say, 'You want me to pick you up?'

Harry then said 'My' and the adult would pick him up. Soon Harry began saying 'My' spontaneously when he wanted to be picked up, and then moved towards saying 'Bit an up.'

At the same time, his expressive vocabulary began developing rapidly, which led him to use more strategies to get what he wanted, including saying, 'No! That's mine,' if a child wanted to take something from him. (This was progress, as he had stopped crying and hitting.)

This was one of several approaches that the staff used to develop Harry's communication.

The manager of the pre-school and Harry's Key Person met with Harry's mother and described and modelled the strategy that they had used. Harry's mother was grateful for the advice, and was able to use this type of interaction in the street or at home when Harry wanted her to pick him up.

The next stage of the intervention was to influence Harry's Home Learning Environment, by involving Harry and his parents in 'drop in' sessions, where children, parents and local Family Workers explored play activities together and discussed how these might be continued at home.

Harry's speech and language delay and his difficulties with socialising with other children were a result of limited experience of positive interaction and play at home. The involvement of the speech and language therapist led to the practitioners developing a strategy that worked. Harry's Key Person was able to share these and other ideas with the parents, and these practical activities were reinforced by the Family Workers at the local Children's Centre. This 'joined up' approach to supporting families came about as a result of training initiatives provided as part of the local ECaT project.

CASE STUDY 5.2

'Sign 4 Feelings and Behaviour': talking and signing to express feelings

Sue Thomas and Katja O'Neill, who initially met while working on Luton's ECaT project, were aware of the need to help children develop their vocabularies, so that the children could adequately express what they already knew, and to explore new ideas. Using Katja's knowledge of British Sign Language (BSL) and Sue's experience as an early years consultant, they have developed several schemes, collectively called 'Sign 4 Learning'. These improve children's comprehension and expression of key ideas in storytelling, maths, writing and general language development. Practitioners attend training where they learn key signs from BSL and then use them with children, e.g. through stories, songs and activity ideas produced by Sign 4 Learning.

In 'Sign 4 Feelings and Behaviour', the children are introduced to key signs from BSL that help them describe accurately how they feel. Activities include making friends with two dolls provided as part of the scheme, and through stories and songs helping the dolls make 'good choices' and exploring their own feelings. Julia Miller, head teacher of Chapel Street Nursery School & Children's Centre in Luton, gave very positive feedback about the influence of the programme on children's behaviour and wellbeing:

> We have noticed with our two-year-olds in particular that they are more relaxed. I feel this is because the use of signs like 'worried' and 'frustrated' give an accurate description of how they feel. So, instead of asking a child, 'Do you feel sad?' you can be much more specific, and so can the child. If someone has taken your bit of Lego and you are getting upset about it, you and a member of staff can talk about how you truly feel. Because we all know the sign for 'angry', we can use it in its proper context with the children. This is more accurate than talking about feeling 'sad'. This supports their vocabulary development too. Feelings are also positive, and it's great to be able to describe that you are very 'excited' and not just 'happy'.

> Julia attributes the low incidence of tantrums in the setting to young children being able to sign and talk about how they feel. Talking and signing can also improve young children's understanding and expression, which increases confidence and wellbeing.

The Sign 4 Learning projects were developed out of recognition that all children need a well-developed vocabulary in order to achieve well in school and beyond. Sue Thomas and Katja O'Neill also understand that practitioners need support to provide children with that vocabulary. Data from the schemes shows that this targeted vocabulary development is having an influence on children's achievement throughout the curriculum areas involved as well as on the children's social development.

Conclusion

Whatever one's views about Bernstein's codes, the use of dialect, or whether or not language in the setting is richer than at home (or vice versa), all children need to have as detailed a vocabulary as possible. This provides children with an opportunity to explore ideas, describe their feelings and talk effectively with adults and other children. Practitioners have a duty to move children forward in the quality of their language. This can come about through ensuring that adults use language that is appropriate to the child's level of development, and using strategies such as those identified in this and subsequent chapters.

There are many reasons why children have limited experience of language. Key factors include the quality of interactions and the amount and type of language children are involved in with their parents. Poverty, parental social class and educational background may have strong influences on how adults talk with their children. Many young children in the UK attend full-time childcare, and most will attend early years settings. Therefore, the type of language that they experience in these settings will be crucial for children's success in school and beyond. Of particular importance is children's ability to be able to use language to talk about objects and events out of context. Parents have a responsibility, and practitioners have a duty, to ensure that children are exposed to language that is appropriate to their developmental level, and to be involved in conversations that are stimulating and move their language and learning forward. In Chapter 6, we explore in practical terms what quality conversations might look like.

Points for reflection and discussion

The ECaT project was based on reports that highlight major differences in children's experience of language at home and the potential impact of 'language impoverishment'.

Do you agree that language impoverishment exists, or not?

Parents' excessive use of smartphones, too much exposure of children to television and computers, and families no longer sitting round a table at mealtimes, are often quoted as reasons for a possible decline in children's language development. What are your thoughts on this?

'What parents do is more important than who parents are' (Sylva et al., 2004). Do you agree?

Thinking of your own experience as a learner, did how your parents speak have an influence on your achievement?

Further reading

Clegg, J. and Ginsborg, J. (2006) *Language and Social Disadvantage: Theory into Practice*. Chichester: Wiley.
Wood, D. (1998) *How Children Think and Learn*. Oxford: Blackwell Publishing.

Useful websites

Sign 4 Learning
www.sign4learning.co.uk (accessed 25 May 2015)
This website gives detailed information on training courses to develop children's use of key signs and talk, to promote wellbeing, positive behaviour, language, literacy and numeracy.
Talk4Meaning
www.talk4meaning.co.uk (accessed 7 August 2015)
My own website, with information about language development and ideas for developing children's communication.

CHAPTER 6

QUALITY TALK IN EARLY YEARS SETTINGS

This chapter will

- Explore examples of effective conversations with children at various stages of speech and language development
- Introduce the concept of 'Sustained Shared Thinking' (SST)
- Reach a conclusion on how to identify effective communication and SST

Identifying quality interactions: Sustained Shared Thinking (SST)

Riley and Reedy, in their review of key research into language and its impact on learning in the early years, point to the need for 'real conversations' and 'sensitive interaction' (Riley and Reedy, 2007). Wells, in his reflection on the Bristol Study, describes how it is the children themselves who work hardest at constructing their own language, but adults maximise children's understanding by responding to the meaning of what children say and adjusting the way they talk to them (Wells, 2009). These observations on effective communication with children, including with those who are very young and difficult to understand, echo the work of Wood and Wood (1984), researching how different conversational styles increase communication with children with profound hearing loss, described in Chapter 4 (p. 77). This includes adults assuming that the child has something important to say, taking time to respond and focusing on the meaning that the child is trying to convey, as opposed to how they say it. In summary, the adults respond to the child, which is reflected in the adults' responsive interactive style.

The Effective Provision of Pre-school Education Project (EPPE), a comprehensive longitudinal research project, explored the progress that children made across many varied settings. The data found that some exceptional settings enabled children to make greater progress than other settings, despite certain children's very different developmental levels at the start of the research (Sylva et al., 2004). The Researching Effective Pedagogy in the Early Years (REPEY) project was designed to investigate why and how some settings were more successful than others in promoting children's learning.

The REPEY team looked at a small sample of the most effective settings in the EPPE project. They noted that children were learning within rich, detailed and largely spontaneous conversations with practitioners. The conversations typically originated from the children's interests and involved the adult and child exploring what the child was doing, in a way that allowed new information and knowledge to be generated and absorbed by the child. These conversations were long enough and detailed enough to effectively support the children's thinking and learning. In essence, the adults were involving children in the type of intellectual enquiry that Vygotsky described as being ideal for learning and which Bruner called 'scaffolding'. It was this finding that inspired the team to apply the term 'Sustained Shared Thinking' (SST) to these high-quality conversations that enabled learning (Siraj-Blatchford et al., 2002; Sylva et al., 2010). SST is now regarded as one of the most important features of quality provision for young children (Brodie, 2014).

SST is defined as taking place when 'two or more individuals "work together" in an intellectual way to solve a problem, clarify a concept, evaluate an activity, extend a narrative, etc. Both parties must contribute to the thinking and it must develop and extend' (Sylva et al., 2004). The EPPE project focused on children from age three years. By this age, many children are well on the way to becoming confident and effective communicators. Adults and children will already be involving each other in talk, through play and practical activities. Increasingly, however, children will be able to explore ideas through talk alone, e.g. by describing to a practitioner something that happened, or what someone said, at home. It is relatively easy to engage children in conversation if their level of pronunciation is such that all adults are able to understand them, and they have sufficiently complex understanding and expression to allow them to communicate their ideas. As a result, it would be tempting to assume that

SST can only take place with children who are skilled communicators and have well-developed speech and language.

However, both Kathy Brodie and Jenni Clarke suggest that this type of rich and rewarding engagement is possible with babies who are pre-verbal, children with emerging language and older children with additional communication needs (Clarke, 2007; Brodie, 2014). We illustrate in the examples below how practitioners are able to extend the thinking and language skills of children throughout the age range. These examples show how it is possible to engage children through spontaneous conversation, during activities where the children have decided what they want to do, as part of incidental social interaction and in an activity supervised by an adult. However, the question we need to answer is whether these examples actually show SST, with its emphasis on intellectual enquiry and extending children's thinking, or are they examples of conversations where adults have primarily supported children's language and social development?

The distinction between an encounter that essentially supports language development – e.g. through extending the child's vocabulary and grammar – and one that illustrates SST may not always be clear. One could argue that by supporting the child's language, the practitioner is automatically increasing the child's ability to think. However, SST can be identified as a distinct process, because the adult engages the child in a conversation that extends the child's thinking. The adult talking with a child or a small group of children might, for example:

- Discuss how to solve a problem
- Discuss whether their problem was solved or needs another solution
- Think together about an idea
- Talk together about an event or activity that the child and adult are involved in
- Talk about how an activity went, e.g. why it was enjoyable
- Share a story and talk about the plot in detail

Both the child and adult need to feel that they are talking as equals, in the sense that the adult takes the child's ideas seriously. However, the adult is acting as the person who has more knowledge than the child and is able to take the child's thinking forward, e.g. in the way that he thinks about a particular problem or in his understanding of the world and the people in it.

Because SST involves talking in detail, which involves uninterrupted time, it is not something that can be noted all day, every day, in settings. As Jeni Riley explains:

> The reason why SST is comparatively rare, even in the most effective settings, is that it cannot be planned for. It is about knowledgeable adults seizing opportunities, whenever they arise, to have an extended conversation with a child.

For Riley, 'knowledgeable adults' are sensitive to individual children as learners. They also understand how to use children's interests to extend their thinking, and thinking about thinking, through meaningful dialogue (Jeni Riley, personal communication, 2014).

Given this description of SST, we can judge whether the following examples, which show practitioners interacting skilfully and sensitively with children, are primarily extending children's language, or truly engaging in SST.

Example 6.1 Meaningful communication at 12 months: Tom at the window

Tom has attended the Baby Room in his local nursery for three months. His sister Kathleen is 3;9 and is in the 'Pre-School Room'. The Baby Room windows look out onto the outdoor play area. Tom is sharing a book with a practitioner, Mandy. Mandy is a newcomer to the Baby Room and is in the process of 'tuning into' the children.

Tom (pointing excitedly towards the window):	Tata! Tata!
Mandy:	Oh! What's that? Is there something outside?
Tom:	Tata!
Mandy:	Something outside? Shall we have a look?
Tom (slides off Mandy's lap, still gesturing towards the window):	Ta! Ta!
Mandy:	Let's have a look. (Picks Tom up and takes him to the window.)

(Tom points to something outside the window. Both can see a tree, some birds, a car parked in the street and children playing.)

Tom:	Tata!!
Mandy:	What can you see? What did you hear? Is it the birds?

(Tom shakes his head and bangs the window.)

Mandy:	Is it the car? No? What about the tree? Do you like the tree? (Tom is laughing at Mandy and banging on the window.)
Mandy:	I know. I think you can see Kathleen! There she is. Wave to Kathleen!

> Tom
> (banging on
> the window):   Tata!!
>
> Mandy: Did you hear Kathleen playing outside? You are a
>   clever boy. Let's wave to Kathleen and see if she
>   can see us. Say, 'Hello Kathleen!'
>
> Tom: (very excited) Tata!
>
> Tom and Mandy stayed at the window for another three minutes, by
> which time Kathleen had slipped out of sight and Tom could hear the
> Baby Room door opening. This distracted his attention and Mandy
> took him back to finish looking at the book together.

Here we see an adult and child working hard to tune into each other.
Everything that Mandy does lets Tom know that she will do her best to
find out what it is he wants to communicate:

Mandy's words	Mandy's message
'Shall we go and have a look?'	I have time to spend with you.
'What can you see? What can you hear?'	I want to understand you and my talk is at the right level.
'I think you can see Kathleen.'	I'm giving you words to express your thoughts.
'Did you hear Kathleen "playing outside"?'	I'm introducing two new words.
'You are a clever boy.'	I'm praising your efforts.
	I like talking with you.

Tom wants to solve a problem: 'I think that is my big sister Kathleen
playing outside. How can I find out whether or not it is her? I will try
talking and see what happens.' When they go to the window, Mandy's job
is to help Tom to solve another problem, i.e. 'How can we communicate
with each other?' Mandy was able to understand what Tom was saying
because she knew about his older sister Kathleen. As a result, she 'put two
and two together', and was able quickly to interpret Tom's message
correctly. But how would we have judged the conversation if Mandy had
misinterpreted Tom's message? Would it have been a 'failed communication'?
Far from it. If Mandy had failed to realise that 'Tata' meant 'I can hear

Kathleen outside,' she would still have helped Tom learn important lessons about communication:

• If I attempt to communicate here, then adults will respond
• Adults here do their best to understand me
• If we fail to understand each other, it can be a bit annoying, but it's not the end of the world
• This adult responds to me, and is willing to interrupt what we are doing to follow what is clearly more interesting for me
• We didn't get it right this time, but this adult makes me feel good, so I will try again another time

It was Tom's exclamation that made Mandy leave the book-sharing and go with Tom to the window. And it was her use of an exclamation, 'Oh! What's that?' as a response to Tom's excitement, which showed that Mandy intuitively knew that if a very young child exclaims with excitement then she should respond accordingly.

This information came from a five-minute chance observation of mine. I use the word 'intuitively' to describe what Mandy did, because her behaviour was an automatic response to Tom's communication. However, Mandy is a very experienced and committed practitioner who knows that her main role is to develop children's wellbeing, language and learning. Over the years, she has learned through observation, mentoring and getting things wrong and right, so this type of response is part of her professional approach. Plus, she thoroughly enjoys her work!

While this is an excellent example of a child and adult successfully tuning into each other in order to reach joint understanding of a shared meaning, it is not SST.

Example 6.2 Solving a problem through talk at 18 months: Priya, two adults, the water and her welly boots

Priya has just woken up from her sleep in the Baby Room. Lisa picks her up and carries her outside to where the other children are filling up buckets with water taken from a water butt. Lisa was on duty indoors while Priya was asleep. It is a warm day, but the children have wellington boots on, as the ground around the water butt has become quite muddy and slippery.

Priya (pointing excitedly to the children playing):	Water! Water!

Lisa:	Yes! The children are playing with the water!
Priya (struggling to be put down):	Water! Priya! Water!
Lisa (putting Priya down and crouching down to be at Priya's eye level):	Do you want to have a go? Do you want to play with the water?
Priya:	Yeh! Yeh!
Lisa:	You want to play? OK. Let's find your wellies first.
Priya:	No! No!
Lisa:	Your shoes will get wet and muddy. We need wellies.

(Lisa leads Priya by the hand back indoors. Priya begins to protest.)

Lisa:	It's OK. We'll put your boots on and then play.

(Lisa turns around with Priya and gives Priya's hand to another practitioner, Josie.)

Lisa:	Priya, stay with Josie. You watch the children with Josie. And Lisa will get your wellies.
Priya (to Josie):	Priya! Water! Boots!

While Lisa goes to get Priya's boots, Josie talks with Priya about what the children are doing: going to the tap, splashing in the water, filling their buckets, look how muddy they are getting, etc. During this running commentary, Priya doesn't say anything, but watches the children and listens. (Perhaps she was wondering why Lisa was taking so long, or even whether she would return at all!)

Lisa returns and Josie goes back to the other children. Lisa talks with Priya while she helps her put her boots on: 'These are nice boots. They will keep your feet nice and dry. Can you help me put them on? You are a good girl for waiting,' etc.

Priya is very definite that she wants to join in with this activity, and makes her thoughts clear by exclaiming and using single words. Once again, the adult opens up the possibility of a conversation, by responding to Priya's excited voice with an equally excited response. Lisa's response, 'Yes! The children are playing with the water!' is a statement that expands Priya's single word, 'Water!' It also confirms to Priya that Lisa knows what she, Priya, is talking about. Lisa waits for Priya to respond, which she does by shouting, 'Water! Priya! Water!' Lisa then confirms that Priya means that she wants to play with the water. This leads to a conversation about the problem that they need to solve between them, needing to wear boots.

Lisa is able to pass Priya to Josie, and Josie continues the conversation as a 'running commentary' on what both adult and child can see happening. This provides Priya with a model of language to match her thoughts, as well as giving Priya an all-important sense that 'this adult cares enough about me to stay with me while Lisa goes to get the wellies'. As with Example 6.1, this conversation could have had some very different outcomes: Priya could have refused point-blank to put on her boots; Lisa could have failed to locate the wellies; or the manager might have appeared at the door and spoken to Lisa for a few minutes, thus delaying the delivery of the boots. Again, this would not have been an example of a 'failed communication' as long as the adults talk about the emerging problems: e.g. 'I wonder where Lisa has got to?' or 'Lisa couldn't find your wellies, but here are a spare pair. Let's try these on. They do look nice! Look, there's a frog on each boot. What picture have you got on your wellies?'

Is this Sustained Shared Thinking, or just a successful interaction? Are adult and child 'working together in an intellectual way to solve a problem'? 'Needing to wear boots otherwise you can't join in' is a very big problem. The adults use language to explain what the problem is, and how to go about solving it. Priya indicates that she doesn't want to go inside, so the adults (there are now two of them) use language to explain what they can do to solve this new problem, i.e. Priya is not going in to get her boots, therefore she can wait with another adult. The adults and child are certainly working together, and the problem is on the way to being sorted.

But is there an 'intellectual' aspect to this interaction? Priya protests, because she doesn't want to put on her wellies, which leads the adult, clearly and with appropriate language, to set out the problem and the solution: 'We need wellies so your shoes don't get wet and muddy.' The adults have used language to present Priya with a link to a cause and effect: water and mud with no boots equals messy shoes. This has engaged Priya cognitively/intellectually and provided her with reassurance and a sense of wellbeing. It has also taken her another step further in developing her understanding of language. If the child and the adult return to a similar situation and are able to engage in another conversation about the need for wellies, with the adult taking the conversation further, then we could judge that this would be SST.

However, as it stands, this is an example of language being used primarily for social and emotional development.

This conversation was successful on several levels because there were enough adults available at the activity for Josie to leave what she was doing and stay with Priya. Lisa was able to hand Priya over temporarily to Josie. This avoided a potential confrontation with Priya, but equally allowed Josie to continue the conversation. Josie showed real intuitive skill by crouching down: to be as near Priya's eye level as possible and to talk about what both adult and child could see, i.e. providing joint attention. The way that the adults worked together is an indication of a high degree of professionalism. This includes a shared awareness of how a positive use of language can stimulate emotional wellbeing, language development and learning. The conversations in Examples 6.1 and 6.2 were incidental, in the sense that they took place spontaneously, but there were enough adults available to ensure that sustained conversations like these could take place in an unhurried manner. (We return to the subject of adult deployment and its impact on language, learning and social development in Chapter 7.)

Conversations with advanced talkers

In the following examples, Aiden was aged 3;9 when this recording was made in a nursery school. Fifteen months later, after an academic year in his local primary school, Aiden was given a diagnosis of Asperger's syndrome. The main features of this condition, which is one of a series of Autism Spectrum Disorders (ASD), are a difficulty with understanding social relationships and particularly non-verbal signals such as facial expression and tone of voice. Children with Asperger's syndrome may also have an obsessive interest in certain topics, well-developed speech and language skills and may show signs of above-average cognitive abilities (Attwood, 2008). This was certainly the case with Aiden when this observation was made.

Example 6.3a Aiden, Francesca and a jar of Marmite

Aiden is sitting at the snack table with Sam, who is the practitioner on duty this morning. Sam has no other duties for the next 30 minutes other than to engage the children in conversation while they prepare a sandwich. There are several fillings on offer, including slices of cucumber, tomatoes and cheese. There is a jar of Marmite, which Aiden loves. NB: there is no peanut butter.

Aiden:	I detest peanut butter. It's slimy and brown and looks like diarrhoea.
Sam:	I quite like it, actually.

(Continued)

(Continued)

Aiden:	I detest it so much. Lots of people detest it and it's full of microbes.
Sam:	Microbes? Would you like some cucumber then?
Aiden:	Microbes can kill people. Microbes are germs that are everywhere but some are harmful while others are harmless. Microbes are everywhere but most of all they are on people's hands and dishcloths that have not been disinfected.
Sam:	Disinfected? You disinfect your hands? Like with bleach?
Aiden:	Bleach is dangerous. You have to dilute it.
Sam:	But you can just wash your hands carefully with soap and water …
Aiden:	Soap and water to wash your hands, that's …

(Enter Francesca, who sits on Sam's lap. Francesca is 4;4. She is wearing a 'Snow White' dress.)

Sam:	Hello, Francesca. Are you hungry, or have you just come for a cuddle?

(Francesca puts her thumb in her mouth.) Aiden and I were just talking about what he wants to put in his sandwich. Weren't we Aiden? I can guess what he wants.

Aiden:	Francesca has to wash his hands.
Sam:	Francesca? Yes. If she wants to make a sandwich, then she has to wash her hands. Let's ask her, shall we?
Aiden:	No. He has to wash them.
Sam:	Let's ask her if she wants a sandwich. Aiden, you ask Francesca if she wants to make a sandwich.
Aiden:	I'm having Marmite. Marmite is made from yeast.
Sam:	Yes. I know. Aiden, you say to Francesca, 'Francesca, do you want to make a sandwich?'
Aiden:	Where's the Marmite? Marmite is very good for you and I want to have some. It is delicious for me and …

Sam:	Aiden, ask Francesca, 'Do you want to make a sandwich?' If she says 'Yes,' then she can go and wash her hands.
Aiden:	Francesca, wash your hands and make a sandwich.
Francesca:	I don't want to make a sandwich because I might get this dress dirty and I don't want to take it off.
Aiden (raising his voice):	Wash your hands. Where's the Marmite? Wash your hands. Where's the Marmite?
Sam (talking to Francesca and ignoring Aiden):	I see what you mean. Are you worried that someone else will want to take the dress? We could always get an apron for you to put on.
Francesca:	That's a good idea. Aiden, can you get me an apron, please?
Aiden:	Yes.
Francesca (looking at Sam):	Uh?

Sam was well aware of Aiden's tendency to talk in detail about his own particular interests, and how this has an impact on his ability to build relationships with other children. One of the challenges when working with children with ASD is being able to have a conversation that is satisfying for both participants, i.e. where there is 'a meeting of two minds on a topic of mutual interest' (Brown, 1973). Aiden's expressive language is highly developed, with precise pronunciation and phonology, grammar and very advanced vocabulary. For such a young child, Aiden does have in-depth knowledge about various subjects. What he has to say is interesting, but not after he has been able to talk about the same topic many times. Sam has been involved in this type of interaction several times, where Aiden seeks to embark on a monologue about his favourite topics of peanut butter, Marmite and microbes. The challenge is to keep a balance between helping him to engage in genuine conversation with adults and other children, while preventing him from dominating and slipping into a lengthy monologue.

Sam does this skilfully, by acknowledging what Aiden has said, and then bringing the subject to something that is relevant to what he is supposed to be doing. For example, when Aiden begins a monologue about microbes, Sam turns the subject to hand-washing, which is part of the routine for making a snack. Sam is also aware that, like many children with ASD, Aiden confuses pronouns; e.g. when he says, 'his hands' instead of 'her hands' and 'he has to' for 'she has to', so she tells him exactly how he should construct his question to Francesca. But was this extract an example of SST? Not exactly. Sam was working to help Aiden talk with Francesca (even though Aiden was doing his best to resist). Aiden was certainly clarifying a concept in an intellectual way. His ongoing difficulty is that he approaches everything in an intellectual way, and fails to notice people's emotional signals through facial expression and tone of voice. However, there is important learning going on here for Aiden:

- Sam wants to listen to my interests and will respond
- Sam can set boundaries about what I talk about
- I can talk with other children, but sometimes I might need adults to help me

And what about Sam's response to Francesca? Sam's responses give the impression that she is able to automatically adjust her communicative style. She changes from needing to be in control of how Aiden is talking – to avoid monologues that soon become meaningless for Aiden and the listener – to being much more responsive to Francesca. In other words, Sam can switch her style from controlling to being responsive, within the same conversation.

However, Example 6.3a primarily illustrates language being used to aid a child's social development, rather than SST. The conversation continues below and illustrates how Sam, having assisted Aiden with the social aspect of having a conversation with Francesca, is able to focus the children on a short piece of intellectual enquiry.

Example 6.3b Aiden, Francesca and a discussion about Marmite

Francesca now has an apron on and is sitting on a chair next to Aiden.

Aiden:	I can't open it! I can't get the lid off!
Sam:	Aiden, would you like me to help you?
Aiden:	Help. Yes. Help.
Sam (unscrewing the lid half way):	Aiden, you can do the rest now.
Francesca:	That really stinks! I hate that smell!

Aiden:	I love Marmite. I don't detest it. It is made from yeast and is good for you …
Francesca:	It smells really yucky. I don't want any.
Aiden:	Marmite is delicious.
Francesca:	My Dad likes Marmite. Do you like it Sam?
Sam:	Yes, I really love it. I like to spread it on toast.
Francesca:	But it's so horrible. It burns my tongue.
Sam:	Yes. It's strange, isn't it? Some people can love the smell and taste of food, while other people can't stand it.
Aiden:	Mummy detests milk.
Francesca:	What does 'distist' mean?
Sam:	If you detest something, it means you really, really, really don't like it.
Francesca:	Everyone likes milk. I love it.
Sam:	Not everyone likes milk. Aiden's Mummy hates it.
Francesca:	Oh.

(There is a break in this part of the conversation while Sam helps the children choose what they want to put in their sandwich.)

Francesca:	My brother hates cheese, but me and Mummy love it.
Sam:	I wonder why that is?
Francesca:	My brother says cheese gives him a runny tummy.
Aiden:	Peanut butter looks like diarrhoea.
Sam:	Maybe it's just the taste and smell that we don't like? Shall we ask Ruth what she thinks about Marmite? (Ruth, the head teacher, walks past.)
Sam (to Francesca and Aiden):	Show Ruth some Marmite and ask her if she likes it.
Francesca:	Smell that Ruth. Do you think it is horrible?
Ruth:	It's got a very strong smell, and a very strong taste, but I do like it. But only a small amount spread on some bread. My Granny used to make gravy with it.
Francesca:	Oh.

In Example 6.3b, both children have clear pronunciation, so Francesca in particular can convey complex ideas to Sam and Aiden without anyone needing to stop her and ask her to repeat what she has just said. This helps the *conversational flow*. This example shows the beginning of SST. Francesca and Sam, and to a certain extent Aiden, are grappling with the idea that one person can love a taste and smell like Marmite, yet someone else can find it repulsive. By saying, 'Yes. It's strange, isn't it?' Sam demonstrates expertly that she, too, is curious to know why this should be. The thinking is sustained, albeit briefly, because, after a natural break in the conversation, Francesca returns to the idea that is clearly puzzling her, by telling Sam about her brother not liking cheese. Sam responds with: 'I wonder why that is?' This 'thinking out loud' again shows the adult's genuine interest, and models for the children how to think about thinking, e.g. by asking yourself 'I wonder why …?'

At the end of each exchange, Francesca says, 'Oh.' We can't know exactly what is going through her mind when she says this, but the first 'oh' seems to suggest that she is trying to work out a possible solution to the problem. After making her sandwich, she comes back with an observation, and the discussion ends with another 'oh'. This suggests that the little girl is likely to go away and think more about this subject, which has clearly intrigued her. The adult's task is to make a note of this conversation and find ways of returning to it, so that adult and child can continue their thinking together.

Sustained Shared Thinking in reality

We see from Examples 6.3a and 6.3b that the adult is able to take time to respond to the children's interests and talk at length, and in depth. This gives the children the time they need to use language socially and develop their ideas. These conversations took place in a very busy open-plan room, where there were many children involved in different activities. It was fortunate at this time that there were no interruptions from other children, or that the adult's attention was not drawn away to an incident or event taking place nearby. It is the nature of busy settings that there will be many demands placed on the practitioner's time and focus, so as a result many promising conversations never really get going. An informal snack time in this setting is part of the daily routine, where a practitioner is stationed at the snack table, with no duties other than to supervise the children and engage them in conversation.

We don't know what happened the next day, but this enquiry could be extended and sustained by the same practitioner planning to do the following:

- Talking with Francesca and her parents at the end of the session, about the interesting conversation they had earlier about food preferences. This might lead to parent and child talking about this subject at home
- Talking to Francesca the following day, at snack time, about her likes and dislikes. The conversation could begin with: 'Francesca, do you remember when we were talking yesterday about how you hate Marmite and Aiden loves it? And about how you and Mummy love cheese but your brother can't stand it? Well, I've been wondering about this ...'
- Involving Francesca in setting up a small survey using Marmite, to find out what each child and adult in the room thinks about the smell and taste of this spread, that people seem to either love or hate. This could give Francesca the chance to take the enquiry further, and perhaps invite other children into the discussion. (See Case Study 7.4 in Chapter 7 for a practical exploration of SST through a whole class survey.)

Example 6.3b is an example, for Francesca, of the beginning of Shared Thinking. Whether this thinking becomes 'sustained' will depend on how Sam and colleagues (and to a certain extent Francesca's parents) talk with her on this subject in the days that follow.

Children's differing language development and Sustained Shared Thinking

Francesca and Aiden in Examples 6.3a and 6.3b both come from families where talking together is valued highly. As a result, the children are able to use language to explore ideas and extend their thinking, even though one of them has a significant additional learning need. This is not to say that children from different family backgrounds, or those with additional learning needs or learning English as an additional language, can't have these types of conversations. However, it may take more prolonged support from practitioners to bring the children's conversational skills and vocabulary to the point where they can be involved in mutually satisfying and detailed conversations. This reminds us of Steven in Example 5.3 in Chapter 5 who clearly has the ability to explore ideas, but needs the vocabulary to express himself fully because he is brought up in a dialect-speaking home environment. However, the adult's sensitive involvement provides Steven with the chance to have a discussion that stimulates his enquiring mind, while giving him the tools to explore his ideas verbally.

Conclusion

It is important to be able to identify quality in our interactions with children. The standards that are set by management for how adults talk with children are an indication of how effective learning will be in the setting. In England, settings are judged by the quality of interactions and conversation between adults and children (Ofsted, 2013). Practitioners need to be aware of the effectiveness of their communication and of the different approaches they can use to ensure that all children are being involved in interactions that extend their language development and learning. Talking effectively with children is a skill that can be learned. It comes with practice, observation and a willingness to be sensitive to children's needs. This sensitivity shows itself in the practitioner being willing to experiment with adjusting his or her language level, to ensure that children understand what is being said. This sensitivity is also shown by the adult being willing to spend time in ensuring that the children are able to express themselves fully. Whether practitioners are actually able to spend time to do this is an issue of intense debate on training courses exploring language and learning. Chapter 7, therefore, looks in detail at how adults can plan for effective talk through adult organisation, so that extended conversations can take place in busy settings.

 Points for reflection and discussion

Is effective talking with children intuitive, or can it be taught?

Can we only have SST with children who have rich language?

The children in the examples were using language for different reasons, and because an adult was already with them nearby. How do you judge whether to involve children in conversation or to leave them to be absorbed in their play?

 Practical activities

Think about a conversation that you have had recently with a child or small group of children, where you came away satisfied that there had been an element of learning involved.

How involved were the children in the conversation? Did they enjoy it?

What did the children gain from the conversation?

The next time you have a fascinating conversation with a child, think about how you can get that conversation going again the next day. (Try choosing a time when you are free to talk without too many interruptions. You could start with, 'I've been thinking about what you said yesterday about the troll in the Billy Goats Gruff story. Shall we share the story again and talk about it some more?' and after you have had your conversation, perhaps you could draw other children in, e.g. 'Shall we ask Roshni what she thinks about the troll?')

Further reading

Dowling, M. (2006) *Supporting Young Children's Sustained Shared Thinking*. London: Early Education.

Siraj, I., Kingston, D. and Melhuish, E. (2015) *Assessing Quality in Early Childhood Education and Care: Sustained Shared Thinking and Emotional Well-Being (SSTEW) Scale for 2–5-year-olds Provision*. London: IOE Press/Trentham Books.

CHAPTER 7

TALKING EFFECTIVELY WITH GROUPS OF CHILDREN

This chapter will

- Explore approaches that help children to enjoy talking with an adult and other children ('Sharing Adults')
- Describe ways to plan for adults to be able stay in one place long enough to have conversations
- Describe approaches that create opportunities for children to focus effectively during group sessions

In Chapter 6, we looked closely at what effective conversations with children in settings might look like. These include conversations where the focus and outcome were promoting children's language and social development, as well as one that began to involve Sustained Shared Thinking (SST). These outcomes are the product of conversations that take place spontaneously, as part of everyday life, routines, spontaneous play and adult-led activities. The interactions also develop when adults are sensitive to individual children and who adopt a responsive interactive style.

Many children approach adults spontaneously and become involved in conversations – often because they are confident communicators. However, practitioners will be concerned to actively engage children who might be reluctant to approach adults, or need specific support with communication. This may be because they are of a shy disposition, have speech and language delay or are learning English as an additional language (EAL). I describe these children as being 'vulnerable' because they are unable to express adequately how they feel or otherwise use language to control their environment. For example, Luke, aged 3;0 with speech and language delay, often became tearful and aggressive towards other children while playing at the sand tray, because he was unable to make the other children understand that he didn't want them to knock over the sandcastle he had just made. This type of reaction had become habitual for Luke, and children were reluctant to approach him for fear of upsetting him, or being hit.

The examples in Chapter 6 illustrate what can happen when an adult has uninterrupted time to explore children's ideas. However, life within busy settings, or at home where there is more than one sibling, is full of interruptions and distractions. As a result, interactions can be short, disjointed exchanges that often seem not to lead to any conclusion. Wells, in his exploration of the data taken from conversations at home in the Bristol Project, concluded that:

> to be most helpful, the child's experience of conversation should be in a one-to-one situation in which the adult is talking about matters of interest and concern to the child, such as what he or she is doing, has done, or plans to do, or about activities in which the child and adult engage together. (Wells, 1987: 44).

Wells also suggested that effective conversations were more likely to take place when children were talking on their own with an adult or with one other child during 'focused group work'.

While it is ideal to engage children individually, it can be difficult to make this a reality on a regular basis. It is possible to have interesting conversations that are sustained, involve intellectual challenge and are mutually rewarding for adults and children, even though we have more than one child who wants to talk to us. However, achieving this goal requires the adults to develop certain attitudes and skills and to plan approaches and activities that help children to enjoy interacting and talking together.

Sharing adults

Vulnerable children often find it very difficult to compete for and maintain an adult's attention, particularly when more confident children talk their way into a conversation and inadvertently dominate it (Johnson and Jones, 2012). Adults in this situation can find themselves automatically turning their attention away from the younger or less confident child, and giving total attention to the newcomer. This can undermine the confidence of the vulnerable children, who will often quietly walk away. All children benefit from help with sharing adults, in order to avoid the children feeling the need to compete for attention. Examples 7.1 and 7.2 are a composite of a series of interactions that I was involved in while making advisory visits to a pre-school, where we were focusing on involving vulnerable children in conversation. At the same time, we explored together how we could involve more confident children in conversations without them feeling the need to take over. The examples illustrate how adult responses to confident children, who interrupt a conversation, can either undermine children's confidence or be used for the benefit of all children in the group.

Example 7.1 Alma at 3;9, Mrs Reynolds and the mud kitchen

Take 1

Alma is learning English as an additional language and has been in her setting for five months. Alma and her best friend Delphine have been making 'pies' outside in the mud kitchen. They have taken soil, pieces of gravel, some small pebbles, grass and water and mixed it all up in a bucket and placed the mixture carefully in an old muffin tray. They have made an 'oven' out of a large hollow wooden unit block, with a 'door' made from a discarded offcut of timber they found nearby.

Practitioners are aware that Alma and Delphine don't usually approach adults to engage them in conversation, so the adults use every opportunity to talk with them. Mrs Reynolds comes over to engage the children in conversation.

Alma:	Look. We is pies.
Mrs R:	Oh! You've been baking pies. I can smell them. They smell lovely!
Alma:	They is pies.
Mrs R:	You have baked pies, have you? Can I open the door to see if they are ready?
Alma:	Is very hot.
Mrs R:	Oh! The door is hot? Are the pies very hot, too? I will be very careful.
Alma:	Pies is …

(Enter Mustafa from behind Mrs Reynolds. He taps Mrs Reynolds repeatedly on the shoulder.)

Mustafa:	I have got something to show you.
Mrs R (turning away from Alma):	What is it Mustafa?
Mustafa:	I have wet my shoe. I trod in a puddle. My shoe is all wet.
Mrs R:	How did you get it wet?

(Mustafa tells Mrs Reynolds his story. Alma and Delphine talk with each other and then walk away.)

Mrs R:	Oh! The girls have gone. Come on Mustafa, let's see if we can find you some clean shoes.

This conversation was just getting going when another child interrupted and diverted the adult's attention. As a result, the girls walked away. If one were to ask Mrs Reynolds why she stopped talking with the girls, she would probably say that this was an inevitable consequence of not having enough adults to follow conversations through to a natural conclusion. However, Mrs Reynolds' attention wasn't diverted by Mustafa: she chose to pay attention to him. By doing so, she inadvertently signalled to the girls that talking with them was less important than talking to Mustafa. They got the message and left. Example 7.2 suggests three possible alternative responses.

Example 7.2 Mrs Reynolds and the mud kitchen (again)

Take 2

Mustafa:	I have got something to show you.
Mrs R:	Hold on, Mustafa. I'm talking to the girls. Wait a minute and then I'll talk to you.
Mustafa (tapping Mrs Reynolds more vigorously):	My shoe is wet.
Mrs R (more stridently):	I told you to wait. Wait until we have finished talking and then I'll see to you.

(Continued)

(Continued)

Mustafa (becoming more agitated):	My shoe is wet. My shoe is wet.
Mrs R:	Sorry girls. I need to sort this out. I'll come and talk to you later. (Exits with Mustafa. The girls walk away.)

Take 3

Mustafa:	I have got something to show you.
Mrs R (to Alma and Delphine):	Stay there girls. (She turns her head towards Mustafa.)
Mrs Reynolds:	Mustafa, Mrs Reynolds is talking with Alma and Delphine. They are making pies.
Mustafa:	My shoe is wet.
Mrs R (firmly):	There is a grown-up indoors. Go and tell her and she will sort you out.

(Mustafa goes indoors. Mrs Reynolds turns her head back to the girls.) Right girls. You were telling me about those hot pies …
   (Both children look slightly nervous and Alma stops talking.)

Take 4

Mustafa:	I have got something to show you.
Mrs R:	Hello, Mustafa. Mrs Reynolds is talking with Delphine and Alma. They are making cakes. They are telling me all about it.
Mustafa:	My shoe is wet.
Mrs R:	Oh, yes. Do you want to listen to what we are talking about? Or go indoors and ask a grown-up to change your shoes?
Mrs R (to the girls):	Alma and Delphine. Show Mustafa our cakes. He's got a wet foot. He's getting cold. Maybe your nice hot cakes will warm him up.

Delphine:	Mustafa, show me your shoe. My God! What happened?
Mustafa:	I was carrying a bucket of water. I dropped it. It fell on my shoe and all water spilled out.
Alma:	You want pie?
Mrs R (to Alma):	Sorry, Alma. I said it was a cake. It's a pie.
Mustafa:	I'm full up. Can I have a burger?
Alma:	Yes. (To Delphine) You is burger make?
Delphine:	We haven't got any burgers, but we can make meat pies with chips.
Mustafa:	OK.
Mrs R:	Mustafa. Your shoe is not so bad. We can change it when we have finished talking to the girls.

(The conversation continues.)

'Take 2' is still unsatisfying for all concerned. Mrs Reynolds gives Mustafa mixed messages, by telling him to 'hold on' and 'wait a minute'. When Mustafa does neither of these, the adult clarifies what she means: 'Wait until we have finished talking and then I'll see to you.' However, it is too late, as Mustafa has become agitated, and Mrs Reynolds has put pressure on herself and the girls to hurry their conversation along, so that she can 'see to' Mustafa's shoe. This created anxiety for the girls, which had an impact on their ability to participate.

In 'Take 3', Mrs Reynolds' language is more accurate, and gives Mustafa a clear message about what he should do. However, the girls, and Alma in particular, have picked up on the irritation expressed in the adult's voice when telling Mustafa to go away. This affected their ability to talk in a relaxed way. 'Take 4' is the most successful interaction of all, because Mrs Reynolds skilfully draws Mustafa into the conversation as an equal. At the same time, she shows him how he can involve himself in a conversation that has already started. The girls have had their self-esteem boosted by the adult remaining with them, which allows them to talk together and to include Mustafa. The practitioner also draws Mustafa into the imaginary play, which he responds to with pleasure. Because Mustafa and Delphine are more experienced English-speakers, they are able to act as role models for Alma.

Example 7.3 Taking turns to talk and listen: one adult and five children discussing their bags and shoes

Michael is visiting a setting. He is aware that Lucy, aged 3;11, is shy and quiet and would benefit from sensitive conversation about a topic that she is interested in. Michael is helping Lucy hang her coat on her peg after having been playing outside. Lucy has a new 'Hello Kitty' backpack.

Michael: I like your bag, Lucy.

Lucy: … (Enter Josh.)

Josh: I got new trainers.

Michael: Hi, Josh. Listen to what Lucy just told me about her bag. (Turns to Lucy.) Lucy was telling me that she has a new Hello Kitty bag. Now Josh, it's your turn.

Josh: I got new Spiderman trainers. And I got a Spiderman bag.

Michael: Great! So Lucy, you've got a Hello Kitty bag and Josh has got a …

Lucy: Spiderman bag.

(Enter Khalid, who pushes Josh.)

Khalid: I got …

Michael: Hello, Khalid. We are talking about Lucy's and Josh's bag and trainers. Do you want to find out what they have to say? Let's hear about Lucy and Josh first. (Turns to Lucy.) Lucy has got …

Lucy: Hello Kitty bag.

Michael: Josh has got … (turns to Josh)

Josh: A Spiderman bag and Spiderman trainers.

Michael: And Khalid (turns to Khalid) has got …

Khalid: Ben 10 trainers and a new light sabre and …

Michael: Let's see if I can remember. So Lucy has got a Hello Kitty bag, Josh has got a Spiderman bag and trainers and Khalid has got Ben 10 trainers. (Michael turns to Lucy.) Now it's

> Lucy's turn again. Have you got anything else? That's a nice T-shirt you are wearing.
>
> Lucy: My Mummy bought it for me.
>
> Michael: Lucy has a nice T-shirt and her Mummy bought it. Josh. It's your turn now.
>
> Josh: I got …
>
> Two more children arrive and immediately Michael explains that we are talking about our bags and shoes. The conversation, which has now become a listening and memory game, continues, as the two new children take turns to talk.

This example shows how children can be encouraged to talk with, and listen to, each other. If Lucy was able to articulate how she felt about this short conversation, and particularly how it raised her self-esteem, she might say, 'I feel better having spoken with Michael because:

- He is spending time with me, helping me to talk about something I know about
- He gives clear messages to me and other children
- He does not allow other children to interrupt and dominate the conversation
- He talks to other children in a friendly way, using clear instructions
- He gives me the chance to talk with other children
- This makes me feel more confident
- The more confident children now know that I have lots to say
- I feel more confident about talking with them'

It also showed the other children how it might be preferable to listen to each other, rather than compete for attention by trying to be louder and more forceful than each other. In settings where adults give mixed messages by using phrases like, 'Wait a second,' or who automatically turn to a child who is interrupting a conversation, it is possible that children develop a belief that the only way to get an adult's attention is to be forceful and talk loudly. I refer to this as 'Survival of the loudest talker.' If children are not supported to talk positively with each other, then settings can become dominated by children who shout a lot and habitually interrupt conversations and group times in order to get the adults' attention. When adults work together to develop consistent, positive responses, children will have space to take turns in listening and talking. This teaches social skills, reduces anxiety and promotes language development.

Points for reflection and discussion

We often inadvertently tell children to 'hang on' 'wait a minute' or 'hold on'.

What do you and your colleagues say to children who interrupt adults when they are talking?

Is it possible to introduce a standard response that all adults use that is accurate and positive? (E.g. 'I'm talking with X right now. Do you want to join in? Or maybe listen? Perhaps another grown-up could help you?')

 Practical tasks

Plan to experiment with the strategy illustrated in Example 7.3.
How did the children respond?

The 'planted adult'

A major barrier to interaction and conversation between adults and children occurs when adults are distracted by incidents taking place nearby, e.g. a child falling over, needing help with wiping his nose, a dispute over a toy or someone being stuck on a piece of equipment. In these circumstances, the adult in conversation can't ignore the other children and will need to stop listening and talking so that she can lend a hand. This is frustrating for adults, who feel that they can't give children the detailed and prolonged attention that they need. It is frustrating for children, who soon realise that adults are only likely to pay attention for very short periods of time.

One solution is for staff to plan for one adult to be available for uninterrupted conversation. For a given amount of time, this adult has no other duties in the setting, other than to stay 'planted' in one place and be available for conversation. This could be at an adult-led activity, at the snack table, at the playdough table, or outside playing in the sand or digging area. The concept of the 'Planted Adult' has been developed by Debbie Brace and Bhavna Acharya, as part of their advisory work leading the 'Let's Talk Together' project in settings in Hounslow, to the west of London (Jones, 2013). Their experience and observations show that children's involvement in conversation increases when an adult is able to give uninterrupted time to interacting with children while they are playing. They also note that an adult who is available for conversation is likely to attract children to them, and particularly those children who may be vulnerable. The potential for mutually rewarding conversations is maximised when the Planted Adult is able to use strategies for effective conversations with more than one child, including those illustrated in Example 7.2 'Take 4' and Example 7.3. As a result, children and adults are more likely to have the time to focus on quality conversation and Sustained Shared Thinking.

In order for the Planted Adult to be able to give uninterrupted time to listening to children, other adults need to have a clearly planned role. The team will agree before the start of the session that the other practitioners will be operating in a more supervisory role with other children, and moving around the room or outdoor area. They will also be aware that during this period, their interactions with children are likely to be relatively brief. In settings where the ratio of children to adults is high, it may only be possible to plan to achieve this level of interaction on certain days and at certain times. However, it is an important strategy that can be used to meet the needs of children who require support, as well as ensuring that all children have an opportunity to be involved in detailed conversations.

CASE STUDY 7.1

The Planted Adult: how can we involve boys in painting?

I was visiting a busy nursery class in a primary school. The class has a higher than average number of vulnerable children. There is a well-resourced painting, cutting and sticking area, where children can independently peg a large piece of paper onto an easel, complete a painting and then put it on a rack to dry.

Practitioners had observed that it was mainly the girls who visited the area and asked me to suggest ways that boys could become more involved in independently painting, cutting and sticking. My main suggestion was to 'plant' an adult in the area for half an hour, while the other practitioners and I were involved in supervising children indoors and outside. One practitioner, Christine, 'planted' herself in the area and almost immediately a boy called Raphael asked for help to peg up a piece of paper. Christine stayed with Raphael and talked about his painting: what colours he was choosing, what the picture might be, and what might he paint next?

I asked another boy, Sean, if he would like to do a painting as well. I helped him to find an apron and to get his paper ready. Sean was unsure how to proceed, so I suggested he pop his head round the easel and talk

(Continued)

(Continued)

to Raphael about what he was doing. This led to a conversation between the boys, supported by Christine, about how Raphael was making different-coloured vertical strokes with his brush, to represent each member of his family. Sean had quite significant speech difficulties, and seemed unsure how to ask Raphael the right questions. Christine prompted him by saying, 'Say to Raphael, "Raphael. What are you painting?"' Sean did this and Raphael explained about his strokes. Sean copied him, but he explained that his brushstrokes were all cats.

Christine, who was now talking with Sean, prompted him to tell Raphael about his picture, by saying, 'Say to Raphael, "Raphael, look at my painting."' Raphael had a look, and Christine prompted Sean again: 'Raphael, look at what Sean has been doing. Sean, tell Raphael about your cats.' This led the boys to ask for fresh sheets of paper and they spent the next 10 minutes painting and talking about what each one was doing, supported by Christine.

While this conversation was taking place, I had reverted back to my supervisory role nearby (while listening intently to the conversation!)

In discussion after this session, Christine was clear that by having no other duties in the room for that 30 minutes, she was able to comfortably support children who needed help with the practicalities of organising themselves to paint. Because Christine was planted in the area, I could send over a vulnerable child in the knowledge that he would be involved in quality interaction. Through Christine's skilled involvement, the children were able to have an extended conversation with each other. They had both learned how to use the painting area independently and, because of the success and pleasure they gained from the experience, would be much more likely to return in the future. We discussed how Christine could plan to encourage Sean back into the painting area during the days that followed in order to build his confidence in using the area, develop his creativity and involve him in talk with other children.

Sharing books, sharing adults and sharing ideas

Being able to share a book with a child provides possibly the greatest opportunity for child and adult to explore ideas through conversation, because the structure of a book-sharing session provides a framework for sharing ideas.

As part of the Every Child a Talker (ECaT) projects in Bedford Borough and Thurrock, settings were involved in giving their book areas a 'makeover'. The number one priority was to ensure that adults had planned time in the book area. During that time, the adult had no other duties in the setting, other than to share books with children. This immediately increased the number of children who visited the area. One consequence of practitioners spending time in the book area was a realisation that certain things needed to improve, including the quality of seating for both adults and children (Jones, 2011). We discussed how the book area could be made to look more attractive, and more comfortable and appealing for the children who would hopefully became regular visitors. A crucial aspect of improving the space was to take a critical look at the number and type of books available.

Book area surveys showed that the vast majority of books on offer, for children aged over 18 months, were fiction. For many children, and particularly those who are vulnerable, non-fiction books can be more appealing than fiction. If one is sharing a storybook with a child, the book can only make sense if it is read from the beginning, with each page being followed in sequence until the story is finished. Adults might try to 'just talk about the pictures' with a child, but it soon becomes clear that the book will need to be read in order to make sense to both the adult and child. The one exception to this observation is if the book is already familiar to the child and adult. Non-fiction books, on the other hand, have the advantage that a child can open the book on any page and start talking meaningfully about the illustrations. This is particularly the case if the book is on a subject that the child is already keenly interested in.

An important piece of unpublished research by Emma Nicolls pointed to the clear advantages for language development and literacy of regularly sharing non-fiction books with children (Nicolls, 2004). Non-fiction books for children have either colour photographs or line drawings, and are designed to describe facts or ideas that appeal to young children. They have specialist language and are usually written in the present tense. Although the written text may often be complex, books can be opened at any page without the child or adult losing a sense of context. For these reasons, very young or vulnerable children may find them more appealing than books with a story.

As well as looking at the type of books that children were being offered, Nicolls focused on what adults did with them. In many cases, what was described by adults as 'book-sharing', was actually teaching a child the mechanics of reading. True book-sharing takes place when the adult:

- Asks the child what book they would like to share
- Offers the child the choice of holding the book or for the adult and child to hold it together
- Asks the child if she would like to talk about the pictures, or whether the adult should read

Given this set of choices, from my observation and experience, a child with a storybook will almost certainly ask the adult to read. A child with a non-fiction book will be more likely to want to lead a discussion about the pictures.

Nicolls suggests that the dynamic at work here is one of 'power'. If the child is holding the book, then she has the power to look at any page she likes, and to lead in the talking. However, if the adult has the book, then the child may adopt a passive role as listener and respond only to what the adult says. While this may not be a problem if the adult is sensitive to the child, there could be potential for a vulnerable child either to lose interest or feel under pressure to concentrate or respond to questions that she may not be able to answer.

While the Planted Adult is in the book area, it is unlikely that he will be able to share an entire book without being interrupted by another child. However, there can be distinct advantages for having two, or even three, children comfortably sharing the adult's attention, with a book as the main focus. This allows the adult to share ideas with a small group of children, and for children to be able to respond to and learn from each other in a sustained way.

CASE STUDY 7.2

The Planted Adult in an 'Instant Book Area'

An 'Instant Book Area' is a crate that contains a colourful rug, some wicker baskets and a selection of books and toys based round a theme, e.g. transport, animals, or books linked to children's TV programmes and films. The books will be a selection of fiction and non-fiction. With the crate are six small plastic seats for the adult and children to sit on. There may also be a 'Welcome' doormat for the children to put their shoes on. (My observation is that when children take off their shoes in the book area, it has the effect of calming children and helps to create a relaxed atmosphere.)

With the children's help, the 'Planted Adult' sets up the book area, involving them in sorting out the books and toys into the various baskets. These are placed on the rug, and the seats are placed in a semi-circle around the rug. Children are encouraged to take off their shoes and to come and share a book. They can either sit on the seats or on the rug. The adult sits on a seat and begins to share a book with a child. When another child arrives, she can be offered the choice of sitting on a spare seat and joining in the book-sharing session with the first child or waiting until the adult is free. If the child decides to wait, the adult may suggest that she might like to go and find a friend to choose a book and toy to play with.

In some cases, there may be too many children for the Planted Adult to deal with effectively. In this case, he has either of two options: to call for another practitioner to join the group, or to set up a 'waiting list'. This can be written down, explaining to the children that, 'there are too many visitors in the book area at the moment. But when Jenny has finished then she will be sent to go and get the person who is next.' As long as the adult is able to keep this promise, then this relieves stress: for the child who desperately wants to join in, and for the adult who needs to focus his attention. This system also helps the child sharing the book to relax, as she knows that she is not under any pressure to finish talking with the practitioner.

Setting up an exciting area, with an adult available to spend a planned amount of time sharing books with children, in a way that stimulates their interests, creates a situation where children and adults can talk in depth and in a sustained way, either individually or as part of a small group.

 Points for reflection and discussion

How do you plan for adults to share talk with 'vulnerable' children?

Could 'planting' an adult at the playdough table be a good place to explore the effectiveness of this technique?

NB: The practitioner's aim is to be fully involved in conversation. This includes not taking notes. It may be useful for the manager to experiment with this activity first (making sure that he/she is not interrupted and remains focused!). The manager can then lead by modelling the technique. (See Chapter 8 on managers leading by example.)

 Practical tasks

Plan to be the 'Planted Adult' in an area where there is a 'child-initiated' activity, e.g. home corner or at the playdough table. (All adults in the room need to cooperate in ensuring that you have no other tasks at this time. It is helpful to have one colleague who is the 'room supervisor' who moves around the room.)

(Continued)

(Continued)

Were you able to avoid the temptation to talk with children who were at activities nearby?

Was there a difference in the quality of conversations you were involved in?

Sustaining concentration and talk in whole-group sessions

Any room with a large number of children in it is bound to be noisy. Even when the practitioners have settled the whole group down for a quiet activity, there can be a significant amount of background noise that distracts the group's attention. In a typical baby room, during a group activity, children's and adults' concentration might be interrupted by at least one of the following:

- A parent arriving with a child
- The manager popping her head round the door to ask a question or show a visitor round
- A washing machine on its spin cycle in an adjoining alcove
- An adult singing to herself as she prepares the snack
- A CD player on in the background
- The internal phone in the room ringing
- An adult noisily preparing for the next activity

A practitioner leading a story or song session with a group of older children can often experience a similar amount of background disruption.

If our aim is to engage a group of children, then children and adults need to have the minimum amount of distraction possible. This allows the adults to create what I call the 'Magic Bubble', when a group of children and adults are so absorbed in what they are sharing that they do not realise that time is passing. Ground rules for creating the Magic Bubble for all children in a room, e.g. at story time, include:

- Planning for the activity to take place at the same time every day
- Choosing a time of day where children and adults will be unhurried
- Having all adults who work in the room focusing on the activity
- Giving one adult the role of 'disruptions manager' to deal with unavoidable disruptions, which allows other adults to have uninterrupted focus

If these rules are consistently adhered to, then children will be more likely to able to concentrate and become absorbed in the activity that the adults might be leading, e.g. a story, a singing session or a discussion about what we would like to do tomorrow.

CASE STUDY 7.3

The Magic Bubble in a baby room

Practitioners in a baby room with children aged 9 months to 18 months were concerned that they could not engage the babies and toddlers in a group session for enough time for the children to benefit in terms of language development and learning. The sessions included group singing and book-sharing and 'heuristic play', where the children were encouraged to explore collections of objects such as pine cones, wooden spoons or containers full of jam jar lids (Goldschmied and Jackson, 2004). On observation, it was discovered that most of the background distractions mentioned above were taking place. Additionally, children would concentrate for a short time, then wander off and play with other toys that were readily available. An adult would then get up and encourage these children to come back to the group. Consequently, there was never a sufficient length of uninterrupted time when the children could concentrate fully on what the adults were hoping would excite their interest.

The adults made the following changes that created 'Magic Bubbles' and greatly improved the children's participation:

The session was held between 9.30 and 10.15 every morning

A sign was put on the door asking for quiet and for adults to avoid interrupting

All adults were involved in the session, apart from one who was 'disruptions manager'

The adults placed a large colourful rug on the floor

All other toys were either removed from the area, or cabinets nearby were covered with large cloths

If any children moved away from the activity, they were not encouraged to come back, but were observed by the disruptions manager. Children often returned to the activity of their own volition

Once the activity was finished, the rug and resources were put away and the room returned to its familiar state

(Continued)

(Continued)

Putting these changes in place created the opportunity for 'Magic Bubbles' to develop, leading to an increase in children's involvement in the activities, as well as improving the quality and quantity of interactions between individual children and adults. In addition, children spent more time copying each other, and there were more instances when children talked together.

The practitioners felt that a group session would be most successful when all the adults were present and able to give their full attention to the children. By rotating the role of the 'disruptions manager' each day, all adults had a chance to be involved in quality interactions within a group activity. Children benefited from being able to focus their concentration because they were with adults who could give their full attention. Children who were not so focused were able to play quietly in another part of the room without 'bursting the Magic Bubble'. Laying down the rug at the beginning of each session gave the children the feeling that something exciting was going to happen in that space. The rug also defined the area that the children were expected to stay in as a group.

Engaging children in small groups in busy rooms

Most settings are likely to have vulnerable children, including children with developmental delay or significant additional learning needs that have an impact on their communication. These additional needs can include children with Asperger's syndrome or other forms of Autism Spectrum Disorder (ASD) and children who have delayed speech and language development because of intermittent hearing difficulties caused by otitis media, which is often known as 'Glue Ear' (Peer, 2005). Many of these children benefit from individual attention, and regular one-to-one work with a practitioner is often recommended by professionals, such as speech and language therapists. One dilemma for the practitioners is how to implement this advice within a busy setting. Another challenge for practitioners comes when practitioners plan to lead groups of children, including those with additional needs, in busy rooms. Here, it can be difficult to achieve a level of concentration and involvement that is conducive to learning.

As part of the Every Child a Talker (ECaT) project, my colleagues and I experimented with various approaches that addressed the issue of how to wholly engage children in small groups, where the focus was planned and led by an adult. Adult-led activities range from 'focused learning' which involves adults guiding children in 'playful, experiential activities' to those where the activity is structured in such a way that the adult directs almost entirely what children do (DCSF, 2009b). One successful approach involved two practitioners working together in adult-led groups, where the children were involved in focused learning. In these cases, one adult acted as the 'manager' of the activity, while the other was the 'Planted Adult'. The manager introduced the resources, addressed the children as a group, moved around and talked to other children who wanted to join in. The Planted Adult stayed in one place and was available for detailed conversations.

The following case study involves a visit to a setting to explore this approach. This type of activity encapsulates a key message of this book: that detailed conversations can take place in busy settings, and particularly when adults organise themselves effectively in order to make this a reality. For this reason, the case study and analysis that follows are more detailed than any other in this book.

CASE STUDY 7.4

The Nursery Rhyme Survey: a successful small group at Chapel Street Nursery School, Luton

Chapel Street Nursery School serves an area of Luton with a diverse population, including families where English is spoken as an additional language (EAL). The nursery school also receives funding from the Local Authority to include children with identified significant additional learning needs. Children in the setting are aged from two to five years. There is no separate provision for two-year-olds, who are involved in the rooms along with older children. Together, we explored how to create an adult-led activity within their main group room, involving two adults in order to spontaneously attract all children, and maintain their interest, involvement and learning. (This was in spite of the other exciting activities on offer in the room.)

The activity we led, the 'Nursery Rhyme Survey' (Jones and Belsten, 2011), aims to involve each child individually in a conversation, where they decide which nursery rhyme is their favourite then illustrate their choice and share their results as a group by creating a block graph.

Resources

A small coloured bag of finger puppets, representing each of six popular nursery rhymes

An iPod and speaker, or CD player with a song for each rhyme

(Continued)

(Continued)

Blank postcard-sized pieces of card

Felt-tipped pens

A small box to put the cards in

An iPad or digital camera for taking photos of the children during the activity

The activity

Each child in turn is asked to play with the puppets, listen to the music and decide which rhyme they like the best. Once they have made their choice, each child draws a picture representing their rhyme on a piece of card, and has a go at writing their name. Once they have finished, they put their card into the box. When all the children have been involved, the whole group sit in a circle or semi-circle and an adult brings the cards out one at a time to create a block graph on the floor.

The planning

Both adults sat at a table in the middle of the room, close to a busy role play area. We had previously decided that I would be the 'manager' of the resources, explaining to the children what to do, having the initial conversation with each child, and encouraging other children to join in or watch while they were waiting for their turn. My job also involved taking a photo of each child while they were involved in the activity. The other adult's role was to be available to talk with each child as they drew their pictures, and to help them write their name.

We also agreed that we would only take photos of the children with their permission, and stop them while they were drawing their pictures, so that they could look at the photo I had taken and comment on it. Before I took a photo, I explained to each child that we wanted to take a photo of what they were doing, so that we could talk about the photos the next day, as well as use them as part of a wall display, so that they could talk about the activity with their parents. We planned to lead this activity over a morning and afternoon session, and to return the next morning to talk with the children about the photographs that we had taken.

We agreed that neither of us would take any notes, as we wanted to ensure that our attention was given entirely to what the children were doing or saying.

What happened

We played the music and were immediately joined by two children, who became actively involved in singing the songs and talking with the adults and to each other. We set up a system where I encouraged up to four children to join in, by taking turns to hold the bag of puppets and to take the right puppet out of the bag as soon as they heard its song. This held the children's attention while they waited.

One child, with additional learning needs that include delayed language development, remained at the activity throughout the entire 90 minutes (apart from a short break to go to the toilet and have a snack). He returned in the afternoon and the following day. Another child, in the early stages of learning EAL, was equally absorbed, while other children stayed at the activity for an average of 20 minutes. Over two sessions, all the children in the room, bar two, became involved in the activity.

The children's differing responses

We needed to adapt what we had planned, as the younger children were interested in playing with the puppets and talking about them and singing the songs, and less willing to be involved in the mark-making aspect of the activity. Once we had decided that children didn't need to do any drawing if they didn't want to, these two-year-olds became more relaxed and involved.

Four children stayed at the activity for at least 50 minutes, waiting for their turn, joining in and then staying to see what other children were doing. This was a significant achievement, bearing in mind that our table was right next to a busy role play area, while other exciting activities were taking place throughout the room. Our view was that these children became absorbed to such an extent that they were able to block out all other distractions. Two of these children were in the early stages of learning EAL, but were able to understand most of what the adults were saying. By waiting their turn and listening to what the other children said and watching how they responded to me, the children were able to become fully involved in the activity when it was their turn. They stayed on after their turn to listen to what other children were saying, to join in with discussions or to talk to me, as the 'manager', about their thoughts and observations.

Observation, recording and taking photographs

There was concern about the embargo on practitioners taking notes. How would they remember what had happened and what children had said? What evidence would we have of the children's involvement? I discourage adults from making notes about what children are doing and saying, because this leads the practitioner to temporarily withdraw their focus from the activity, which has the potential to 'burst' the Magic Bubble of their involvement. This equally applies to a practitioner who steps out of the activity temporarily to take photos of what the children are doing. One way to do this was for the practitioners to talk to each other during the activity. This ensured that we were able to remember how the children had responded.

For example, Tony had just said something very interesting, so I interrupted Claudette, the Planted Adult, to tell her about what Tony had said. Tony, was aged 3;8 at the time and learning EAL. He was normally quite quiet and reserved, but spoke to me at length:

Tony:	I think 'Humpty Dumpty' is the best song. Because it is funny when he fall off the wall and bump his head.
Michael:	Oh. That's very interesting. Claudette is busy talking with Marsha at the moment. But can I tell her what you have just said?
Tony:	Yes.
Michael:	Claudette. Excuse me. . Are you busy? Can I just tell you what Tony has said? It's very interesting.
Claudette:	Yes Michael. You can..
Michael:	Tony has just told me that he likes 'Humpty Dumpty' best, because it's funny when Humpty falls off the wall.
Claudette:	I like that nursery rhyme, too. It makes me laugh as well, but I feel a bit sorry for poor old Humpty.
Tony:	They couldn't fix him.
Claudette:	No, they couldn't. All the king's horses and all the king's men couldn't put him back together again!

Claudette then returned her attention to Marsha (who had been listening intently) and I continued talking with Tony.

Claudette and I were struck by how animated Tony had been and how clearly he had expressed himself. This was an unusual moment for him, so we made a note of it after the session had finished. Using this method to communicate with each other as the activity was taking place ensured that we had both made a mental note of a significant new aspect of Tony's behaviour. Granted, we couldn't remember word for word what he had said, but this was unnecessary, as our observation, which would be recorded in his observations file, was about his newfound animation and ability to use English as part of a group. By interrupting Claudette in quite a formal way ('Claudette. Excuse me.. Are you busy?') I was conveying two messages to the children in the group:

- What you have to say is important
- Saying, 'Claudette. Excuse me. …' is a good way to get an adult's attention while she is talking to another child

The decision only to take photographs with the children's permission came from an observation that children talk at length about photographs if they have been involved in taking them, and are encouraged to talk about them immediately afterwards. Far from disrupting the child's concentration, this method can help children to describe what they are doing and gives the practitioner a valid reason for joining in the children's play. To explore this principle we used an iPad. The advantage of the iPad camera is that the screen is large, there is excellent picture resolution and children can touch the screen to expand the photographs in order to look at detail. A typical exchange when taking a photo went as follows:

Jessica, aged 3;2 is involved in drawing a picture of her favourite rhyme, 'Twinkle, Twinkle.'

Michael places the finger puppet in front of Jessica so that it will appear in the photo:

Michael: Ooh, Jessica! Sorry to interrupt you. I can see that you are busy drawing and talking to Claudette. But can I take a photo of you drawing Twinkle, Twinkle?

Jessica: Yes please.

(Michael takes the photo and immediately shows it to Jessica.)

Michael: Look, Jessica. What are you doing?

Jessica (very excited about the photo):   There's Jessie. I'm drawing Twinkle.

Michael: Yes. That's right. Shall we show that photo to Mummy and Daddy? We want to put this photo on the wall. Then you can talk to Mummy and Daddy about it.

Jessica: Yes please.

Michael: And what will you tell Mummy and Daddy about the picture?

Jessica: I like Twinkle, Twinkle. Tamsin likes Twinkle, Twinkle as well.

(Jessica carries on drawing and talking with Claudette.)

Following up the activity

We now had an excellent photo of Jessica drawing. We planned to use this and other photos over the days that followed, as we involved the children in individual follow-up conversations about the photographs. Our aim was to see if they could talk about an activity that had already taken place. It is relatively easy for children to talk about events as they occur, but more challenging to describe something using past tenses. Our aims in talking with the children about the photos we had taken, of themselves and of other children, were:

- To assess their ability to describe an activity
- To write down what they had said, for our records
- To use the conversation to model appropriate grammar and vocabulary
- To write down 'accurate' responses and use them as captions for the photos and drawings, as part of a large wall display

A typical conversation could be as follows, with Emmanuel, an EAL learner who is aged 4;2:

Michael: What did you do yesterday?

Emmanuel: I am draw Baa Baa Black Sheep.

Michael: Yes. You drew a picture of Baa Baa Black Sheep.

Emmanuel: Machin him draw spider.

Michael: Yes, Machin drew Incy Wincy Spider. Let's write about what you did, so we can read your words when we look at the pictures on the wall. Then you can talk to Mummy and Daddy about what we did.

(Michael begins to write.)

Michael: We can say, 'I drew a picture of Baa Baa Black Sheep. Machin drew a picture of Incy Wincy Spider.'

(Emmanuel watches Michael write each word and they read the caption together.)

Here I have fulfilled my need to record accurately what Emmanuel was able to say. I dated his original comment and added it to his records. I also used the conversation as a way to model an appropriate use of English grammar. It is this caption that will appear on the wall as a model of accurate English. In displaying the photos and captions prominently, at the children's eye level, the aim is to attract the children's and parents' attention. Hopefully, the children and their parents will be drawn to talk about the display regularly when they drop off and collect their children. Practitioners can also talk regularly with the children about this simple, yet exciting, activity, sustaining a conversation over the days and weeks that the display remains in place. When the display is finally taken down, the photos and captions can be added to the children's record folders or sent home for the children and parents to talk about and cherish forever. The photos can also be transferred to a PowerPoint display that children can access independently on the computer in the room.

Evaluation

Each child was able to be involved in a detailed conversation with two adults, for as long as they wanted. The first conversation with me was structured, so that I could explain to each child what we wanted them to do. We had planned beforehand that we wanted to explore with the children the concepts of 'best' and 'favourite', so I asked each child, 'Which song do you like best? Which one is your favourite?' Children who were waiting and observing could see (literally) what they would have to do when it was their turn. Those with language learning needs could successfully link my words to my facial expressions and gestures. This ensured optimum understanding when it came to their turn, including the key vocabulary that we had planned to introduce and reinforce.

The Planted Adult, on the other hand, responded to what the children said as they drew a picture, and during the process of helping them to write their name on the card. Having the freedom to become absorbed in a conversation with an individual child, or two children involved in the same task, enabled the Planted Adult to discuss in detail what the children were doing, answer their questions or respond in an unhurried way to what they were saying. This presented the opportunity for Sustained Shared Thinking. The activity appealed to all the children because it was based on what they already knew. Each child talked with enthusiasm and intensity about their choices, because, like all children in early years settings in the UK, singing and learning nursery rhymes is an integral part of their experience. Because both adults responded with equal passion and intensity, the experience was not only absorbing at the time, but exciting enough for the children to become absorbed in talking about photographs the following day, and for many days to come.

During the follow-up session the next day, it was interesting for us to note that the children were all keen to handle the puppets again, and to listen to the music. The two-year-olds in particular, were excited about being involved in the activity again (although without the drawing), as were the children with additional learning needs. This underlines the importance of planning to repeat activities in order to continue to develop conversation and learning.

Two adults working together

Case Study 7.4 and the detailed analysis of the activity above illustrate the advantages of regularly using two adults in an adult-led activity, where both adults are focused on conversation. This creates a relaxed atmosphere where children can develop their ideas. Two practitioners can plan to spend time at an activity in any area, with the express purpose of engaging the children in conversation. This includes having two adults taking part in activities that are described as 'child-initiated', where the children choose to develop their own play activities, based on resources that adults have made available (DCSF, 2009b).

Children also benefit from two adults spending time at the activities that are available daily and that typically draw children into repetitive and relaxed exploratory play. These 'continuous provision' activities include playdough and sand and water play. In many settings, one might observe practitioners spending a short amount of time at the playdough table, then moving on to areas where closer supervision may be needed. However, from my experience, when two adults 'plant' themselves in areas with continuous provision, children can become involved in very detailed and lengthy conversations. These conversations are often completely 'open-ended', in the sense that there is no objective other than to explore ideas that children bring up themselves. This has the impact of drawing vulnerable children to the activity and ensuring that they remain there for enough time to take part in conversations of length, depth and interest. While there might be brief reference to what the children are doing, e.g. making 'biscuits' with playdough, the conversation often turns to topics such as 'what we do at home', 'what my little brother did' or 'what Mummy said to Daddy'. These types of 'decontextualised' conversations are valuable for developing children's conversational and social skills, as well as being vital for literacy development (see Chapter 9). It is important to point out that both adults working with child-initiated, open-ended activities, such as in the home corner and role-play areas, would be acting equally as Planted Adults in conversation with children, as there is no need for either to 'manage' the activity.

Two adults can be involved in activities that require a high degree of adult direction, e.g. using tools at a woodwork bench or making a Victoria sponge cake. In these cases, the 'manager' organises the children to use the resources appropriately or follow a sequence of instructions. The Planted Adult can be available for detailed conversations and explanations with individual children, while they are taking part in the activity. If the adults work together as described above, any photographs that they take with the children can be used to create opportunities to further extend the children's language, e.g. in homemade photo-books that the children and adults can share.

Conclusion

Interacting and talking with small groups of children who are deeply involved in child-initiated play or adult-led activities can be as effective as sharing ideas with children individually. Many children need support to reach the point where they can feel that being part of a group is as rewarding as having individual adult attention. How successful they are in being able to participate in small group conversations will depend on their age, level of social and emotional maturity and communication skills. However, if adults are clear about their aims for involving children in conversation, then children can talk and learn together.

In Chapter 8, we explore in more detail how the collective understanding of how children learn, i.e. the pedagogy of the setting, influences how adults can plan for talk, so that children and adults can talk and learn together effectively.

 Points for reflection and discussion

Asking two adults to work together at an activity is a huge investment of time. Is it a valid strategy for your setting, to meet the needs of 'vulnerable' children?

Do you have concerns about not making written notes in 'real time'?

 Practical activities

Plan an adult-led activity with two adults working together as in Case Study 7.4. How did the children respond?

Plan for two adults to be at a child-initiated activity. Was there a difference in the quality of conversation?

Evaluate this strategy and report back in detail to the manager and colleagues.

'Plant' an adult in your book area. Does this have an impact on the number of children visiting? Is there a difference in the quality of book-sharing?

Further reading

Jones, M. and Twani, J. (2014) *Let's Talk About Maths!* Cambridge: Lawrence Educational/Yellow Door.

Useful websites

National Literacy Trust Book Corner Audit
www.wordsforlife.org.uk/questionnaire/index.php?option=Book+corner+audit (accessed 25 May 2015)
Provides a comprehensive interactive resource for assessing the current status of your book area, as well as practical suggestions for how to make improvements.
Talk4Meaning
www.talk4meaning.co.uk/every-child-a-talker/give-your-book-corner-a-makeover/ (accessed 25 May 2015)
Further information and practical ideas for transforming book areas.

CHAPTER 8

PEDAGOGY AND PRACTICE THAT INFLUENCES TALK

This chapter will

- Suggest that the pedagogy of the setting influences how adults talk with children
- Describe how practitioners have adapted the way they interact to meet children's changing needs
- Describe how settings have made changes to the systems they operate to improve wellbeing and language

In Chapter 7, we made reference to the continuum of activities that exists in settings, from unstructured and child-initiated play, through activities planned and led by adults, including those that are highly structured (DCSF, 2009b). In any setting, decisions made by adults dictate what the balance between these approaches will be. These decisions reflect what the practitioners working in the setting know about child development, and their beliefs about how best to meet children's needs, to aid development and to stimulate learning. The shared belief of managers and practitioners, their pedagogy, has a direct influence on the types of activities that children are involved in and how adults interact with them (DCSF, 2009b). The definition of the pedagogy of a setting also includes how adults adapt to the unique needs of particular groups of children (Siraj-Blatchford, 2010). Evidence from detailed case studies from the Effective Provision of Pre-school Education Project (EPPE) suggests that in the settings that were judged to be most highly effective, the practitioners' pedagogy led them to provide a balance between child-initiated and adult-led activities. Practitioners within these settings were more likely to be able to engage children in detailed conversations and Sustained Shared Thinking, which provided the framework the children needed to scaffold their learning (Sylva et al., 2004).

Pedagogy also directly influences how adults plan the physical environment, including outdoor areas, resources and furniture. This can have a significant impact on the way that children are able to play, explore and talk together, which influences their wellbeing and what they talk about (Community Playthings, 2013; White, 2014). What happens within that environment, including how the children are taught and the learning that stems from that teaching, is also directly influenced by pedagogy. The Early Years Foundation Stage (EYFS) recommends that the key features of effective early learning and teaching involve children playing and exploring, actively learning, creating and thinking. Children should be encouraged to investigate and experience, concentrate and keep on trying, while they develop their own ideas and ultimately enjoy their achievements (DFE, 2012). Nancy Stewart, in her book *How Children Learn* (2011), asserts that these features of effective teaching depend on the quality of interactions that adults have with children.

In the UK, significant changes in society have led practitioners in settings to make changes to their practice, in order to meet children's language and learning needs. Enlargement of the European Union has led to an increase in families moving to the UK, and often settling in rural areas. Here, settings that have not previously had experience of supporting children learning English as an additional language (EAL) may now support several children whose parents are new to the country, and whose children are in the very early stages of learning English.

One national government policy change that has had a significant impact on practice has been the inclusion in settings of two-year-old children who are judged to be 'vulnerable'. This 'vulnerability' may stem, for example, from the family's adverse social circumstances, or issues that contribute to difficulties with parenting. Many of these children will need support with social development and communication. Settings have also had to adapt to changes within society, where more children are judged to have 'language impoverishment'. In many cases, these children's reduced progress in language development is due, in the main, to limited experience of talk at home (I CAN, 2006).

This chapter will focus on settings where practitioners have worked together to adapt or radically change aspects of their practice, in order to meet children's changing language and learning needs. This impulse to change has come from the practitioners' shared beliefs about children's development, i.e. the adults' collective pedagogy.

Setting a standard for adult talk

In Chapter 5 (p. 88), we explored the possibility that some children and adults may use a 'Restricted Code', including using a smaller range of vocabulary than those who use an 'Elaborated Code' (Bernstein, 1973). Whether or not we agree with Bernstein, it is clearly important to take every opportunity to enrich all children's vocabularies. In Example 5.3, we see a teacher enriching Steven's vocabulary by suggesting that what he calls 'the 'ump' could be referred to in another way, i.e. by using the word 'annoyed'. This is enriching his language. He can still talk about 'having the 'ump', but now has another word that will help him communicate better at home, and at school with children and adults who don't share his family's dialect.

Many settings decide to enrich children's vocabularies by practical interventions that include adult-led activities, e.g. small groups aimed at stimulating children's interests and talk. Others take as their starting point a focus on the *adults'* language. In some settings, for example, practitioners work on reducing the amount of local dialect that they use when talking with children, while increasing their use of Standard English. It is important to state here that practitioners were not changing their *accents* or trying to influence children's accents. However, in these settings, practitioners might habitually use only the local dialect, i.e. the variation of English, which would only be fully understood by local people (e.g. 'Geordie' in Newcastle or 'Scouse' in Liverpool). Practitioners made a conscious decision to use mainly English that would be recognisable to any speaker in the UK, and any child in the setting.

CASE STUDY 8.1

Changing greetings and how adults talk to groups of children

A local authority advisor visited a setting where a significant number of children were judged to be showing signs of 'language impoverishment'. The manager suggested that in many cases, the children's difficulties were due to the lack of interaction between parents and their children, as well as the restricted range of the parents' vocabularies in everyday conversations. The advisor noted that practitioners would greet parents and children alike in the morning with, 'You alright?' which was a typical greeting in the local community. During feedback to the manager, the advisor pointed out that greeting children and parents were valuable opportunities to improve

(Continued)

(Continued)

children's language. For example, practitioners could use phrases such as, 'Good *morning/afternoon*. Hello. How are you *today?/* Are you *well?* Did you sleep well? What *have you had/* what *did you have* for *breakfast?* Did you have a nice *lunch?*' This would model a style of greeting that was more reflective of Standard English, as well as opening up the possibility for a brief conversation between parents, practitioner and child.

In the same setting, it was common for staff to shout, 'Listen up guys!' when they wanted to gain children's attention. It was pointed out to the manager that telling children to 'listen up' might be confusing, and that no one in the setting was a 'guy', as there were only women and children in the building. As an alternative way of getting a group of children's attention adults could say, 'Listen *children/girls/boys/* boys *and* girls. *Everyone pay attention/* Look at me, etc.'

The manager could see that the advisor had an interesting point; particularly as both had recently visited a local primary school where all of the staff greeted the children using Standard English, as well as taking every opportunity they could to model a more 'elaborate' use of English when talking with children. This view was put to the staff in a follow-up training session on language development. There was a heated debate about the pros and cons of practitioners using words from the dialect, which reflected how many people in the community spoke. At the end of the meeting, the manager and deputy agreed to use less dialect themselves and to observe what effect this had on the children's language. An immediate consequence was that children in the early stages of learning EAL showed a marked increase in their use of the words 'morning' and 'afternoon'. The staff attributed this change to their greeting the children using these key words. This made a big impression on the practitioners, who followed the managers' example and set about changing this aspect of their interaction with children and parents.

It might seem that the advisor in Case Study 8.1 was making a value judgement about one type of English being 'better' than another. An alternative view is that children need to be aware that different registers exist within English, and when and with whom it is appropriate to use them. For example, children in school become aware that some of their peers might use *slang,* or even swear, in the playground. Slang is an informal register that children might use at home or when playing amongst themselves. Sometimes it is part of a local dialect, and is often consciously used by older children and adults to indicate that they are part of a particular group.

For example, children in a setting in the North East of England were heard to tell each other to 'Shut your gob' (be quiet) while playing outdoors. One of the children later said this to a practitioner, who suggested that it wasn't such a nice thing to say. The child explained that his Daddy said this a lot, and particularly when they were involved in rough-and-tumble play. The practitioner explained that it was fine to use this type of language at home, as long as Mummy and Daddy don't mind, but we shouldn't say it to each other in nursery, and especially not to grown-ups.

Children learn about swearing in the same way. If children swear, adults can help them, through discussion, to understand that swearing is not a good thing to do. Four-year-old Faye, for example, used a very offensive word to describe her best friend, Lauren, when they were arguing over which one of them should wear the much-coveted Snow White dress. Lauren was so shocked that she immediately told her teacher what Faye had said. The teacher took Faye and Lauren to one side and explained that some people do use 'strong words', but it's not nice to do this, and we should certainly never use these words in school. This led Faye to explain exactly where she had heard this word being used, by whom and in what context, i.e. 'My Daddy said it to my next door neighbour, because his cat keeps coming into our garden and pooing.' These types of discussions are very important, because they provide children with a sense that language is not only made up of words, but that it can be used in different ways.

Practitioners often use imaginative play, e.g. with puppets or in the role play area, to explore the concept of register and dialect. Giving puppets personalities that use different dialects and accents not only makes children laugh, but opens up the possibility of talking about how people use English in different ways. For example, adults often talk about the same things, but use different types of English to say what they mean. For example, children often realise that when a puppet is made to say, 'And I was like, "Chillax Dude", and he was like, "That's totally awesome, Dude,"' the puppet is using the same 'Surfer Lingo' as 'Crush', the turtle character in Disney's film *Finding Nemo*. While playing with a group of three-year-olds in a day nursery, where we were busy changing and feeding several realistic-looking newborn baby dolls, I tried an experiment to see if the children had an appreciation of different registers. I spoke to one little girl in 'Motherese'. She was horrified and told me, 'I not a baby! I a big girl!' Another little boy said, 'My not a kitten!' It took me a while to realise what he meant, as cat owners often use the same type of register as 'Motherese' when addressing their pets. These very young children were clearly aware of the uses of different registers.

Wood (1998) makes the observation that some children who are judged to have language difficulties when they start school may, in actual fact, be failing to understand what teachers are saying to them. This, according to Wood, is not due to a fundamental problem with verbal comprehension, but because the type of talk that teachers sometimes use, i.e. their register, is unfamiliar.

Example 8.1 'Teacher talk'

Talia, a child who was age 4;6 and had attended a reception class in a primary school for six months, enjoyed playing 'schools' at home. She was overheard saying to her 'class' of teddies and dolls sitting on the carpet in front of her, 'Do you know, Red Class, I'm really rather disappointed with the behaviour of some of you.' Talia attended a school where the majority of the children were learning EAL, and it would be quite possible that some of them would be rather bemused by this example of what I often refer to as 'teacher talk', that Talia was imitating. There is nothing wrong with using the word 'disappointed', as it is a true reflection of how the teacher feels, but her grammar is complex and potentially confusing. In this case, it might have been better for the teacher to use simpler language that is guaranteed to be understood by most of the class, e.g. 'Some children in our class have not been behaving nicely. This makes me feel disappointed.'

 Points for reflection and discussion

Do you use dialect, or words from dialect, with children? Should all practitioners in the setting use Standard English?

 Practical tasks

You may be aware that some parents, or colleagues even, are using a register or level of language that is creating a barrier to communication. They may, for example, be using language that is too complex or even have the very bad habit of using sarcasm, e.g. 'What do you think you are doing?' or 'You wouldn't do that at home would you?' Their register may be too simple, e.g. using a tone of voice and grammar with older children that you might expect to be used with younger ones. For example, one parent trying to stop her almost five-year-old from hitting his younger brother, said in a high-pitched, 'sing song' voice, 'Oh, please don't fight. Mummy will get upset.'

How can you help?

Experiment with modelling an appropriate register, e.g. 'Leon, stop fighting.'

Accuracy of adult talk

If we accept that children with limited vocabulary are at a disadvantage in school, then it is the practitioners' duty to help all children have as rich a vocabulary as possible. Adults can do this by using accurate vocabulary when talking with children. For example, I had helped a little girl from Lithuania get ready to go outside on a freezing cold day, and told her how much I liked her coat. The head teacher pointed out to me that what I had been referring to as a coat was, in fact, a jacket. By being inaccurate, I had inadvertently reduced this child's potential for learning English, as well as missing an opportunity to introduce a new word, 'jacket'. This head teacher was very clear that she, her colleagues and all visitors need to be aware of how they talk with children. By leading from her own example, she set a standard for talk with children, and her favourite saying was: 'All learning starts with language.'

Example 8.2 Talking about toggles with Donna

Donna, aged 2;5, has a new duffle coat. She is very pleased with it, but finds the toggles very difficult to manage. Over three days, she is involved in discussion with her Key Person, Scarlet, as she helps Donna put on her coat.

Day 1

Scarlet:	I like your new coat! It is lovely and big and looks very warm.
Donna:	Me like it. Me like it warm.
Scarlet:	Shall I help you do your coat up?
Donna:	Me not do buttons.
Scarlet:	Yes. They are very big. We call them toggles.
Donna:	Toggles.
Scarlet:	Those toggles are very hard to do up.
Donna:	Buttons. Big buttons.
Scarlet:	Let's have a go at doing up those toggles.

(Continued)

(Continued)

Day 2

Scarlet: Let's have a go at doing up those toggles again.

Donna: No toggles. Button.

Scarlet: It's a big toggle. Toggles.

Donna: Big button.

Scarlet
(laughing):   You call it a big button. I call it a toggle.

Donna: Mummy say button.

Scarlet: Mummy calls them buttons does she?

Day 3

Donna: Me like new coat.

Scarlet: I like it too.

Donna
(pointing to
a toggle):   What that?

Scarlet: That's a toggle.

Donna: Me like buttons.

Scarlet: Is that because buttons are easier to do up? Are toggles
                    very hard?

Donna: Toggle hard. Yes.

Here we see a real exchange of ideas, and a very young child standing her ground about what she wants to call something, because that's what her Mummy calls it. Scarlet expertly acknowledges that neither Donna nor her Mummy are 'wrong'. However, Scarlet is equally determined, in the nicest possible way, to point out that you can also call this very large (and annoyingly difficult to do up) fixing a 'toggle'. By the end of the third conversation, Donna has the word 'toggle' as part of her vocabulary. Whether or not she chooses to use it is another matter!

Another approach to improving adult accuracy of language in order to expand children's vocabulary has become known as 'Five for One'.

Practitioners are encouraged to actively increase each child's vocabulary fivefold. Practitioners engage children in conversation and make a mental note about how children refer to various items in the environment, e.g. footwear. If 'shoe' is part of a child's expressive vocabulary, adults aim to introduce five more ways of accurately naming what people wear on their feet, e.g. trainers/sandals/wellies/slippers/flip-flops. This could be done as part of a daily routine of helping children put on their shoes, e.g. commenting, 'I like your sandals. Were you wearing trainers yesterday?' In addition, vocabulary can be introduced or reinforced as an adult-led maths and language activity. For example, children in a small group are presented with a big bag of various types of footwear. They are helped to match them up and sort them into different sets, e.g. slippers/trainers/plimsolls/sandals. The activity can be extended by re-sorting the pairs into sets of indoor and outdoor footwear.

CASE STUDY 8.2

Five words for 'top'

One of the first actions in settings involved in the Every Child a Talker (ECaT) project was to designate a member of staff to be the Early Language Lead Practitioner (ELLP). That person's role was to lead initiatives in the setting related to language development. In one setting, initial monitoring of all children's language showed that many children needed support with developing their expressive language. The ELLP observed that most parents, and some practitioners, referred to their children's jumpers/sweaters/cardigans/hoody tops/fleeces as 'top'. After discussion with the head teacher, the ELLP then discussed the issue with all the staff and collectively they decided to convert the role play area into a clothes shop. This included a wall display with various clothes items, with captions accurately labelling what they were called, including 'boxer shorts/knickers/tights/polo shirt/T-shirt and jumper'.

Staff also made a concerted effort to use correct vocabulary when talking with children as part of everyday interactions. Because staff came from a range of language backgrounds, there was often discussion about what certain items were called. These often took place in front of the children. For example, two practitioners were leading a story session during the summer and children were all looking very hot. Mrs Lopez, a Colombian practitioner whose first language is Spanish, asked the children to take off their 'tops'. Mrs Gregory, whose first language is German, started a conversation about what the individual items of

(Continued)

(Continued)

clothing were called. Both were undecided about what to call a jumper with a hood. After much debate with the children, the matter was settled by the ELLP. Her daughter worked in retail and could confirm that it is accurately known in the garment industry as a 'hoody top'. This then led to a discussion about what children call a 'jumper' at home, both in English and their home languages.

The decision to improve the children's vocabulary in these informal ways was shared with parents through the setting's website and newsletter, as well as by the Family Worker in parents' workshops.

These types of activities are beneficial for all children, as they increase children's awareness of the language that is spoken in the setting. They also create opportunities for adults and children to have conversations about language and languages, including about vocabulary. This not only increases children's vocabularies, but promotes children's ability to think about language. The collective decision to improve adults' language, for the benefit of the children, is a very positive example of how the setting's pedagogy influenced children's progress. All practitioners were keen to find ways to improve their interactions, because there was a collective understanding that this is the most effective way to develop children's communication and language.

Meaning what you say

Parents and practitioners use conversation with young children to develop their social skills and to help them understand how to behave appropriately at home, in public and when in the setting. These important lessons are learned from interactions that result from everyday routines, and incidents that occur as part of young children and adults sharing time together. Unfortunately, the way that adults talk with children can sometimes create confusion, which can lead to some children displaying what is described as 'challenging behaviour'.

Example 8.3 George and the bikes: adults giving mixed messages

George is aged 3;7 and has speech and language delay associated with having otitis media ('Glue Ear'). Glue Ear develops when fluid builds up in the space behind the eardrum (the middle ear). This often leads to hearing loss. Because this hearing loss can be intermittent (it tends to be worse when a child has a cold), it can be difficult for children to adjust, and adults may not always be aware that the child can't hear normally (Peer, 2012). George's behaviour can become quite unpredictable during the periods when he has a cold, ear infection and hearing loss. Before the full extent of his problem was diagnosed, George's parents described him as being 'defiant' when he didn't respond to instructions.

An advisor for children with hearing impairment visited the setting to observe George and give advice on how to support practitioners to meet his needs, and particularly when he occasionally displayed 'challenging' behaviour. Practitioners were already aware of the need to talk with George individually when giving instructions, and to make sure that he can see the speaker's face.

Event 1

George was outside playing with a group of other children on the bikes. George was observed to repeatedly crash his bike into the back of another child's bike. A practitioner, Yvonne, approached George:

Yvonne: George. Would you mind not doing that? You are going to hurt Ryan. OK?

(Yvonne moves away and George continues bumping into Ryan.)

Event 2

It begins to rain and Yvonne tells the children to go indoors:

Yvonne: Shall we go in now? It's raining! OK?

(All the children, apart from George, leave the bikes and head indoors. Yvonne approaches George.)

Yvonne: George. I'd like you to come in now. OK?

George: No. Me want stay here!

Yvonne: I've just told you to go in. OK?

George: No! No! (George puts his hood up and cycles away from Yvonne.)

(Continued)

(Continued)

Yvonne looks at the advisor with a facial expression that says, 'See what I mean? What shall I do now?'

The advisor suggests that Yvonne tries saying, 'George. (Point to the sky.) Look. It's raining. (Point to George's trousers.) You are getting wet. It's time to go in now. (Point to the classroom door.) I'll help you bring the bike in.' Yvonne did this and George helped her put the bike away and they both went indoors.

In discussion, the advisor and practitioners explored the need for adults (including parents) to give children clear messages. When Yvonne said, 'Shall we go in now? It's raining! OK?' she was lucky that any of the children went indoors. What she thought was an instruction was actually two questions, i.e.: 'Shall we go in?' and 'OK?' The children who went indoors were aware of Yvonne's true meaning, but George took what she said literally, i.e. 'She has asked me if we should go in, or not, so I can choose what I want to do.' Yvonne compounded the problem by tagging the question 'OK?' on the end of 'It's raining!' When Yvonne said, 'OK?' she meant, 'Do you understand?' However, George interpreted her meaning as, 'What do you think about that idea?' (To which he replied, 'No!')

By saying, 'I'd like you to come in now.' Yvonne is making her message clearer. However, by using the statement 'I'd like you to …' she runs the risk of making the incident very personal. If George refuses, then he is going against Yvonne's express wish, with the potential for a major confrontation. By adding 'OK?' she is again suggesting that George can now tell her what he thinks about her instruction.

George complied with Yvonne's wishes when he was given a very clear and brief explanation of the problem ('It's raining and you are getting wet') and a neutral explanation of what will happen next ('It's time to go in now'). Because she stopped tagging 'OK?' onto the end of her instructions, George got the message that this was not a situation where he could negotiate. Yvonne then made a suggestion about how she could help George solve his problem, by telling him that she will help him bring his bike in. It is important to note that Yvonne did not say, 'Shall I help you?' as this would have suggested to George that there was some leeway for discussion.

Incidents like these are common, and may occur because adults inadvertently give children 'mixed messages'. This confusion is caused by adults typically framing an instruction as a question, e.g. saying, 'Shall we?' when we mean 'Let's' or 'We must.' By changing how she framed instructions, Yvonne supported George's behaviour. By being clear about what needed to happen, i.e. her brief explanation of why he needed to go in ('You are getting wet.'), Yvonne also potentially helped boost George's vocabulary. This successful interaction gave them both something to talk about as they walked indoors together. They also had something in common to talk about later as Yvonne changed George's wet trousers. Yvonne talked about how George had got his *jeans* wet and that they had a spare pair of *jogging bottoms* in a *carrier bag* hanging on his peg.

Children with advanced language skills are often able to interpret what adults mean when they politely ask, 'Would you mind not doing that?' (i.e., 'Stop it') or exclaim, 'Excuse me!' ('Stop it!') or ask, 'Do you mind?' ('Stop it!'). It can even be fun to bring these different meanings to children's attention through role play, e.g. in the home corner or with puppets. Very young children, however, or those vulnerable because of learning EAL, or with language delay, or who are very shy, often become confused and anxious when trying to interpret mixed messages and benefit from clear instructions and brief explanations (Johnson and Jones, 2012).

As a follow-up to this session, practitioners were asked to observe each other when interacting with children, and to help colleagues to eradicate tag questions and frame instructions more clearly. The manager reported an improvement in George's behaviour and an overall reduction in 'challenging behaviour' throughout the setting. George's Key Person was able to report this positive change to George's mother, who could see that many altercations that she and George's Dad had with him were due to her giving mixed messages. She visited the setting on several occasions and staff modelled to her how to give clear instructions. The collective pedagogy of this setting included an understanding that staff would make adjustments to practice, in order to meet children's individual needs, where possible. This enabled the advisor to make suggestions that were followed through by the staff, with benefits for all children in the setting.

Saying what you mean

Adults who give children clear instructions when helping them develop positive behaviour not only improve children's social skills, but can also boost language development and learning. When adults are unclear, e.g. by using inaccurate language, they can have the opposite effect, particularly on children's behaviour. For example, one often hears practitioners telling children to 'share' toys or equipment. Parents can often be heard to be more direct, or even aggressive, when they declare, 'You need to learn to share!' What the adults really mean is that they want the children to 'take turns', which is not the same as 'sharing'. The following examples show George again, displaying 'challenging behaviour' towards another child. Take 2 provides an alternative suggestion for how the incident could have been approached, with a very different outcome.

Example 8.4 George, Kishan and the bikes

George is out on the bike again. It is a single-seater. George has been on the bike for 10 minutes and Kishan, aged 4;0, asks him to get off. George pushes Kishan and Kishan attempts to grab the bike. George punches Kishan, who starts to cry. Alex, one of the practitioners who is supervising outdoors, comes over to see what all the fuss is about:

Take 1

Kishan:	He hit me!
George:	Kishan push me!
Alex:	Are you both fighting about the bike?
George:	It my bike! It my bike!
Alex:	George. What have we said about sharing? You need to learn to share. You have been on the bike for a long time now. You get off so that Kishan can get on.
George (shouting and trying to ride away):	No! No!

Take 2

Alex:	Are you both fighting about the bike?
George:	It my bike! It my bike!
Alex:	We have to take turns with the bike. (To Kishan.) It's George's turn now. It's his go. When George has finished then you can have a go. Look. There's a car over there. Do you want to have a go in that?
Kishan:	No. I want a go on the bike.
Alex:	I have an idea. Go and get the car and see if you can swap it with George.
(Kishan goes to get the car.)	
Alex:	Kishan, say to George, 'Do you want to swap? Do you want to swap the bike for the car?'

> Kishan: George (pointing to the car). You wanna swap?
>
> (George jumps off the bike and jumps into the car.)
>
> Alex   Well done! That was good swapping. Now it's
> (to George   Kishan's turn on the bike and George's turn in the
> and Kishan):   car. Look! Lily is waiting for the bike. Kishan, when
>   you have finished, tell Lily that it's her turn. Can
>   you do that? (Kishan nods.) Great!

Alex, in Take 1, was talking incorrectly. He told George to 'share' but he really meant 'take turns'. George was being asked to do something that was impossible, because you can only truly share a bike if it has two saddles. Furthermore, by saying, 'You need to learn to …' Alex failed to give George any indication of how he could comply with this impossible demand. George, who does not have enough language to be able to explain how he feels or to ask what he should do, panicked and tried to ride away. What Alex was trying to do, and achieved in Take 2, was to explain about *taking turns*. Sharing and taking turns are quite different things and are often confused. To 'share', in this example, means to sit on the bike and manoeuvre it as equals. This is not possible. To 'take turns' means to agree that one person will have a turn, or 'go', then at an agreed time he will move away from the bike, so that another child can have their 'turn' or 'go'.

By saying exactly what he means in Take 2, Alex has stopped the children from fighting and shows the way for a possible solution. When this doesn't work, Alex introduces the concept of 'swapping', which is acceptable to both children. By using accurate language, Alex has enhanced the children's language development, by reinforcing important concepts and linking them to vocabulary. Children in this setting play the 'Swapping Game' regularly during adult-led group sessions. Each child is given a toy at random. If a child doesn't like his toy then he can try and swap it with another child, for whatever they have. Children who don't want to swap, because they are happy with what they already have, are encouraged to say, 'I'm fine, thank you.' In this case an adult might suggest that both children could 'play together' with the toy, or 'take turns to play with it.' This may involve the adult supporting them to succeed in doing this. If both children want the same book, then it is quite appropriate to ask them if they would like to 'share' it. When we use the word 'share' in this sense, we mean 'hold the book together and decide which pages you would like to look at together, or take turns to look at a page each'. Again, it is likely that an adult will need to model what 'good sharing' looks like.

These types of interactions, which might seem on the surface to be merely a question of playing with words, can have a significant impact on children's social and language development and wellbeing.

However, all practitioners need to work together to ensure that everyone uses the same language and actually says what they mean. These techniques can be shared with parents, in order to support them to develop their children's social skills and language at home.

In this particular setting, the practitioners have a shared understanding that children learn through experience. An important part of learning involves social development, where children learn to play, interact and learn from each other. A key element of this shared pedagogy is an understanding that children will, at various times in their lives, meet some significant challenges that can have an impact on their development. This could include conditions such as 'Glue Ear'. In these situations, there is a shared understanding that practitioners, either individually or as a group, would be expected to seek advice and do their best to incorporate this advice into their everyday practice.

 Points for reflection and discussion

Does how you give instructions influence how children respond?
    Could children's 'challenging behaviour', e.g. not following instructions, be improved by you and your colleagues 'saying what you mean and meaning what you say'?

 Practical tasks

Observe a colleague who you consider to be an effective communicator with children. Are there certain features of what s/he says that you could adopt? Observe if this has a positive impact on children's understanding and behaviour. If so, adopt this into your interactive style!
    Listen out for parents and colleagues who use the word 'share' when talking with children.
    Are they using the word correctly? Or do they really mean 'take turns'?
    Discuss with your manager and colleagues how you might collectively use accurate language to model for parents how they can talk positively with their children.

Adults interacting positively

The examples and case studies above illustrate how adults can change certain aspects of how they talk with children to enrich vocabulary and influence children's behaviour. In some cases, adults need support to change fundamental aspects of their *interactive style*. This may be because they are not used to working with a particular age group or because of insufficient initial training or experience. Often adjustments can be made through observing more experienced colleagues who interact successfully with children. In these cases, the less experienced member of staff will be aware of the need to change and will consciously make an effort to copy the aspects of interaction that work. For example, a teacher used to working with classes of nine-year-olds was assigned to work with a class of four-year-olds. He quickly realised that the way he spoke with the class as a whole group was too advanced. After observing his colleague, he reduced his overall language level, including making his instructions to the whole class shorter and simpler.

In some cases, practitioners may be aware that they are not communicating successfully, with individual children or with groups, but are unclear about which areas to improve or where to start. In other cases, adults may not be aware that they have a problem.

Making changes in how we work, and in particular how we interact with other people, can create a high degree of stress in the person who is making the change. If the process is to lead to lasting changes, then the practitioner will need positive support and encouragement. Early years consultant Debbie Brace and speech and language therapist Bhavna Acharya lead training known as Positive Interaction. This includes practical work in settings, when practitioners are supported to improve their interaction with children. This could include one or more key Positive Interaction strategies, e.g.:

- Watching, waiting and listening for the child's verbal or non-verbal initiation, which acts as the trigger to invite the adult in to an interactive moment
- Reducing questioning
- Increasing the number of comments that adults make about what the child is doing, to clearly model language at the right level

Part of the process of making changes includes practitioners videoing each other interacting with children. Following this, each member of staff is released one at a time for a video feedback session. Naturally, adults can initially react with embarrassment when looking at clips of themselves. However, the trainer's role is to help practitioners to focus on what went well and the positive aspects of what they were doing together with the child or children. This leads the practitioner to set their own goals, including identifying a Positive Interaction strategy they feel they could use more frequently, to make their interactions more effective. For example, one practitioner working with two-year-olds realised that she was asking the children several questions in a row, without allowing the children the chance to think about the first question, think of a response and then reply. This realisation led the practitioner to focus on increasing her use of the 'watch, wait and listen' strategy, as well as commenting on what the child was doing, rather than asking questions. Observations of subsequent video clips of the same adult interacting more responsively pinpointed a change in the way that the children behaved. For example, when the practitioner spoke less and waited more, the children talked more. As the adult responded to what the children said, so the children responded more and this led to an effective conversation, as opposed to a string of questions.

Changing systems to meet changing needs

Practitioners, either individually or as a whole staff, can make a commitment to change their interactive style to meet children's communication, language and social needs. They can also act collectively to adjust or radically change the way that they organise themselves, including the systems they have in place to help children learn. These systems can include how support staff are utilised, how adults lead groups of children and how children are helped to separate from their parents and register at the beginning of sessions.

CASE STUDY 8.3

Changing the role of second-language support practitioners

Over a period of two years, the number of children learning EAL in a large nursery school increased from 10 per cent to 50 per cent. The majority of these new children were from Polish families who had recently arrived in the UK. Two Polish-speaking practitioners were employed to support the Polish children in their learning of English. At the end of the academic year, it became clear that while some children had made significant progress in developing English, many had not shown the same gains in understanding or expression. Some parents were becoming concerned about their children's relatively slow rate of learning English. Staff had noted that many of the Polish children played together and talked almost exclusively in Polish, which may have had an impact on their learning of English.

The setting's Local Authority advisor met the head teacher to discuss possible ways to improve the situation. An early years advisor who was a specialist in language development was asked to advise the staff, in order to develop an approach that would best support children with EAL. After observations and leading activities with the children and support staff, the advisor noted that the Polish-speaking practitioners were acting, in the main, as interpreters for the children. For example, in a group activity led by an adult in English, the Polish staff would automatically interpret what was said into Polish. This was based on an assumption that the children would learn English if what was said to them in English was immediately interpreted into Polish.

The advisor felt that this use of support staff was inadvertently hindering learning. She proposed an alternative approach and set up an adult-led activity in order to demonstrate how another system might be more beneficial. This activity involved the children being based at a table, making a farm using miniature farm animals and an assortment of natural materials, including pine cones, sticks and wool. The advisor asked a support practitioner to sit slightly behind the group, allowing the children to have free access to the table and to be able to talk with each other. The advisor spoke to all the children in English and told the support staff to do the same. If it was clear that a child did not understand what was being said, the advisor would use other methods to clarify her meaning, including simplifying her language and using gesture. If the child still didn't understand, the advisor might ask the support practitioner, 'How do you say that in Polish?' and then repeat this phrase to the child (much to the children's amusement!).

If a child spoke to the support practitioner in Polish, the adult agreed to respond by answering the question in English first, using gesture and facial expression to maximise understanding. If the child still did not understand, then the adult would explain in Polish what she meant. The following example illustrates this technique. Beth is the advisor, Milena is the Polish-speaking practitioner and Mateusz is the child. Mateusz has collected all the dogs in one hand and seems to be making a field out of sticks to put the dogs in.

Beth:	Mateusz. What have you made? What's that?

(Mateusz looks confused and turns to Milena. Milena looks at Beth.)

Beth:	The dogs. (Pointing to the dogs.) What are you doing with the dogs?

(Mateusz turns again to Milena and speaks to her in Polish.)

Beth (to Milena):	Milena. How do you say 'dogs' in Polish?
Milena:	Psy.

(Continued)

(Continued)

Beth (gesturing to Mateusz and with exaggerated facial expression):	The dogs! Psy!

(Mateusz talks excitedly to Milena and Beth in Polish.)

Milena (to Beth):	Mateusz is explaining that the dogs are dangerous and he needs to make a fence to stop them from chasing the other animals.
Beth (to Milena):	How do you say 'dangerous' in Polish?
Milena:	Niebezpieczny.
Beth (to Mateusz):	Your dogs are dangerous? Niebezpieczny psy?
Mateusz (laughing and very excited):	Yes. Yes. Bad dogs! Very bad dog! Niebezpieczny!

Mateusz was one of the children who had made least progress with learning English and who spoke mainly Polish with other children. After the session, the head teacher, the Polish staff, advisor and the deputy head discussed the impact of this approach and how it differed significantly from interpreting for the children. It was agreed that purely interpreting was having a limited impact on children's language learning, because the children knew that if they didn't understand then they could automatically rely on an adult to interpret. Their motivation to learn English was therefore reduced.

The approach modelled by the advisor involved the children actively trying to communicate in English, with support from adults when needed. This practical approach began the change from the support staff being used mainly as interpreters to being able to facilitate the children's progress in English. Observations showed that the children's spontaneous use of English, with adults and other children, increased once they began to achieve success in understanding English and communicating their ideas.

This change in practice came about because the manager and staff had identified that current approaches were not facilitating children's learning. All practitioners were willing to try new approaches for the benefit of the children. The advisor actively involved the staff in a joint problem-solving approach, by saying, 'I have seen an approach that works in other settings that are similar to yours. Let's see what happens if we try it here. We will make time to discuss it with the head teacher afterwards.' These sentences conveyed several important messages to the staff, who were taking a risk by changing their practice:

- I understand what the problem is
- I have observed a possible better way of working
- I will work with you to see if it is successful here
- This is an experiment, so let's see what happens
- You are involved in making changes that will have an impact on your work and the children's progress

The head teacher ensured that the staff had time to meet immediately after the session, which involved her deputy head, who had the responsibility for leading practice to benefit language development of all children in the setting. The head, deputy and advisor drew up an action plan that included setting up a meeting for all parents, where the staff and advisor led a presentation about children's language development. The key messages were:

- Parents can support their children's language and learning at home by involving them in conversation
- Parents should talk with their children and read with them in their home language

There was a lively discussion, where parents expressed the wish to improve their own proficiency in English, but were concerned that the family could eventually lose their ability to communicate in their home language. They were told, most emphatically, that research shows that children who have a strong grounding in their home language go on to develop proficiency in English that enables successful academic learning in school (Cummins, 2000; Baker, 2007). Parents were encouraged to explore ways to maintain their children's home language while extending the English of all their family members, e.g. by borrowing from the setting's supply of dual-language books, written in English and a variety of home languages.

Changing registration at the beginning of a session

How young children separate from their parents at the beginning of a session influences their sense of wellbeing, which in turn influences their ability to explore, communicate and learn in a relaxed way (Goldschmied and Jackson, 2004). A setting where the pedagogy gives a high priority to maximising children's wellbeing will be one where thought, planning and experimentation have created a framework for parents and children to separate positively from each other.

CASE STUDY 8.4

Registration of children aged from 3;6 to 5;0 in a nursery class in a primary school

Staff in this nursery class decided to make a series of changes to the way that children began their morning session. For many years the system was as follows:

> Parents entered the lobby and helped children hang their coats up. A practitioner waiting at the door ushered the children onto the carpet area, where children were encouraged to sit and look at books and talk to other children and practitioners. When the majority of children had entered the room, the practitioner in charge on that day 'took the register'. This involved, for example, Mrs Morgan saying to James, 'Good morning James,' who was encouraged to answer, 'Good morning Mrs Morgan.' One member of staff supported the lead practitioner by sitting with the children and encouraging them to join in. Registration was followed by counting the number of children on the carpet and focusing on a chart where adult and children discussed the day of the week, the month, the weather and activities that were available for children to explore. A child who had brought an object in from home on that day might be encouraged to show it to the assembled group, while the adult asked him questions about it. During this time, the adult at the door would be dealing with latecomers or involved in discussion with parents and children who were finding separation difficult.

> A new team leader observed that many children were showing signs of stress at the beginning of the session. Some children were highly active and disruptive, and needed extra encouragement to sit still and 'pay attention'. Others, often of a shy disposition, were unable to answer their names, which created a sense of anxiety. Many children sat passively during these sessions, which could last up to 20 minutes. All the practitioners described themselves as feeling stressed during these prolonged registration sessions. They agreed that a change was needed. The team leader described a system that had operated in her previous setting and it was agreed to phase in these changes over the summer term. The aim was to introduce a completely new system at the beginning of the new academic year. The proposed changes were discussed with parents, including asking for their cooperation while everyone took time to adjust to the new system and to make 'tweaks' where necessary.

The new system now works as follows: Children are assigned to one of three 'family groups', each led by a designated adult. Each group has a name and symbol, e.g. 'squares', 'triangles' or 'circles'. There are 10 children in each group. Two practitioners are assigned to 'meet and greet' parents and children when they arrive. One of these adults has a specific duty to mark a child as 'present' in the register as the child enters the room. The other adult has a brief conversation with each child and carer and is available to respond to any concerns, e.g. children who might be upset or a child who may have a health issue or need to leave early to attend an appointment.

Each child has a laminated card with their photograph, name and family group symbol on it. At the beginning of the session, all the cards are placed on a table near the entrance. As the children come in, they go with their carer to find their card and stick it on a wall display board in the area designated for their family group. The carers then say 'goodbye' to the children, who begin to take part in child-initiated play and adult-led activities. After 30 minutes, each child goes to their family group area and takes part in an adult-led group activity, sitting in a circle on the floor. The groups always include a song where the children and adults sing 'hello' to each other in turn, and a short activity focusing on either mathematical or language development. After the group, children are able to access the outdoor area and have a snack at the 'snack bar' if they wish. At the end of the session children meet again in their family groups to get ready to leave.

From an individual child's point of view, the benefits that the new system brought could be expressed as follows:

- Finding my name card with Mummy is fun
- We can talk about my name and see which other children are in nursery
- I am learning to read my name
- I can go and play straight away
- This all makes it easy/easier to say goodbye to Mummy

There were benefits for adults, too:

- Meet and greet allows parents to discuss any problems that staff need to know about immediately, e.g. about the child's health or wellbeing
- The parents have a 'ritual' which empowers them to successfully separate from their children
- If parents need to stay to settle their child, they can do so as part of the initial play session

- Parents can take part in the process of helping their children become literate
- Practitioners can immediately interact with children in child-initiated activities
- The smaller, mid-morning group activity is more relaxed, and children interact and learn more in the planned language and maths activities
- Meeting together in the family group at the end of the session allows for a more relaxed way to end the session

Independent 'self-registration' and family groups are particularly beneficial for settings that cater for two-year-olds and older children together. One setting found that having a specific family group for the two-year-olds allowed the staff to plan language activities that were designed to be of shorter duration and aimed at the children's level of cognitive and language development. For example, the very young children delighted in bringing in a toy from home and partially hiding it under a basket so that the other children could guess what it was. They never seemed to tire of this activity, while older children found it interesting once or twice and then needed an activity that was more stimulating.

Leading pedagogy for talk and learning

The England-wide Every Child a Talker (ECaT) project, which to date has yet to be officially evaluated, established the position of Early Language Lead Practitioner (ELLP) in every setting that took part (DCSF, 2008b). The ELLP was often a member of staff who wanted to take on the role of developing language and communication in the setting, in much the same way that a teacher would have responsibility for a curriculum area in a primary school. With outside support from a local consultant, the ELLP worked with leaders and colleagues in the setting to monitor all children's progress and to identify children at risk of language delay. This led to introducing approaches and activities that had an impact on all children's communication, but particularly those judged to be at risk of delay in their speech and language development. From my experience of working as a consultant for ECaT projects in 90 settings, the creation of the ELLP was a major factor in creating change and innovation in settings. Through attending local training events and networking with ELLPs in other settings, these practitioners were enabled to influence practice that had an impact on children's language development. Although ECaT ceased to have national government funding in 2011, many local councils have continued funding similar projects, including the 'Let's Talk Together' project in Hounslow and 'Keep On Talking' in Hampshire (Jones, 2012c).

It was the vision and actions of the manager, however, which influenced whether lasting change would take place. Settings that were involved in major innovation were those where the manager had a clear vision of the pedagogy for the setting. Additionally, part of this leadership role is to encourage innovation and collaboration (O'Sullivan, 2009).

CASE STUDY 8.5

A manager leading change based on observation

Mary Field, head of Millington Road Nursery School in Cambridge, which at the time of writing had recently been declared 'outstanding' after an Ofsted inspection, seeks to make changes as a result of observation. These observations may originate from her own viewpoint, from her colleagues, or from outside support such as visits from advisors and training. Mary explained to me:

> I often make observations of practice and try and look at what is happening from the children's point of view. Then I work with colleagues to implement changes by asking, 'Would this be better for the children?' This includes reviewing the effectiveness of systems we have for organising children, such as registration at the beginning of the session.

Equally, Mary explained, innovation can come from making changes to practice and resourcing as a result of training:

> I found the training particularly useful when Michael came into our setting and worked with the children and practitioners during practical activities. For example, he led a mark-making activity where children were encouraged to talk about characters that they were familiar with from TV programmes and films. We could see that children were highly animated because they were talking with authority about a subject that meant a lot to them, and was related to their life at home. In discussion with the trainer and colleagues after the session we could see the benefits of investing in resources, such as books and toys, which reflect this aspect of children's culture.

Conclusion

Making changes to interaction can have a rapid impact on children's responses to adults, with subsequent improvements in children's wellbeing and language development. The process of making changes, and particularly to how we talk and behave, can be challenging, but also highly rewarding. The main reason for making changes should be the positive impact it has for children. However, these changes can only take place if colleagues are able to work together positively. This includes working in an environment where practitioners are encouraged to support each other constructively as they attempt to make changes to their personal interaction. Introducing some of the approaches suggested in this chapter can potentially involve changes to the adults' wellbeing. This can include temporary feelings of vulnerability as they move from the 'comfort zone' of one way of working to a different system. The manager has a crucial role to play in providing the vision for change, leading the change and supporting colleagues who have a vision. This can include modelling appropriate interaction and experimenting with new approaches, e.g. introducing the Planted Adult and two adults working together and then evaluating the relative benefits of new approaches. Local consultants and advisors have an important role to play in providing training, leading initiatives, supporting managers and lead practitioners, as well as in sharing good practice between settings.

 Points for reflection and discussion

Some systems, like registration, organising children for snack time or how you share stories with large groups of children, become part of traditional practice in a setting. You may be aware that they are no longer effective or would like to make a change. How would you go about this?

 Practical activities

Look critically at one aspect of a system in your setting, e.g. registration, mealtimes and group sessions. Imagine that you are looking at them from a child's point of view (including literally getting on your knees to see what they actually see!). What impact does this system have on children's communication and language? What changes could be made?

Useful websites

The Hanen Centre
www.hanen.org/Home.aspx (accessed 25 May 2015)
A Canadian not-for-profit charitable organisation committed to supporting parents, early childhood educators and speech-language pathologists in their

efforts to promote the best possible language, social and literacy skills in young children.

Mantra Lingua

www.mantralingua.com/mantralinguachoosecountry.html (accessed 25 May 2015)

Provides a wide range of dual-language books and resources to support the development of bilingual learning.

Siren Films

http://sirenfilms.co.uk/product/the-two-year-old-at-home-at-nursery/ (accessed 25 May 2015)

The Two-Year-Old at Home & at Nursery

This series of filmed observations illustrates the drama of initial separations of child and parents when first attending a pre-school and the positive benefits of successful communication between child, parents and the Key Person.

Video Interaction Guidance

www.youtube.com/watch?v=YRVaL_ZlxHs (accessed 25 May 2015)

Provides information on the techniques and rationale behind this approach to developing practitioners' and parents' interaction with children.

CHAPTER 9

COMMUNICATING COMPLEX IDEAS

This chapter will

- Explore how children convey complex meanings from a very young age
- Explore how practitioners can support children throughout the early years to use language to develop and express their thoughts
- Make the link between 'decontextualised language' and literacy development
- Describe the need for sensitive teachers

Example 9.1 Simone at 4;6: is Elvis real?

'Is Elvis real?' This is possibly the most bizarre question I have ever been asked. About 20 years ago, I was visiting a reception class just before the end of the Christmas term, sitting at a table with Simone and her friend Carl, making Christmas cards. The conversation went something like this (I can picture the scene, even now, because it was so memorable):

Simone:	Michael. Is Elvis real?
Michael (after a long pause):	Why do you ask?
Simone (taking a deep breath):	Well. My big sister says that Santa is not real. So I asked my Dad and he says that Santa was a nice man once who went round people's houses and give them presents but he's dead now.
Michael:	Ah.
Simone:	So if he's dead, how does he come down the chimney?
Carl:	Is he a ghost? Has he got super powers?
Michael (to Simone):	So why do you ask about Elvis?
Simone:	Well. My Dad likes Elvis. He plays his music all the time in the car. My Mum don't like Elvis. She likes other music.

(There is a pause while Simone goes off to ask her teacher for some glitter. Simone returns and carries on the conversation.)

Simone:	My Dad says Elvis is dead. We can still hear him singing and watch his films on video. So is that like Santa then? Is Elvis real, like Santa?

I had no idea what to say, so I stopped Mrs Langley, the teaching assistant, who was walking past.

Michael:	Mrs Langley, Simone is asking me some very interesting questions.
Mrs Langley:	Is it about Santa and Elvis? Simone, you've been asking everyone about that this week, haven't you?

And so she had. Clearly the question about whether Santa was real or not had been occupying Simone's thoughts for some time, and she was looking for an answer that would satisfy her. The adults, including myself, were unclear how to respond, because parents have very strong views about what children should be told about Santa and, quite frankly, the whole subject of Father Christmas and his reality can be a minefield.

(Continued)

(Continued)

Simone is using language to express an extremely complex set of ideas:

People say Santa is real. My sister says he is not. My dad says he is dead. Elvis is dead, but we can still hear him and see him on videos. Therefore if Elvis is 'real' (because we can still see and hear him) is Santa 'real' (because we see his image everywhere and we see him in films and we are told he comes down the chimney and gives us presents)?

Children communicating relatively simple meanings

Four-and-a-half years previously, Simone would have been communicating an important message, although this time through crying, i.e. 'I'm hungry!' Now she can give expression to some of the most important questions asked by humankind, i.e. 'What is the nature of death?' This is also an example of a young child being able to use language to share ideas that are 'decontextualised'. In most cases, this would be to talk about an event with someone who was not there when it took place. In Simone's case, she has gone several steps further and is able to discuss abstract ideas. This ability, as we shall see, is thought to be directly linked to later literacy development. How has Simone come so far in such a short time? Once again, adults play a crucial part, through conversation, in facilitating this process.

We have already looked at how children develop their communication skills early on. Continuing with this, many children by age four can tell their parents that they are 'hungry' when they want food and 'thirsty' when they would like a drink. One four-year-old, with particularly advanced language, said to her Mum, 'I'm hungry, but can we have something different to eat today, because we had pasta yesterday and I'd quite like to try something else? Please?' To which Mum replied, 'Not really, because we've got some pasta left over' (by which she meant, quite simply, 'No'!). The ability to communicate the message has advanced rapidly, but the message, 'I'm hungry' remains the same.

Linguist Halliday (1975), whose work we introduced in Chapter 1 (p. 21), suggested that young children use talk to fulfil different functions. The message, 'I'm hungry!' fulfils an 'instrumental' function; its purpose is to get the child what he needs and, once he can make a choice, what he wants. Crying fulfils this purpose for the baby, but once they are physically and cognitively able, children use words and phrases, and then complex sentences, to get their needs and wants met (although many occasionally return to crying when words fail!). In the same way, children seek to control what we do to them, and let us know what we need to do for them. A baby who cries because he is hot, a two-year-old who shouts, 'No hat!' because he is hot and a four-year-old who asks, 'Can I have a hottie (hot-water bottle) tonight 'cos my feet get cold in bed?' are all communicating messages that Halliday describes as having a 'regulatory' function. Language is also used in an 'interactional' way when children make contact with other people and build relationships, while the 'personal' function exists for the child to be able to talk about how they feel.

Of Halliday's seven proposed functions for communication through language, he suggests that the 'instrumental', 'regulatory', 'interactional' and 'personal' functions are used primarily to satisfy a child's physical, social and emotional needs. Indeed, from my observation, many of the first words and phrases that children use in conversation help them to get what they want, make contact and express how they feel. Children and adults maintain these functions when they talk, but the way that they express them becomes, with experience, ever more sophisticated.

Children communicating complex meanings

Halliday's other three functions of language exist to help the child to understand his environment through exploring complex ideas. We explore these functions in detail through the following examples, to illustrate the vital role of effective conversation with adults in developing children's ability to express complex meanings.

Example 9.2 Stacey at 4;5: do cats poo? – the 'heuristic' function of language

Stacey lives in a block of flats and attends her local community day nursery. She is going for a walk to the local market with staff and children from the 'pre-school room'. She is in conversation with Kelly, who is holding her hand as they walk along the street:

Kelly: Mind the dog poo, Stacey.

Stacey: There's a big poo near our block.

Kelly: Oh dear, that's not very nice for owners to let their dogs do that.

Stacey: Do cats poo?

Kelly: Yes, they do. Why do you ask?

(Continued)

(Continued)

Stacey: I was just asking. Because I never seen one. I seen a dog do a poo, but not a cat.

Kelly: All animals have to poo.

Stacey: Oh. And a goldfish. My goldfish does it, too. What about a hedgehog? What about a snake? What about a spider? What about a chicken? They lay eggs.

Kelly: All living creatures need to poo and wee.

Stacey: Oh. Look at that bus!

Here, Stacey is using language 'heuristically', i.e. to find out about her environment. On the surface, her question is simple, in the sense that there are three simple words. However, the thinking behind the question is complex: 'I know that dogs poo, because I have seen one do it. I haven't seen a cat do that. Cats are animals, too, so I wonder if they poo as well. I will ask Kelly and see if she knows.'

Kelly, for her part, handles the question beautifully. She gives a straightforward answer, 'Yes, they do.' Then she follows with something that is quite risky: she asks, 'Why do you ask?' It was an automatic response and a question that, perhaps if used with a younger child, might not have gained a response, or even put the child off. But Kelly knows Stacey well. She knows that Stacy asks lots of questions. She's a girl with a strong sense of curiosity. By saying, 'Why do you ask?' Kelly is giving Stacey several messages:

- I think that that is an interesting question
- I want to know what your thinking is behind that question
- I want to talk to you more about your thinking
- I have time to listen to you
- Let's see what happens in this conversation!

One could say that this short conversation was an exercise in intellectual enquiry, in the sense that both minds were engaged on exploring the same idea. Kelly has, intuitively, tuned into Stacey's train of thought, i.e. 'I'll make a list of some of the animals I know. A chicken lays eggs. Is that pooing?' Kelly introduces accurate vocabulary to describe everything on this list, 'living creatures', and the concept that eliminating waste is necessary. Stacey was just getting into her stride, thinking about where hens' eggs fit into the scheme of things, when she was distracted by a large bus. One suspects that she will return to that subject on another day!

Example 9.3 Christian at 2;4 on the telephone: the 'imaginative' function of language

Christian is on the phone to his Auntie. Normally, before she speaks to Christian, Auntie checks with Mum what Christian has been doing recently so that she can understand what he is saying and have a long, meaningful conversation. On this occasion, Christian has picked up the phone first, so Auntie has to go into the chat 'cold':

Christian: Hello!

Auntie: Hello, Christian. It's Auntie Nicola. What are you doing?

Christian: Sleep.

Auntie: You're sleeping?

Christian: No. No sleep. Goin' sleep.

Auntie: Oh. You are going to go to sleep?

Christian: Yes. My go sleep. My jacket. Muddy. My fall down.

Auntie: Did you fall in a muddy puddle?

Christian: Yes. My fall muddy puddle. Finger got blood.

Auntie: Oh. Did you cut your finger?

Christian: Yes.

Auntie: And did Mummy put a plaster on your finger?

Christian: Yes. Leg got blood. My fall. Leg got plaster.

Auntie: Oh. You fell over and cut your leg? What did Daddy say?

Christian: 'Whoops a daisy.' Daddy say, 'Up you get.'

Auntie: And what did Mummy say?

Christian: Mummy shout.

At this point, Mum took the phone and explained exactly what did happen. To use Mum's words: 'Christian is telling porkies.' True, there was a small amount of mud on his jacket, and he had fallen

(Continued)

(Continued)

over. But he had not cut his finger or leg and certainly hadn't been given a plaster.

His older brother had, on separate occasions, recently cut his finger and leg in school, and had come home each time with a plaster covering his cut. Christian had been very impressed by the plasters, and asked if he could have one.

It looks like his Auntie's line of questioning helped Christian say something which wasn't quite true. This could be interpreted, using Halliday's terminology, as an early example of the use of the 'imaginative' function of language.

Christian's Auntie used questioning to help her nephew to tell a story, or 'create a narrative'.

It is her fault that he started to tell untruths, because she asked him, 'And did Mummy put a plaster on your finger?' Had she not done so, Christian may have tried to tell her about what happened to his brother. But this would have been a narrative only, with no imaginative element. In the event, Christian showed that, with Auntie's help, he is able to do several things:

- Talk in a 'decontextualised' way
- Talk on the phone, with no visual clues about what is being said to him
- 'Repair' a conversation, by correcting his Auntie when she suggests that he might have already been to bed: 'No. No sleep. Goin' sleep.'

At this age, there is a wide variation in children's vocabulary and level of grammar, but there is no doubting that Christian is starting to use what language he has in an 'imaginative' way. As he matures and grows in experience, this will also include the ability to tell stories, make jokes and eventually create imaginary worlds.

Example 9.4 Holly at 3;8 shares two books: the 'representative' function of language

Holly is with her Childminder, Sue. The two younger children Sue cares for are asleep, so Holly has a chance to share a book with Sue, with no interruptions (until the others wake up.) She chooses *Mr Gumpy's Outing* by John Burningham (Burningham, 2001), a story about two children and a collection of animals who jump into a boat and eventually sink it, before going to Mr Gumpy's house for tea.

Holly:	I know what a baby dog is. It's a pubby.
Sue:	Ah, yes. A puppy.
Holly:	And a baby cat is a kitten. And …
Sue:	A baby chicken?
Holly:	I forgot.
Sue:	A chi …
Holly:	A chi …
Sue:	A chi …
Holly:	A children! (They both laugh.)
Holly:	It's a chick. A little baby chick.

They finish the story (Sue reads and Holly interrupts to talk about the pictures on each page.)

Sue has another book at hand, a non-fiction book about animals and their babies. It is a 'touchy-feely' book with various textures to feel on each page.

Holly:	I know this one. I have same one at home.
Sue:	Oh. You have the same one at home? So do you want to share another one?
Holly:	No. I like this one. I knows the pictures.
Holly (touching a furry rabbit):	This one is soft and furry. (Turns the page.) This frog is lumpy. I calls it lumpy. Mummy calls it bumpy. What does you call it Sue?
Sue:	I would call it a bit lumpy and a bit bumpy.

This conversation lasted for another 10 minutes, with Holly very much taking the lead to talk about each page and ask Sue questions. In discussion with Sue after the session, she described Holly as being very keen on facts, and how Holly would often turn a storybook-sharing session into a discussion about what was happening on each page.

If we were using Halliday's classifications, we would describe Holly as using language in these sessions primarily in a 'representative' way, to share facts and information.

The adult's role in helping children to express meanings

Returning to Simone in Example 9.1, we can see that her Dad said something very puzzling. This has set Simone off to explore a complex idea. In the same way that 'heuristic' play involves young children exploring objects and what can be done with them (Goldschmied and Jackson, 1994), the 'heuristic' function of language is to explore ideas. Simone is grappling with her ideas in a sophisticated way, as she tries to understand the meaning behind her father's use of words in relation to Santa and Elvis. As a visitor to the class, I had time to explore her ideas with her (even though I was unsure of my subject). Stacey in Example 9.2 was also using language heuristically, and, again, an adult was available to extend her thinking. Stacey's enquiry only lasted a relatively short time, but she had explored the subject in as much depth as she had needed. In all of the examples above the children were helped to express meanings because the adults saw developing children's language as a priority, and were able to provide a total focus on the conversation. The following short vignettes suggest ways that adults can model how to use language in thinking.

Example 9.5 Adults 'thinking aloud': modelling talking about thinking

A group from a pre-school visited the playground in the local park. There was an old baby buggy high up in the branches of a tree. Several of the children had noticed the buggy and the practitioners said, 'Goodness. That is a surprise! How did that buggy get up there? And how might we get it down?'

A group of four-year-old children are walking with their teacher outside the front of the school. It has been raining heavily and there is always a large puddle by the school entrance. A van that was parked there has just driven off. One of the children notices that there are what he calls 'rainbow colours', in the puddle, from an oil leak. The teacher stops to look and asks, almost to herself, 'I wonder how that happens?'

It is a sunny day in May, and the entire pre-school are playing outside. Suddenly, the sky darkens and just as the children get inside, there is a very severe hailstorm. One of the practitioners, looking out of the window with the children, says, 'Well! I didn't expect that to happen. Did you?' another replied, 'Yes. It was a surprise. I wonder if we will be able to go out again this afternoon.'

These experienced practitioners all use spontaneous events to model for the children how to go about thinking. They may know the answer to some of the questions, but by expressing surprise and saying, 'I wonder/ How did that buggy get up there?/I didn't expect that to happen. Did you?' they are inviting children to get involved in thinking about an interesting event or phenomenon. They are also signalling that they have time to listen to what the children might have to say in response.

 Practical tasks

Look again at Example 9.4. Like Sue, share a fiction and non-fiction book on the same subject, with several children, one at a time. Is there a difference in the types of conversations you have about each book? (You may find, for example, that you talk more about feelings when talking about a story, as opposed to discussing and answering questions about facts with a non-fiction book.)

Is there a difference in the types of question that children ask?

Do children of different ages and stages of language development respond differently to fiction books? For example, might younger children be more inclined to talk about non-fiction?

Decontextualised language: moving from the 'here and now' to the 'there and then'

At several points in this book, I have highlighted the importance placed on children's ability to use language in a decontextualised way, where children are involved in the 'sharing of events that have not been experienced by anyone present' (Riley and Reedy, 2007). Riley also lists the ways that adults can help children talk about a subject out of context by involving the children in:

- Explaining what the children mean
- Recounting their own experiences
- Making up stories about fantasy worlds
- Being able to do the above with relative strangers, e.g. someone visiting the setting

Catherine Snow and colleagues, in evaluating the Home School Study of Language and Literacy Development, found that children who had developed the skills associated with decontextualised language showed increased reading comprehension abilities in the middle grades of school (Snow, 1991).

Other studies make a similar link, e.g. Sénéchal et al. (1998) and Sénéchal and LeFevre (2002). They suggest that there are two broad types of exposure to books at home in the early years: those where parents focus more formally on skills; and those where parents are more concerned with informally sharing a story and talking about what is happening. Conversations in the latter category of interactions will include sharing the meaning of the story, encouraging and enabling the child to ponder, wonder and predict. The five-year longitudinal study of 168 children showed that the children whose parents had focused mainly on reading and writing skills achieved well early in school when developing those skills further. The inference we can take from these studies is that adults sharing books, including exploring the ideas within them through talk, is vital if children are to become effective, active readers. This is particularly important for their understanding of books that they will read and think about for themselves as they develop literacy skills and experience of reading.

Through sharing books, children come to realise that writing is spoken language written down. They also learn that the language of books is not the same as the language that we use to talk with each other, in the same way that they learn that there are different spoken registers that can be used, depending on who you are talking to. These realisations come through repeated, positive experiences of sharing books with adults. These conversations also lift children from talking about 'concrete' experiences in the present, to being able to explore complex ideas in a more abstract way.

Sensitive teachers, sensitive interactions

In Chapter 6, we explored in detail how children can be encouraged to talk by being involved in what Riley describes as 'real conversations' and 'sensitive interaction' (Riley, 2007: 68–9). Chapter 7 looked at the challenges adults face in being sensitive to children and having the types of conversations that help children talk about what they are doing, to explore ideas and use talk to learn. As children settle into the life of school, many of these conversations will take place within a large group. Typically, a teacher will lead a discussion with up to 30 children sitting on the carpet in front of him. Teachers use the whole class group as a forum for discussing ideas. Here, it is important for children to be able to use and understand language out of context, including exploring ideas, feelings and describing what has happened and what will happen. This is largely achieved through talk, where children will focus on the teacher, what he is holding in his hand or pointing at.

Once children become confident in being involved in large groups, these groups can be an effective forum for developing learning, and particularly if the teacher is skilled at engaging children's participation. In our final example, we look at a child who has plenty to say at home, in the playground and when talking with friends, but finds participation through talk within a large group quite overwhelming.

Example 9.6 Harrison, Sanghita and the bird table

Harrison is 4;1 and Sanghita is 4;7. They have been attending their reception class in a primary school for three weeks. The class teacher, Mr Cooper, is encouraging children to explore the topic of 'Ourselves'. His aim is to develop the children's ability to talk and share what they know, including through early writing and as part of developing the children's identity as a class group.

Harrison knows a lot about birds. He has a bird table in his garden and he likes to watch the birds feeding. His favourite bird is the blue tit. He has known Sanghita since he was a baby, as they are neighbours and attended the same local pre-school. Harrison is very quiet during whole class sessions on the carpet. Mr Cooper has told the class that he would like everyone to paint a picture of their favourite thing, so the paintings can be part of a big wall display about 'What We Like'. Mrs Evans, the class Teaching Assistant (TA), is sitting with Harrison, Sanghita and two other children, talking about their favourite things. Harrison has just described in detail how he likes blue tits and Sanghita has talked about her teddy. The children help Mrs Evans to cover the table with newspaper and each child has a large piece of paper for their painting.

Harrison watches the other children paint, but doesn't do anything himself. He tells Mrs Evans, 'I can't paint birds.' This leads to a discussion between them, including about what colour the bird might be. Is he fat or thin? Has he just been eating lots of seeds? Can you see his wings? What do his legs look like? Is he a robin? Harrison explains that it is a fat blue tit and you can't see his wings. He paints a large blue blob with some brown in the background (i.e., 'A blue tit on the bird table').

(Enter Mr Cooper.)

Mr Cooper: My goodness, Harrison. That is a marvellous painting!

(Harrison looks at Mrs Evans. Mr Cooper looks at Mrs Evans. The message Mr Cooper conveys through his facial expression is: 'What is it?')

Mrs Evans: Harrison has been busy telling us all about the birds in his garden, and he has painted his favourite bird. Haven't you Harrison? (Harrison nods.) Shall we see if Mr Cooper can guess what kind of bird it is?

(Continued)

(Continued)

Mr Cooper (a look of slight panic crossing his face):	I think I know, but Harrison, can you give me a clue?
Harrison:	It's blue.
Mr Cooper:	Well, it can't be a robin or a blackbird, so it looks to me like a blue tit! Am I right? That's marvellous. Can we show that to the other children when it's time to sit on the carpet?

(Harrison looks alarmed.)

Mr Cooper:	It's alright. Sanghita and Mrs Evans can help you tell us what bird it is. Can't you Sanghita? (Sanghita nods enthusiastically.) And you can help Sanghita tell us about her ...
Mrs Evans:	Her teddy. Her teddy, Mr Cooper.
Mr Cooper:	Oh, yes, of course.

After Mr Cooper had moved away, Harrison asked Mrs Evans, 'What does 'marvellous' mean?' Mrs Evans explained that it meant, 'Very, very, very, good.' To which Harrison replied, 'I thought so.'

Mr Cooper is aware that Harrison is quite shy and this is particularly evident when he is in the whole class group. Later, when the paintings had dried, the class were all sitting on the carpet. As many children as possible talked about their paintings. Harrison was very shy, so the teacher proceeded as follows:

Mr Cooper:	This is a marvellous painting by Harrison. It's so bright! Harrison has already talked to me about it. It's a bird. Does anyone know what kind of bird? (Harrison is looking down and has begun blushing. Several of the children give suggestions, which are mainly 'eagle' or 'robin'.)
Mr Cooper:	Well, I wasn't sure at first, but there's one big clue ... The colour. Harrison, would you like to tell us what it is? (Harrison looks down. Mrs Evans puts her hand up.)
Mr Cooper:	Yes, Mrs Evans?

Mrs Evans:	Well Mr Cooper. Sanghita, Harrison and Mrs Evans were talking about this, and I think that Sanghita would like to tell us what kind of bird it is.
Sanghita:	Blue Tit!! (Harrison smiles.)

In Example 9.6, the teacher's working relationship with his TA is strong, in the sense that they have an understanding of how best to work together, in order to engage these young children in conversation and learning. Both adults, through the way they respond to the children, show genuine pleasure in talking with the children. Mr Cooper describes how, when he was in training, he was often reminded by his tutor that 'talking is working': i.e., that teachers should engage children in conversation, that this talk should be pleasurable for adult and child and that 'talk is the child's work and the teacher's, too.'

Another TA, Mrs Ryan, and teacher colleague shared a similar approach to working jointly. This was reflected in the way that they discussed talking with children. For example, the teacher would say to the children, 'Who would like to *share a book* with Mrs Ryan?' Other teachers might say, 'Mrs Ryan is going *to hear* readers.' These are two very different messages: the former is inviting children to talk about books, while the latter is instructing children to read. The two sentences are completely different and reflect two very different approaches to talk and books.

 Points for reflection and discussion

Look again at the way that the TA and teacher work together in Example 9.6. There seems to be a 'division of labour', where the teacher has planned for the TA to use the small group for discussion. The teacher then visits the group and gets information that the children can share with the whole class. How effective is this approach?

Thinking about large group activities in your setting, how much do the adults contribute to the discussion, modelling responses and encouraging children to participate?

 Practical tasks

Do you talk about 'hearing readers' or 'sharing books'? Or do you say to children, 'Shall we read a book together?' as opposed to 'Shall we share a book together?' Does the difference in words used by you and your colleagues reflect differences in your approach to talking with children using books?

Conclusion: learning with young children

We began thinking about babies, from birth, communicating with their parents, and we end with 30 children sitting on a carpet talking with one adult. This book's title is *Talking and Learning with Young Children*. Through all the interactions that they have, children learn about themselves and the world and their place within that world. But an equally important part of the process of interaction and conversation is that *adults* are learning about the children at the same time. We learn about what children need and what they want and what they are thinking about. We learn to 'tune into them', particularly when they are very young and their speech is quite difficult to understand. We want to tune into them so that we can understand the meaning of what they are saying, or trying to say. Adults also learn about the best way to teach children: from watching and listening to how they respond to things we do and say. This applies equally to children who develop language rapidly and those who struggle to make sense of communication and language.

Finally, let's return to the sentence in the Introduction that summed up the main message of this book:

> Conversation is the place where children develop as talkers – through learning about language, themselves, the world and their place in that world.

In front of the word 'conversation', insert 'Enjoyable'.

GLOSSARY

Accent   A typical way of pronouncing speech sounds in connected speech that is associated with a particular region or country or social class.

Articulation   The physical production of a speech sound.

Attachment   The relationship that the child has with her main caregivers. Attachments can be 'secure', where the child feels confident that an adult will care for her, or 'insecure', where the child has not been able to make a strong attachment.

Attachment Theory   The concept that infants need to develop a positive, loving relationship with their primary caregivers. This influences their future social and emotional development, including how to regulate their feelings.

Auditory feedback   The ability to hear oneself speaking. This can be restricted if a child has a hearing impairment, influencing the development of their speech.

Behaviourist   A perspective that is primarily concerned with behaviour that can be observed, rather than focusing on what might be occurring within the child, e.g. their thinking or what motivates them. Psychologists and other professionals who are influenced by behaviourism work with children with behaviour difficulties by promoting positive behaviour through reward and reducing negative behaviour by ignoring it.

Bilingual   Being able to understand and use two languages. Children who are bilingual may be able to use one language more confidently than another, but this can change through life, depending on experience.

Bonding   The positive feelings that a primary caregiver has for a child. Bonding is closely linked to the infant's ability to form an attachment with that caregiver.

Child Directed Speech (CDS)   A variation or register of talking that adults use with infants who have begun talking and older children with developing language.

Cochlear implant   An electronic advice that is surgically inserted into the inner ear of a person with profound hearing impairment. They provide hearing to people whose deafness is caused by damage to sensory hair cells in the cochleas. The cochlea is part of the inner ear, where sound vibrations are converted into electrical impulses that are then transmitted to the brain to be interpreted. More information about cochlear implants and hearing impairment can be found at: www.ndcs.org.uk/family_support/useful_links_and_organisations/glossary/cochlear_implant.html (accessed 7 September 2015)

Cognitive development   The development of thinking. Cognitive development is influenced by children's innate abilities, experience and how adults and other children guide the child through play and talk.

Communication   How we share meanings. Communication can be verbal, written or non-verbal, e.g. using signs or gestures.

Conversation   A way of sharing meanings, including thoughts and ideas, with other people. Conversation is a two-way process, with those involved listening and responding to each other and taking turns. Conversations can be verbal, or involving signs, e.g. among people with hearing impairment.

Conversational flow   How well participants in a conversation are able to understand each other and express ideas, e.g. through taking turns and encouraging each other to continue by saying: 'I see/really? that's interesting,' etc.

Conversational style   A description of the way that adults involve children in conversation. Some styles can be more effective than others. For example, an adult who listens and allows the child time to express herself and then responds is described as having a 'responsive conversational style'. An adult who dominates the conversation, e.g. by asking lots of 'closed' questions (for instance, 'What's that?' 'What shape is that?' etc.) is using a 'controlling conversational style'.

Developmental delay   Occurs when a child does not reach specific developmental milestones, such as walking or talking, within what is regarded as the normal age range. Delays can be caused by the environment, e.g. lack of experience or illness, or by factors within the child, such as Down syndrome.

Dialect   The distinct form of a language spoken in a certain geographical area. The dialect of a certain area may contain words and phrases that are only used in that region or city. Speakers of a local dialect often use a particular accent associated with the area. Examples are 'Scouse' from Liverpool and 'Geordie' from Newcastle.

Genetically determined   A skill that is decided from the moment of conception. The development of that skill will also be influenced by the environment.

Grammar   A system of rules that describes how words are combined in a language.

Imperative pointing   The type of pointing that young children use to show that they want something. This may be with an outstretched hand or finger (or by using eye pointing or body movements if the child has a physical or sensory disability).

Infant Directed Speech (IDS)   A register that adults use when talking and playing with babies, including highly exaggerated tones of voice; and a type of made-up vocabulary, including words like 'diddums', 'boo', 'wasa-matta?' and 'there, there'. IDS was originally known as 'Motherese'.

Innate   A behaviour or skill that exists and develops naturally, rather than something that is learned from experience.

Interaction   How we respond to each other while communicating. For example, an adult playing and talking with a baby might use turn taking, eye contact and smiling as part of the interaction.

Language   The method we use for communicating. Language can be spoken (verbal), written or using signs, e.g. British Sign Language. Any given language is made up of agreed rules that help the speakers understand each other.

Language acquisition   The idea that children create their own rules of grammar, using a vocabulary that they have learned. These skills are acquired naturally and the process is innate. These concepts are associated with linguist and philosopher Noam Chomsky.

Language Acquisition Device (LAD)   A theoretical concept created by Noam Chomsky to explain how a child acquires the rules of grammar.

Maturation   The process of growth that is determined by innate and genetically determined forces within the child. Maturation can be neurological, where the child's nervous system automatically develops. Physical maturation takes place at the same time, which can include the growth of organs such as the larynx (voice box). The combination of these two types of maturation is crucial for the development of skills such as walking and the child's control of speech sounds.

Neuron   Nerve cells that transmit information in chemical and electrical form around the body.

Non-verbal communication   Includes facial expression, tone of voice and gestures that help the listener understand the messages conveyed by a speaker.

Overgeneralisation   When a child tries to apply a regular rule of grammar to one that is irregular, e.g. by saying: 'I goed to nursery' for 'I went.'

Pedagogy   The educational understanding and beliefs that a practitioner or group of practitioners have. Pedagogy influences how we teach children and how we communicate with them.

Phonology   How speech sounds are linked together to make words in a language. Children's phonology develops in a systematic way as they mature.

Pragmatics   How we use language to convey meanings and to understand what other people mean. This can include an understanding of non-verbal communication such as facial expression.

Primary intersubjectivity   When infant and adult (often primary carer) focus on each other as part of early communication.

Pronunciation   The way that speech sounds are formed, or articulated, in an acceptable way, so that someone can be understood. Pronunciation of speech sounds varies depending on where people live, creating their accent.

Proto-conversation   The type of playful verbal interaction that baby and adult have together that includes listening, turn-taking and responding. Proto-conversations are regarded as providing 'practice' for later conversations when children are able to use words.

Register   A variety or style of language used in a particular situation or with a particular person. Registers can be 'informal', e.g. when talking with children or friends, or 'formal', e.g. at a job interview or when talking with parents.

Scaffolding   The support that adults provide young children to progress in their learning. Scaffolding includes using language to help children develop skills and to help them express their thoughts and explore ideas.

Schema   Patterns of repeated behaviour which can often be noticed in young children's play, including throwing, spinning and wrapping up objects.

Secondary intersubjectivity   When a baby and adult focus on an object together and share an interest in this object.

Semantics   The meaning of the words that we use, including single words and phrases, sentences and stories. Semantics includes what we understand of what is being said to us, and how we are able to say what we mean.

Slang   Words and phrases that are used very informally, and may have been invented to show that the speaker comes from, or wants to be part of, a particular group. For example, someone who wants to be a surfer might use 'Surfer Slang', saying 'That's totally awesome, dude!' to mean, 'That was rather good, my friend.'

Speech   Individual sounds that are used to make up words in a language. This is also referred to as 'pronunciation' or 'articulation'.

Speech and language delay   Where children's understanding, speech sounds, phonological development and expressive language are developing in a similar way to children of a younger chronological age.

Theory of Mind   The realisation that someone else can have thoughts and ideas. Some children with autism are thought not to have this understanding.

Verbal communication   Using talk to communicate with other people.

Verbal comprehension   Our understanding of what is said to us. In normally developing language, children's verbal comprehension will be greater than their ability to express themselves.

Verbal expression (expressive language)   How we express ourselves through talk, using speech, vocabulary and phrases that create sentences that we use to convey meaning.

Vocabulary   Individual words, including nouns, adjectives and verbs, which we use to label objects and ideas and their properties.

Vocal cords   Two mucous membranes stretched horizontally across the larynx (voice box). When they are fully open and at rest, air passes over them without creating sound. When they are almost closed, air passing through them from the lungs causes them to vibrate, creating sound.

Voice   Sounds made from the vibration of the vocal cords: e.g. [g] and [d] are created by air passing over the vocal cords, making them vibrate; while [k] and [t] are made without the vocal cords vibrating.

Zone of Proximal Development   A concept introduced by Lev Vygotsky that describes the difference between what a child can learn on their own, and how they might get to the next step in their learning with help from a supportive adult or older child.

REFERENCES

Apicella, F., Chericoni, N., Ostanzo, V., Baldini, S., Billeci, L., Cohen, D. and Muratori, F. (2013) 'Reciprocity in interaction: A window on the first year of life in autism', *Autism Research and Treatment*, available at: www.hindawi.com/journals/aurt/2013/705895/ (accessed 25 May 2015)

Attwood, T. (2008) *The Complete Guide to Asperger's Syndrome*. London: Jessica Kingsley Publishers.

Baker, C. (2007) *A Parents' and Teachers' Guide to Bilingualism*, 3rd edn. Clevedon: Multilingual Matters.

Baldwin, D.A. (1995) 'Understanding the link between joint attention and language', in C. Moore and P.J. Dunham (eds), *Joint Attention: Its Origins and Role in Development*. Hove: Psychology Press, pp. 131–58.

Baron-Cohen, S. (1989) 'Perceptual role-taking and proto-declarative pointing in autism', *British Journal of Developmental Psychology*, 7: 113–27.

Baron-Cohen, S. (1995) *Mindblindness: An Essay on Autism and Theory of Mind*. Cambridge, MA: MIT Press.

Baron-Cohen, S., Allen, J. and Gillberg, C. (1992) 'Can autism be detected at 18 months? The needle, the haystack and the CHAT', *British Journal of Psychiatry*, 161: 839–43.

Barry, A.K. (2008) *Linguistic Perspectives on Language and Education*. Upper Saddle River, NJ: Pearson.

BBC Radio 4 (2013) 'From Donald Winnicott to the Naughty Step', Archive on 4, 4 May, available at: www.bbc.co.uk/programmes/b01s7v7b (accessed 25 May 2015)

Beebe, B., Knoblauch, S., Rustin, J. and Sorter, D. (2003) 'A comparison of Meltzoff, Trevarthen and Stern', *Psychoanalytic Dialogues*, 13 (6): 809–36.

Berko Gleason, J. and Weintraub, S. (1976) 'The acquisition of routines in child language', *Language in Society*, 5: 129–36.

Bernstein, B. (1973) *Class, Codes and Control*, Vol. 1. London: Routledge and Kegan Paul.

Bishop, D.V.M. (2000) 'What's so special about Asperger Syndrome? The need for fuller exploration of the borderlands of autism', in A. Klin, F. Volkmar and S. Sparrow (eds), *Asperger Syndrome*. New York: Guilford Press, pp. 254–77.

Bishop, D.V.M. and Norbury, C.F. (2002) 'Exploring the borderlands of autistic disorder and specific language impairment: A study using standardised diagnostic instruments', *Journal of Child Psychology & Psychiatry*, 43 (7): 917–29.

Blank Grief, E. and Berko Gleason, J. (1980) 'Hi, thanks and goodbye: More routine information', *Language in Society*, 9: 159–66.

Bloom, P. (2000) *How Children Learn the Meanings of Words*. Cambridge, MA: MIT Press.

Bloom, P. (2004) 'Myths of word learning', in D.G. Hall and S.R. Waxman (eds), *Weaving a Lexicon*. Cambridge, MA: MIT Press, pp. 205–24.

Bowlby, J. (1953) *Childcare and the Growth of Love*. Harmondsworth: Penguin.

Boyce, S. (2012) *Identifying Non-Verbal Communication Difficulties: A Life-Changing Approach*. Milton Keynes: Speechmark Publishing.

Brazelton, T.B. and Nugent, K.J. (1995) *Neonatal Behavioural Assessment Scale*, 3rd edn. London: MacKeith Press.

Brodie, K. (2014) *Sustained Shared Thinking in the Early Years*. Abingdon: Routledge.

Brown, R. (1973) *A First Language: The Early Stages*. Cambridge, MA: Harvard University Press.

Bruner, J.S. (1975) 'The ontogenesis of speech acts', *Journal of Child Language*, 2: 1–19.

Bruner, J.S. (1983) *Child's Talk: Learning to Use Language*. Oxford: Oxford University Press.

Burningham, J. (2001) *Mr Gumpy's Outing*. London: Red Fox.

Camaioni, L., Perucchini, P., Bellagamba, F. and Colonnesi, C. (2004) 'The role of declarative pointing in developing a theory of mind', *Infancy*, 5 (3): 291–308.

Chomsky, N. (1965) *Aspects of the Theory of Syntax*. Cambridge, MA: MIT Press.

Chomsky, N. (1975) *Reflections on Language*. London: Temple Smith.

Chomsky, N. (1980) *Rules and Representations*. Oxford: Blackwell.

Clarke, J. (2007) *Sustained Shared Thinking*. London: Featherstone Education.

Clements, C. and Chawarska, K. (2010) 'Beyond pointing: Development of the 'sharing' gesture in children with autism spectrum disorder', *Yale Review of Undergraduate Research in Psychology*, : 46–63; available at: www.yale.edu/yrurp/issues/YRURP%20Second%20Issue.pdf#page=46 (accessed 25 May 2015)

Community Playthings (2013) *A Good Place to Be Two*. Robertsbridge: Community Playthings.

Conkbayir, M. and Pascal, C. (2014) *Early Childhood Theories and Contemporary Issues: An Introduction*. London: Bloomsbury.

Coupe-O'Kane, J. and Goldbart, J. (1998) *Communication Before Speech: Development and Assessment*. London: David Fulton Publishers.

Cowley, J. (1998) *Mrs Wishy-Washy*. Chicago: Wright Group/Mcgraw-Hill.

Croft, C.E. (2009) 'How can a reflective model of support, enhance relationships between babies, young children and practitioners?', MA dissertation, London Metropolitan University.

Crystal, D. (1989) *Listen to Your Child*. London: Penguin.

Cummins, J. (2000) *Language, Power and Pedagogy: Bilingual Children in the Crossfire*. Clevedon: Multilingual Matters.

Cummings, M.E. and Kouros, C.D. (2009) *Maternal Depression and its Relation to Children's Development and Adjustment*. Montreal: Centre of Excellence for Early Childhood Development.

Dawson, G., Toth, K., Abbott, R., Osterling, J., Munson, J., Ester, A. and Liaw, J. (2004) 'Early social attention impairments in autism: Social orienting, joint attention, and attention to distress', *Developmental Psychology*, 40: 271–83.

Department for Children, Schools and Families (DCSF) (2008a) *The Bercow Report: A Review of Services for Children and Young People (0–19) with Speech, Language and*

Communication Needs. Nottingham: DCSF Publications, available at: http://www.education.gov.uk/publications/standard/publicationdetail/page1/DCSF-00632-2008 (accessed 25 May 2015)

DCSF (2008b) *Every Child a Talker: Guidance for Early Language Lead Practitioners (First Instalment).* Nottingham: DCSF Publications, available at: http://webarchive.nationalarchives.gov.uk/20110202093118/http:/nationalstrategies.standards.dcsf.gov.uk/node/153355 (accessed 25 May 2015)

DCSF (2009a) *Every Child a Talker: Guidance for Early Language Lead Practitioners (Second Instalment).* Nottingham: DCSF Publications, available at: http://webarchive.nationalarchives.gov.uk/20110202093118/http://nationalstrategies.standards.dcsf.gov.uk/node/158181 (accessed 25 May 2015)

DCSF (2009b) *Learning, Playing and Interacting: Good Practice in the Early Years Foundation Stage.* Nottingham: DCSF Publications, available at: http://dera.ioe.ac.uk/2412/7/85679136be4953413879dc59eab23ce0_Redacted.pdf (accessed 25 May 2015)

DCSF (2010) *Every Child a Talker: Guidance for Consultants and Early Language Lead Practitioners (Third Instalment).* Nottingham: DCSF Publications, available at: http://webarchive.nationalarchives.gov.uk/20110202093118/http:/nationalstrategies.standards.dcsf.gov.uk/node/277287 (accessed 25 May 2015)

Dewart, H. and Summers, S. (1989) *Pragmatics Profile of Early Communication Skills.* Windsor: NFER-Nelson.

Dewart, H. and Summers, S. (1995) The *Pragmatics Profile of Everyday Communication Skills.* Windsor: NFER-Nelson.

DFE (2012) *Statutory Framework for the Early Years Foundation Stage: Setting the Standards for Learning, Development and Care for Children From Birth to Five.* London: Department for Education, available at http://webarchive.nationalarchives.gov.uk/20130401151715/https://www.education.gov.uk/publications/eOrdering-Download/EYFS%20Statutory%20Framework.pdf (last accessed 25 May 2015)

Emde, R. and Easterbrooks, A. (1985) 'Assessing emotional availability in early development', in W. Frankenburg, R. Emde and J. Sullivan (eds), *Early Identification of Children at Risk: An International Perspective.* New York and London: Plenum Press, pp. 79–101.

Featherstone, S. (2011) *Setting the Scene: Creating Successful Environments for Babies and Young Children.* London: Featherstone Education.

Fletcher, P. (1985) *A Child's Learning of English.* Oxford: Blackwell.

Gerhardt, S. (2015) *Why Love Matters: How Affection Shapes a Baby's Brain*, 2nd edn. Abingdon: Routledge.

Goldschmied, E. and Jackson, S. (1994) *People under Three: Young Children in Day Care*, 2nd edn. Abingdon: Routledge.

Haggan, M. (2002) 'Self-reports and self-delusion regarding the use of motherese: Implications from Kuwaiti adults', *Language Sciences*, 24 (1): 17–28.

Halliday, M.A.K. (1975) *Learning How to Mean.* London: Edward Arnold.

Harris, M., Jones, D., Brookes, S. and Grant, J. (1986) 'Relations between the non-verbal context of maternal speech and rate of language development', *British Journal of Developmental Psychology*, 4: 261–8.

Hart, B. and Risley, T.R. (1995) *Meaningful Differences in the Everyday Experience of Young American Children.* Baltimore, MD: Paul H. Brookes.

Heath, S.B. (1983) *Ways with Words: Language, Life and Work in Communities and Classrooms.* Cambridge: Cambridge University Press.

Hindley, J. and Benedict, W. (1996) *The Big Red Bus*. London: Walker Books.

I CAN (2006) *The Cost to the Nation of Children's Poor Communication*. I CAN Talk Series, Issue No. 2. London: I CAN, available at: www.ican.org.uk/~/media/Ican2/Whats%20the%20Issue/Evidence/2%20The%20Cost%20to%20the%20Nation%20of%20Children%20s%20Poor%20Communication%20pdf.ashx (accessed 25 May 2015)

Johnson, M. and Jones, M. (2012) *Supporting Quiet Children*. Cambridge: Lawrence Educational.

Jones, M. (1988) 'Lack of verbal stimulation in infancy: Possible effects on language development'. MSc thesis, City University London.

Jones, M. (2010) 'Sign posting', *Nursery World*, 29 July.

Jones, M. (2011) 'Come on in!', *Nursery World*, 24 March.

Jones, M. (2012a) 'Baby room excellence', *Early Years Educator*, 13 (10), February.

Jones, M. (2012b) 'Successful additions', *Early Years Educator*, 13 (11), March.

Jones, M. (2012c) 'Keep on talking!', *Nursery World*, 6–19 March.

Jones, M. (2013) 'Effective talk with babies', *Early Years Educator*, 15 (5), September.

Jones, M. (2014) 'The power of pointing', *Early Years Educator*, 15 (11), March.

Jones, M. and Belsten, M. (2011) *Let's Get Talking!* Cambridge: Lawrence Educational.

Lawrence, V. and Stevenson, C. (2011a) *The Northamptonshire Baby Room Project: Facilitators' Manual*. Northampton: Northamptonshire County Council.

Lawrence, V. and Stevenson, C. (2011b) *The Northamptonshire Baby Room Project – Parents' Course: Facilitators' Manual*. Northampton: Northamptonshire County Council.

Lieven, E.V.M. (1984) 'Interactional style and children's language learning', *Topics in Language Disorders*, 4: 15–23.

Lindon, J. (2012) *What Does it Mean to Be Two?* London: Practical Pre-School Books.

Locke, J.L. (1989) 'Babbling and early speech: Continuity and individual differences', *First Language*, 9 (6): 191–205.

Louis, S., Beswick, C., Magraw, L., Hayes, L. and Featherstone, S. (2008) *Again! Again! Understanding Schemas in Young Children*. London: A & C Black Publishers.

Loveland, K. and Landry, S. (1986) 'Joint attention in autism and developmental language delay', *Journal of Autism and Developmental Disorders*, 16: 335–49.

McDonald, L. and Pien, D. (1982) 'Mother conversational behaviour as a function of interactional intent', *Journal of Child Language*, 8: 337–58.

Melhuish, E. (2010) 'Why children, parents and home learning are important', in K. Sylva, E. Melhuish, P. Sammons, I. Siraj-Blatchford and B. Taggart (eds), *Early Childhood Matters: Evidence from the Effective Pre-School and Primary Education Project*. Abingdon: Routledge, pp. 44–69.

Meltzoff, A.N. (1999) 'Origins of theory of mind, cognition and communication', *Journal of Communication Disorders*, 32: 251–69.

Meltzoff, A.N. and Gopnik, A. (1993) 'The role of understanding persons and developing theory of mind', in S. Baron-Cohen, H. Tagler-Flusberg (eds), *Understanding Other Minds: Perspectives from Autism*. Oxford: Oxford University Press, pp.335–366.

Nicolls, E. (2004) 'The contribution of the shared reading of expository books to the development of language and literacy'. DPhil dissertation, University of Oxford.

Nutbrown, C. (2011) *Threads of Thinking*, 4th edn. London: Sage.

O'Sullivan, J. (2009) *Leadership Skills in the Early Years: Making a Difference*. London: Continuum International Publishing Group.

Office for Standards in Education (Ofsted) (2013) *Getting it Right First Time: Achieving and Maintaining High-Quality Early Years Provision*, Ofsted Report No. 130117, July. London: Ofsted, available at: http://www.ofsted.gov.uk/resources/getting-it-right-first-time-achieving-and-maintaining-high-quality-early-years-provision (accessed 25 May 2015)

Oller, D.K. and Eilers, R.E. (1988) 'The role of audition in infant babbling', *Child Development*, 59: 441–49.

Peer, L. (2005) *Glue Ear*. Abingdon: Routledge.

Pine, J. (1994) 'The language of primary caregivers', in C. Gallaway and B. Richards (eds), *Input and Interaction in Language Acquisition*. Cambridge: Cambridge University Press, pp. 15–37.

Riley, J. (2007) 'The child, the context and early childhood education', in J. Riley (ed.), *Learning in the Early Years 3–7*, 2nd edn. London: Sage, pp. 1–28.

Riley, J. and Reedy, D. (2007) 'Communication, language and literacy: Learning through speaking and listening, reading and writing', in J. Riley (ed.), *Learning in the Early Years 3–7*, 2nd edn. London: Sage, pp. 65–100.

Robin, T. (2000) 'La Rose de Jaipur', from *Ciel de Cuivre*. Naïve Records.

Robinshaw, H.M. (1996) 'Acquisition of speech, pre- and post-cochlear implantation: Longitudinal studies of a congenitally deaf infant', *International Journal of Language and Communication Disorders*, 31 (2): 121–39.

Robinson, M. (2003) 'Role of staff'. Interview on Education Scotland Early Years website, available at: http://www.educationscotland.gov.uk/learningandteaching/early learningandchildcare/prebirthtothree/nationalguidance/conversations/mariarobinson.asp (accessed 7 August 2015)

Saxton, M. (2010) *Child Language Acquisition and Development*. London: Sage.

Sénéchal, M. and LeFevre, J. (2002) 'Parental involvement in the development of children's reading skill: A five-year longitudinal study', *Child Development*, 73 (2): 445–60.

Sénéchal, M., LeFevre, J., Thomas, E.M. and Daley, K.E. (1998) 'Differential effects of home literacy experiences on the development of oral and written language', *Reading Research Quarterly*, 33: 96–116.

Siraj-Blatchford, I. (2010) 'A focus on pedagogy: Case studies of effective practice', in K. Sylva, E. Melhuish, P. Sammons, I. Siraj-Blatchford and B. Taggart (eds), *Early Childhood Matters: Evidence from the Effective Pre-School and Primary Education Project*. Abingdon: Routledge, pp. 8–23.

Siraj-Blatchford, I., Sylva, K., Muttock, S., Gilden, R. and Bell, D. (2002) *Researching Effective Pedagogy in the Early Years*, Department for Education and Skills (DfES) Research Report No. 356. London: DfES, available at: www.ioe.ac.uk/REPEY_research_report.pdf (last accessed 25 May 2015)

Skinner, B.F. (1957) *Verbal Behaviour*. New York: Appleton-Century-Crofts.

Slonims, V., Cox, A. and McConachie, H. (2006) 'Analysis of mother–infant interaction in infants with Down syndrome and typically developing infants', *American Journal on Mental Retardation*, 111 (4): 273–89.

Snow, C. (1977) 'Mothers' speech research: From input to interaction', in C. Snow and C. Ferguson (eds), *Talking to Children: Language Input and Acquisition*. Cambridge: Cambridge University Press, pp. 31–50.

Snow, C.E. (1991) 'The theoretical basis for relationships between language and literacy in development', *Journal of Research in Childhood Education*, 6 (1): 5–10.

Soderstrom, M. (2007) 'Beyond babytalk: Re-evaluating the nature and content of speech input to preverbal infants', *Developmental Review*, 27 (4): 501–32.

Stadlen, N. (2004) *What Mothers Do: Especially When it Looks Like Nothing*. London: Piatkus Books.

Stern, D.N. (1985) *The Interpersonal World of the Infant: A View from Psychoanalysis and Developmental Psychology*. New York: Basic Books.

Stern, D.N. (1998) *The Motherhood Constellation*. London: Karnac Books.

Stewart, N. (2011) *How Children Learn: The Characteristics of Effective Early Learning*. London: British Association for Early Childhood Education.

Stilwell Peccei, J. (2006) *Child Language: A Resource Book for Students*. London: Routledge.

Sylva, K., Melhuish, E.C., Sammons, P., Siraj-Blatchford, I. and Taggart, B. (2004) *The Effective Provision of Pre-School Education (EPPE) Project: Final Report*. London: Department for Education and Skills (DfES)/Institute of Education, University of London, available at: www.ioe.ac.uk/RB_Final_Report_3-7.pdf (last accessed 25 May 2015)

Sylva, K., Melhuish, E.C., Sammons, P., Siraj-Blatchford, I. and Taggart, B. (2010) *Early Childhood Matters: Evidence from the Effective Pre-School and Primary Education Project*. Abingdon: Routledge.

Tizard, B. and Hughes, M. (2002) *Young Children Learning*, 2nd edn. Oxford: Blackwell.

Trevarthen, C. (1977) 'Descriptive analyses of infant communicative behaviour', in H.R. Schaffer (ed.), *Studies in Mother–Infant Interaction*. London: Academic Press.

Trevarthen, C. (1979) 'Communication and cooperation in early infancy: A description of primary intersubjectivity', in M. Bullowa (ed.), *Before Speech: The Beginnings of Interpersonal Communication*. Cambridge: Cambridge University Press, pp. 321–47.

Trevarthen, C. and Daniel, S. (2005) 'Disorganized rhythm and synchrony: Early signs of autism and Rett syndrome', *Brain and Development*, 27 (Suppl. 1): S25–S34.

Trevarthen, C. and Hubley P. (1978) 'Secondary intersubjectivity: Confidence, confiding and acts of meaning in the first year', in A. Locke (ed.), *Action, Gesture and Symbol: The Emergence of Language*. London: Academic Press, pp. 183–229.

Trevarthen, C., Barr, I., Dunlop, A.-W., Gjersoe, N., Marwick, H. and Stephen, C. (2003) *Supporting a Young Child's Needs for Care and Affection, Shared Meaning and a Place: A Review of Childcare and the Development of Children Aged 0–3. Research Evidence, and Implications for Out-of-Home Provision*. Edinburgh: Scottish Executive, available at: www.scotland.gov.uk/Resource/Doc/933/0007610.pdf (accessed 25 May 2015)

Tronick, E., Als, H. and Adamson, L. (1979) 'Structure of early face-to-face communicative interactions', in M. Bullowa (ed), *Before Speech: The Beginning of Interpersonal Communication*. Cambridge: Cambridge University Press, pp. 349–72.

Vygotsky, L.S. (1978) *Mind in Society: The Development of Higher Psychological Processes*. Cambridge MA: Harvard University Press.

Warren, S.F., Gilkerson, S., Richards, J.A., Oller, D.K., Xu, D., Umit, Y. and Gray, S. (2010) 'What automated vocal analysis reveals about the vocal production and language learning environment of young children with autism', *Journal of Autism and Developmental Disabilities*, 40: 555–69.

Wells, G. (1987) *The Meaning Makers: Learning to Talk and Talking to Learn*. London: Hodder & Stoughton.

Wells, G. (2009) *The Meaning Makers: Learning to Talk and Talking to Learn*, 2nd edn. London: Hodder & Stoughton.

Wells, G. and Gutfreund, M. (1987) 'The conversational requirements for language learning', in W. Yule and M. Rutter (eds), *Language Development and Disorders*. Oxford: Blackwell, pp. 90–102.

White, J. (2014) *Playing and Learning Outdoors*, 2nd edn. Abingdon: Routledge.

Wood, D. (1998) *How Children Think and Learn*. Oxford: Blackwell Publishing.

Wood, H.A. and Wood, D.J. (1984) 'An experimental evaluation of the effects of five styles of teacher conversation on the language of hearing-impaired children', *Journal of Child Psychology & Psychiatry*, 25 (1): 45–62.

Yule, G. (2014) *The Study of Language*, 5th edn. Cambridge: Cambridge University Press.

INDEX

accents, 14–15, 147, 187
Acharya, B., 126–127, 161
adult interactive style, 76–79, 160–162
articulation, 5, 187
Asperger's syndrome, 109–114, 134
attachment, 40–44, 187
Attachment Theory, 41, 44, 187
auditory feedback, 54, 187
Autism Spectrum Disorder (ASD)
    attachment and, 43
    babbling and, 54
    groups of children and, 134
    imperative pointing and, 57
    Sustained Shared Thinking and,
        109–114
    Theory of Mind and, 34
    uses of language and, 22

babbling, 51–55
Baby Matters (Luton), 44–46
baby rooms, 44–46
Baby Talk and Play project, 47
behaviourism, 14–15, 187
Bercow Report (DCSF), 96
Berko Gleason, J., 28
Bernstein, B., 88, 147
bilingualism, 7, 29, 187
bonding, 40–41, 44–46, 187
book-sharing sessions, 128–132
Bowlby, J., 41
Boyce, S., 39
Brace, D., 42–43, 47, 126–127, 161
Brazelton, T.B., 43, 44
Bristol Study, 91–92, 101
British Sign Language (BSL), 58–59
Brodie, K., 103
Brown, R., 19
Bruner, J., 27–28, 102

challenging behaviour, 154–157
Child-Centred Interactional Style, 84,
    85–86
Child Directed Speech (CDS), 23–27,
    88–89, 188
Chomsky, N., 8, 16–19, 189
Clarke, J., 103
closed questions, 76–77
cochlear implants, 54, 188
cognitive development, 8, 27–28, 188
communication, definition of, 3, 188
competence, 19
complex ideas
    adult's role in helping children with,
        180–181
    decontextualised language and,
        181–182
    functions of language and, 172–180
    sensitive interactions and, 182–185
concentration, 132–134
contingency, 63
Continuity Hypothesis, 52–53
controlling interactional style (directional
    interactional style), 85, 86–88
conversation, definition of, 3, 30, 188
conversational flow, 114, 188
conversational style, 76–79, 188
cooing, 50–51
*The Cost to the Nation of Children's Poor
    Communication* (I CAN), 95–96
Coupe-O'Kane, J., 38
Croft, C., 44
Crystal, D., 52

declarative pointing, 55–59
decontextualised language, 181–182
developmental delay, 9, 57–58, 134, 188
dialects, 89, 92, 147–149, 188–189

directional interactional style (controlling interactional style), 85, 86–88
Discontinuity Hypothesis, 53

Early Language Lead Practitioners (ELLPs), 153–154, 168–169
Early Years Foundation Stage (EYFS), 146
Effective Provision of Pre-school Education Project (EPPE), 94–95, 102–103, 146
Elaborated Code, 88, 147
English as an additional language (EAL), 10, 146, 162–165
evaluation, 141–142
Every Child a Talker (ECaT) project
  book areas and, 129
  Early Language Lead Practitioners and, 153–154, 168–169
  groups of children and, 134–135
  language impoverishment and, 9, 96
  Sign 4 Learning and, 98–99
extrinsic reinforcement, 14–15

Featherstone, S., 45
Field, M., 169
first words, 59–66
Fletcher, J., 58
fronting, 80

genetically determined skills, 18–19, 189
Gerhardt, S., 41, 44, 46
Glue Ear (otitis media), 134, 154–155
Goldbart, J., 38
Goldschmied, E., 44
grammar, definition of, 3, 189
groups of children
  in busy rooms, 134–137
  children's differing responses in, 137
  concentration in, 132–134
  difficulties in, 118–119
  evaluation in, 141–142
  follow-up conversations in, 140–141
  observation, recording and photographs in, 138–141, 143
  'planted adult' in, 126–128, 130–132, 135, 141, 142–143
  sharing adults in, 119–126
  sharing books in, 128–132
  standard for adult talk in, 147–148
  two adults in, 142–143, 182–185

Halliday, M.A.K., 21–22, 174–180
Harris, M., 41
Hart, B., 95

hearing impairment, 77–78, 89–90
Heath, S.B., 24
Home Learning Environment (HLE)
  Bernstein's Restricted and Elaborated Codes and, 88
  dialect, register and Standard English in, 88–91
  Effective Provision of Pre-school Education Project and, 94–95
  importance of, 91–94
  influence of, 28, 83
  interactional styles and, 84–88
  language development in the setting and, 96–99
  need for action in, 95–96
  social class and, 84, 88
Home School Study of Language and Literacy Development project, 181–182
Hughes, M., 92

I CAN (charity), 95–96
imaginative play, 149
imitation, 14–15, 19, 30
imperative pointing, 38–39, 57, 189
Infant Directed Speech (IDS), 23, 35, 52, 88–89, 189
innate behaviour and skills, 35–36, 189
instinct, 46–47
interaction, 3, 22–28, 189
interactive babbling, 52
intersubjectivity, 34–38
intonation, 52
intrinsic reinforcement, 14–15
Islands of Intimacy, 44

Jackson, S., 44

Keep On Talking project, 168
Key Person approach, 44

language
  definition of, 3, 189
  functions of, 21–22, 172–180
language acquisition, 8, 16–19, 28–29, 189
Language Acquisition Device (LAD), 8, 189
Language Acquisition Support System (LASS), 28
language development, 28–29
language impoverishment, 9, 95–96, 147–149
language learning, 28–29

language learning theories
    Child Directed Speech and, 22–27
    Chomsky and, 8, 16–19, 16–20, 189
    Halliday and, 21–22
    introduction to, 11–14
    role of imitation and rewards in, 14–16
    scaffolding and, 27–28
    social norms and, 28
LeFevre, J., 182
Let's Talk Together project, 126–127, 168

Magic Bubble, 132–134
Makaton signs, 58–59
Maternal Interactive Style, 84–85
maturation, 8, 51, 189–190
Meltzoff, A., 34
mixed messages, 154–157
Motherese, 22–23, 88–89, 149

Naming Insight, 72–73
nativist approach, 19
Neonatal Behavioral Assessment Scale, 43
neurons, 41, 190
Nicolls, E., 129–130
non-verbal communication, 3, 39–40,
    53–54, 190
The Northamptonshire Baby Room Project,
    44–45, 47
notes, 138–141
Nursery Rhyme Survey (activity), 135–142

observation, 138–141
otitis media (Glue Ear), 134, 154–155
overgeneralisation, 17–18, 80, 190

pedagogy
    accuracy of adult talk and, 150–154
    adult interactive style and, 160–162
    beginning of sessions and, 165–168
    changing needs and, 162–165
    definition of, 9, 190
    Every Child a Talker and, 168–169
    importance of, 145–146
    meaning what you say and, 154–157
    saying what you mean and, 157–160
    standard for adult talk and, 147–149
phatic comments, 78–79
phonology, 3, 5, 190
photographs, 138–139, 143
planted adults, 126–128, 130–132, 135,
    141, 142–143
Positive Interaction, 161–162
power, 130
pragmatics, 3, 190
primary intersubjectivity, 36, 190

processing space, 85
pronunciation, 190
proto-conversations, 35, 52, 190

recasting, 63, 71, 75
redundancy of meaning, 85
Reedy, D., 101, 181
reflexive vocalisations, 50. See also
    vegetative sounds
register, 22, 23–24, 88–91, 148–149, 190
registration, 165–168
repetition, 13, 69, 73
Researching Effective Pedagogy in the Early
    Years (REPEY) project, 102–103
Restricted Code, 88, 90–91, 147
rewards, 13, 14–16, 30
Riley, J., 101, 103–104, 181, 182
Risley, T.R., 95
Robin, T., 52
Robinson, M., 45

scaffolding, 27–28, 34, 57, 102, 146, 190
schemas, 69, 191
scribble talk, 52, 54, 69–71, 74–75
second-language support practitioners,
    162–165
secondary intersubjectivity, 36–38, 191
secure attachment, 44–45
self-regulation, 94–95
Semantic-Pragmatic Language Disorder, 22
semantics, 3, 191
Sénéchal, M., 182
sensitive interactions, 182–185
settings, types of, 10
Sign 4 Learning, 98–99
signing, 58–59, 64
slang, 148–149, 191
Snow, C., 22–23, 181–182
social class, 84, 88
social norms, 28
Something Special (TV programme), 58
sound play, 51
speech, 3, 191
speech and language delay, 54, 89–90, 191
Stadlen, N., 42
Standard English, 89, 147
Stern, D., 34, 35
Stewart, N., 146
Still Face Paradigm experiments, 40
Stilwell Peccei, J., 51
Sustained Shared Thinking (SST)
    examples of, 109–115
    in groups of children, 141–142
    language development and, 115
    quality interactions and, 101–109, 116

swearing, 149
Sylva, K., 95, 102–103

talking at home. *See* Home Learning
    Environment (HLE)
tantrums, 68–69
Theory of Mind, 34, 56, 191
Tizard, B., 92
Trevarthen, C., 34
Tronick, E., 40
two-year-olds
    adult interactive style and, 76–79
    development of speech and language,
        confidence and learning of,
        79–81
    experiences of, 68–69
    spontaneous conversation with,
        69–72
    talking with, 76
    vocabulary development and, 72–76

vegetative sounds, 22–23, 50
verbal communication, 3, 191
verbal comprehension, 3, 191
verbal expression (expressive language), 3, 191
vocabulary, 3, 147, 150–154, 157, 191
vocal cords, 51, 191
vocal play, 51
voice, 51, 191
vulnerable children, 146. *See also* groups of
    children
Vygotsky, L.S., 27, 102, 191

Wells (1987), 119
Wells (2009), 92, 101
Wood, D., 79, 92, 101–102, 149
Wood H.A., 79, 101–102
Word Explosion (Word Spurt), 72, 73–74
Word Mapping, 72, 73–74

Zone of Proximal Development, 27, 191